American Film and Society since 1945

American Film and Society since 1945

Third Edition, Revised and Expanded

LEONARD QUART
and
ALBERT AUSTER

PRAEGER

Westport, Connecticut
London

Library of Congress Cataloging-in-Publication Data

Quart, Leonard.
    American film and society since 1945 / Leonard Quart and Albert
Auster.—3rd ed., rev. and expanded.
        p.   cm.
    Includes bibliographical references and index.
    ISBN 0–275–96742–5 (alk. paper)—ISBN 0–275–96743–3 (pbk. : alk. paper)
    1. Motion pictures—Social aspects—United States.   2. Motion
pictures—United States—History.   I. Auster, Albert.   II. Title.
PN1995.9.S6Q37   2002
302.23′43′0973—dc21   2001034630

British Library Cataloguing in Publication Data is available.

Library of Congress Catalog Card Number: 2001034630
ISBN: 0–275–96742–5
        0–275–96743–3 (pbk.)

First published in 2002

Praeger Publishers, 88 Post Road West, Westport, CT 06881
An imprint of Greenwood Publishing Group, Inc.
www.praeger.com

Printed in the United States of America

The paper used in this book complies with the
Permanent Paper Standard issued by the National
Information Standards Organization (Z39.48–1984).

10 9 8 7 6

To my parents
Meyer and Luba Quart
and to my wife Barbara

To my parents
Lazar and Mollie Auster
and to my wife
Susan Hamovitch

CONTENTS

Photo essay follows p. 66.

PREFACE TO THE
THIRD EDITION

Our aim in writing a third edition of *American Film and Society since 1945* was to revise, expand, and update the original and revised editions, which were published in 1984 and 1991. The third edition adheres to the structure and critical premises of the other two; however, we updated the Introduction to account for new theoretical work in film studies and additional brief analyses of a few films.

The most significant change was the updating of the book to include a chapter on film in the nineties, concluding with Stanley Kubrick's final work, *Eyes Wide Shut*. The chapter explores the Hollywood film in the post–Cold War and Clinton era—the longest period of economic expansion in our history. There is no single political and cultural current that nineties' films evoke. Some of the diverse films analyzed include: films reaffirming American patriotism such as Steven Spielberg's *Saving Private Ryan*, critiques of mainstream politics like *Wag the Dog* and *Bulworth*, inner city films like *Boyz N' the Hood*; films dealing with homosexuality and women like *Philadelphia* and *Thelma and Louise*, and a lengthy critique of the cultural significance of *Schindler's List*.

We mean this book to provide students, teachers, and the general public an accessible, synthetic, intradisciplinary approach to American film. Hopefully it succeeds.

ACKNOWLEDGMENTS

Though we often consider the act of writing a solitary one, there are people whose help has been invaluable in completing this edition of the book. Al Auster wishes to acknowledge the love, support, and creative inspiration of his wife Susan Hamovitch. Leonard Quart wishes to acknowledge his wife Barbara, whose love has always sustained him as a writer, helping make him a better one than he ever thought he could be. Finally, a special note of thanks to Chris Brookeman, who helped launch the first edition of this book almost two decades ago.

1

INTRODUCTION

From shadows and symbols into the truth.

John Henry, Cardinal Newman

In 1981, John Houston's almost legendary Second World War documentary about psychologically crippled veterans, *Let There Be Light* (1945), received its first commercial public showing, thirty-five years after it was produced. Originally suppressed by the U.S. Defense Department, which feared its possible pacifistic influence, interest in it was kept alive by film critics—most notably James Agee, who even included it on his best films list of 1946. Unfortunately, time had not dealt well with *Let There Be Light*, and most contemporary film critics found it ingenuous and naive to the point of simplemindedness.[1]

Despite the fact that *Let There Be Light* failed to live up to its critical reputation, it succeeded on another level. In fact, the showing of the film might be compared to lifting the lid on a time capsule—one that provided a clear insight into an era's cultural and social perspective and mood. By contemporary standards, a film that adheres to *Let There Be Light*'s magical faith in the healing power of psychiatrists and Freudianism would be seen as innocent and overly-sanguine. It is a vision of the human condition that would hardly be emulated by today's more cynical (albeit no more sophisticated) films. *Let There Be Light* may have left modern critics unimpressed with its moving portrayal of the plight of shell-shocked soldiers, but it does serve as a useful conduit to help understand the intellectual assumptions of the postwar period.

It is hardly an original point, though it bears repeating, that films have the ability to evoke the mood and tone of a society in a particular era. However, there was a time when a number of historians and social scientists were hesitant to accept this truism. By films one does not mean merely documentaries, which obviously directly capture something of the reality of people's lives and feelings, but also mainstream Hollywood commercial films. It is not only that these films sometimes convey and imitate the surfaces of day-to-day life—the way people talk, dress and consume—though social realism is clearly not an aesthetic that Hollywood usually embraces or has seen as commercially viable. But more importantly, fictional films reveal something of the dreams, desires, displacements, and, in some cases, the social and political issues confronting American society.

Undeniably, films are a powerful and significant art form. As art historian and critic Erwin Panofsky has suggested, their absence from our lives would probably constitute a "social catastrophe."[2] He wrote: "If all the serious lyric poets, composers, painters and sculptors were forced by law to stop their activities, a rather small fraction of the general public would seriously regret it. If the same thing were to happen with the movies the social consequences would be catastrophic."[3] That sentiment obviously overstates the case, but films shown in theaters, on television and video cassettes are clearly one of the prime forms of entertainment for the general public, and one of the most democratic elements in the cultural fabric.

That films give a great deal of pleasure to a great many people does not necessarily connote that they are a significant form of cultural and historical evidence. But the fact that they reach a mass audience signifies that films do connect with some part of the conscious or unconscious experience of the general public or, at least, a large proportion of it. However, the attempt to define the specific relationship between Hollywood film and popular consciousness is a difficult one. One problem is that the writers and directors of films—be they assembly line products like *Risky Business* (1983) or works expressing a complex individual sensibility like Martin Scorsese's *Taxi Driver* (1976)—have no mystical access to the zeitgeist. There are no straight, clear lines to be drawn between the film industry and the popular mind—neither is it a mirror of public feelings and habits, nor can one make the vulgar, mechanistic connection which implies that the industry is some evil empire conspiratorially shaping the social values and political opinions of a supine public. Though there is no question that Hollywood's genius for manufacturing and publicizing seductive images like John Wayne's World War II heroes—icons who had a profound effect on the lives of countless young Vietnam enlistees—should not be minimized. The images often becoming a substitute for reality for their audiences.

The popular mind itself is no monolith. It is divided by age, social class, gender, region, ethnicity, race, and is often fickle and changeable in its response. In a matter of four or five years, during the late sixties and early seventies, the movie audience shifted away from sympathy toward social outlawry of *Bonnie and Clyde* (1967) to the law and order vigilantism of *Dirty Harry* (1971), and it's doubtful that shift corresponded with some radical transformation of popular feeling. Still, it's possible that during that period both responses towards crime coexisted in American society, and the films tapped different audiences. It is also hard to be certain why a film achieves popular success. For example, was the success of *Rambo* based on its political significance—its voicing populist, patriotic, and anti-communist sentiments; or because of Stallone's muscle-headed charisma and the film's nonstop action and violence? The answer is that it is probably a combination of all these elements which helped garner a large audience for the film; and it's truly difficult to distinguish which aspects of the film were the basis of its audience appeal.

All one can say with certainty is that American directors, like Altman or Coppola, most of whose films express powerful personal visions and styles, share some of the same dreams and cultural tensions and influences other Americans do. Consequently, films like *Nashville* (1975) and *Godfather I* and *II* (1972 and 1974) cannot help but convey some of the cultural and social strains the directors hold in common with their audience. And for the rest of Hollywood's output—films which are much less personal in nature—the movie industry spends a great deal of time and money trying to divine popular values and trends, often succeeding in attracting an audience by knowing just how to package those concerns. For example, some of the biggest commercial hits of the summer of 1989 were films like *Field of Dreams* which constructed a mythic American past by nostalgically conjuring up the Chicago Black Sox of 1919 playing on a pristine and bucolic baseball diamond, and the well-crafted sitcom *Parenthood* which views the family as the foundation of American life and consecrates the act of having babies as if family planning never existed. Both of these films lure audiences by shutting out much of the larger social world, and being awash with nostalgia for an earlier America. Clearly film images rarely determine our values, but they are both suggestive signs of and reinforcers of popular feelings.

During the last twenty years a number of historians and culture critics have begun to give films their due as important social and cultural evidence. Among the noteworthy ones are *History/American Film* ed. Jackson and O'Connor, *Movie Made America* by Robert Sklar, *We're in the Money* by Andrew Bergman, *Film: The Democratic Art* by Garth Jowett, *America in the Movies* by Michael Wood, *From Reverence to Rape* by Molly Haskell, *A Certain Tendency of the Hollywood Cinema, 1930–1980* by Robert B. Ray, and *Camera Politica* by Michael Ryan and Douglas Kellner. In fact, the pendulum may have swung so far that for a number of historians films have come to be one of the most important clues to understanding the state of the American mind. As Arthur Schlesinger Jr. has said, albeit in an inflated manner:

Strike the American contribution from drama, painting, music, sculpture and even dance, and possibly poetry and the novel and the world's achievement is only marginally diminished. But the film without American contribution is unimaginable. The fact that film has been the most potent vehicle for the American imagination suggests all the more strongly that movies have something to tell us not just about the surfaces but the mysteries of American life.[4]

Of course, stating this is much easier than defining precisely how we can penetrate those surfaces and reveal those mysteries. Obviously, the political and social significance of explicitly political films ranging from Polansky's Marxist film noir Force of Evil (1948) to Kubrick's sardonic and apocalyptic Dr. Strangelove (1964) to Oliver Stone's mixture of social realism and Manichean melodrama in Platoon (1986) can easily be gleaned. Though, again the relation of the political and social perspectives of even these films to the public's social and cultural beliefs is never a seamless one.

All films, however, can be considered political—for films as varied as On the Town (1949) and Batman (1989) convey a point of view, an implicit ideological perspective, on the nature of American reality. Of course, it is more difficult to discover cultural and social meaning in ostensibly apolitical films like Curtiz's Mildred Pierce (1945) and Spielberg's E.T. (1982). These two works, like the great majority of American films, rarely attempt to consciously illuminate cultural and social patterns. They usually stylize, mythologize, and at times trivialize the social world—primarily aiming to provide glamor, escape, thrills, or a sense of emotional security to a mass audience. That these films, both the explicitly political and the nonpolitical, were and are often bound by institutional forces like the power of the studios or producers to make final cuts, genre conventions, collective screenwriting and rewriting, censorship, and the star system, provides one more difficulty in gleaning the social and cultural perspective of the films. (The film's original intent being blurred by the number of people and industry controls that go into shaping the final product—inadvertently creating conflicted texts in some films.) Given all these variables, the effort to explore the link between these films and the basic premises, values and problems of American society must be by its very nature tentative and touched with ambiguity. There are no absolutes or certainties that underlie this relationship, and there are few films whose social meaning is not open to contesting and contradictory interpretations.

In the act, however, of either displacing or stylizing social reality Hollywood was able to create vital and reverberating images, characters, and dialogue that granted a great deal of insight into the culture. It succeeded in helping to shape the consciousness of its audience by creating mythic landscapes and urbanscapes—the transcendental West of John Ford's Monument Valley, and the magical, neon-lit Broadway of countless musicals—and archetypal figures like the gangster, private eye, and femme fatale. The link between Hollywood and its audience, as stated previously, is a reciprocal one. Frank Capra's humane, harmonious small towns and the New York apartments and night clubs of thirties' screwball comedies like *Holiday* (1938) and *The Awful Truth* (1937) were distinctive Hollywood creations that had resonance for audiences because they reinforced public fantasies and feelings.

The nature of cinematic archetypes and landscapes have changed through the years, but most Hollywood films still follow a set of narrative and stylistic conventions. (Though in the last two decades a number of major directors have played with and veered from them.) The classic Hollywood film was committed to a linear narrative, temporal and spatial coherence and closure, usually centering around a protagonist the audience could emotionally identify with, and through whose actions the narrative would be resolved. Implicitly this narrative tradition, with its emphasis on the patterned and predictable usually reinforced the social status quo. The films were also built around either individual heroism or at least the centrality of the individual—a value that Hollywood has embraced since its beginnings. In fact, most American political films from *Home of the Brave* (1949) to *Platoon* of the eighties define political events in terms of an individual's fate and consciousness. The ideological and institutional context of Vietnam, for example, is left untouched by *Platoon*, the war being basically conceived as a murderous rite of passage and existential drama that one individual soldier goes through.

Hollywood films have also been firm believers in the American success ethic, almost never questioning the viability and virtue of our social and economic system. As a result, films have usually promoted the notion, in a wide variety of genres, that most white males have the ability and opportunity to succeed in America. In recent years, in films like *Working Girl* (1988), some women have been added to the host of Hollywood characters who easily overcome the obstacles of class, ethnicity, gender, even race (at least for a star like Eddie Murphy), and are able to achieve the American Dream.

Socially subversive and anarchic elements obviously exist in popular American films—like the psychopathic gangster and the detective who breaks all the institutional rules. However, despite their deviant behavior, characters like Cagney's psycho gangster in *White Heat* (1949) or Eastwood's vigilante cop, Harry Callaghan, in *Dirty Harry* don't ultimately disrupt the social status quo. Still, despite the fact that classical Hollywood has usually restored the traditional order of things at the film's conclusion, a great many of its films contain camera set ups, snatches of dialogue, elements in the mise-en-scène, and performances that counter the thrust of the narrative and call the conventional world and its values into question. Even amid the familial sweetness of a film like *Meet Me in St. Louis* (1944) there are dark and uneasy images that, for a moment, subvert the film's serene vision.

Hollywood, however, has made films which break ideologically from the status quo. In the thirties King Vidor's low budget *Our Daily Bread* (1934) envisioned a collective farm, where unemployed people would work communally, as an alternative to the harshness of depression poverty and capitalism. But American films that proffer alternative political and social visions are very rare. Films, however, that see the world as dark and murderous—without political or social alternatives—and provide no concluding image of hope or reconciliation are far more common. However, for every film like Stanley Kubrick's *Full Metal Jacket* (1987), a black comic, profoundly pessimistic and genuinely critical vision of the American military and the human condition, there are innumerable *To Live and Die in L.A.*'s (1985) with their pop nihilism and gratuitous violence—conventional films which seemingly have merely inverted the classical Hollywood idea of closure and made the bleak, bloody climax their parallel to the happy ending.

Nevertheless, American films can be clearly politically radical and liberal or conservative, nihilistic, ambiguous, confused, and conflicted ideologically, and the analysis of the relationship between them and the society still remains problematic. For example, can one really link *E.T.*'s affirmation of innocence and distrust of adult authority to the nostalgia-drenched, anti-big-government pieties of the early Reagan years? And what does the audience really perceive that film's ideological intent or more importantly, a film like Spike Lee's *Do the Right Thing*'s (1989) to be? However, despite our wariness about coming up with facile generalizations about the connection between film and society, it is as important to explore that relationship as to study the nature of directorial sensibility and style, the range of Hollywood genres, star biographies, and the history of the studios—not that any of these elements are mutually exclusive.

Clearly, any cultural and social analysis of Hollywood films would have to take into account a variety of theoretical and critical approaches. The auteurist critics' origins go back to French critics-cum-directors like Truffaut, Godard, Rivette, and Chabrol who wrote for *Cahiers du Cinéma* about neglected commercial directors—mostly American—who needed to be explored in depth. They promoted the notion that the basic starting point of film is the personal sensibility, style, and especially the motifs of the director, which give him a "signature"—a coherent world view. And that the best films are those that most clearly bear the "signature" of their creator.

Though more interested in defending, even glorifying, the aesthetic value of the Hollywood studio films than in exploring their social and political meaning, American auteur critics like Andrew Sarris (writing in *Film Culture* and *The Village Voice*), who took their lead from the French, did chart how John Ford's vision of family and community had remained constant through such diverse films as *The Grapes of Wrath* (1940), *They Were Expendable* (1945), and *She Wore a Yellow Ribbon* (1949). Auteur critics were, however, in their unsystematic, polemical (in their homages to individual auteurs they overrated their mediocre work, and almost never mentioned how powerful a role the studios played in producing these films),[5] sometimes defensive manner, primarily interested in demonstrating how a film's visual style was redolent with meaning. They loved to demonstrate just how the mise-en-scène of a Budd Boetticher B western had much greater aesthetic and even intellectual value than the liberal pieties pervading a Stanley Kramer or Richards Brooks social-problem film. As a result, they were able to redeem and sometimes create the critical reputations of directors such as Howard Hawks, Nicholas Ray, Douglas Sirk, and other less deserving figures.

In doing that, the auteur critics granted added luster and cultural importance to commercial Hollywood genres like the western, thriller, screwball comedy, and the woman's picture. These genres themselves were subject to a body of criticism which explored their themes, structures, and iconography. Genre criticism often traced the shifts in the form's conventions and themes (for example, the changes in the western from Tom Mix through John Ford to Sam Peckinpah) or examined the relationship of the genre to its audience. Most genre critics were more interested in analyzing the films as self-contained forms, dissecting the iconography of the musical rather than evoking its cultural and social significance. However, there were critics such as Robert Warshow and Leo Braudy who sought to analyze the link between a genre's popularity and the attitudes and needs that audiences bring to it. For example, Warshow's essay on the gangster film asserting that the vicious, avaricious behavior of the protagonist in films like *Little Caesar* (1930) appealed to the part of the American psyche that rejects official American culture.[6]

There have also been film critics who have directly sought to unravel, by using a psychoanalytic interpretation, the hidden social and psychological meanings of a film. A theorist like Siegfried Kracauer believed that films are never merely the product of an individual artist, but a collaborative expression of mass feelings.[7] For instance, his landmark work, *From Caligari to Hitler*, although marred by too heady a faith in German films' ability to reveal the secrets of the collective mind as well as to predict the rise of Nazism, still yields interesting insight into film as a means of illuminating the "deepest psychological dispositions"[8] of a society. This, coupled with the Freudian notion that films, like dreams, have a latent and manifest content, has proved of some value in wringing social meaning from even the most escapist of films.

Nonetheless, these perceptions are weakened by the fact that they make the meaning of a film dependent on some kind of unconscious activity. It is impossible to demonstrate how the Jungian "collective unconscious" (even if we accept its existence) or the latent content of Freudianism manifests itself in the narrative and imagery of the film. A critic must maintain an almost mystical faith that it does, or more commonly see it as mere speculation and feel it unnecessary to prove its existence. But in writing about notions such as the mass unconscious, there is a tendency to graft elaborate meanings onto the most commonplace of films. As a result, the work of art becomes something secondary, even insignificant; what becomes all-important is the analysis and interpretation, or else, as in the words of Paddy Whannel and Stuart Hall, art—in this case film—becomes merely "sugar on the pill."[9]

In recent years a number of theoretical approaches to film, like structuralism and semiology, have held that film is "a system of conventions and codes, a set of structures dictating and circumscribing the ultimate possibilities of any individual film."[10] According to these theoretical perspectives, it is the underlying cultural patterns, not the individual artist, that create meaning in a film. The emphasis in semiology is on sign systems and in structuralism is on broader organizing principles (e.g., the antimony between civilization and the wilderness that runs through the western film)—rather than the individual artist's vision or the work's aesthetic value or its virtues and weaknesses. As a result, the distinction between high art and popular art, and art and artifact, becomes of little or no interest to the critic—all being equally open to structural and semiological analysis.

In the wake of structuralism and semiotics, there has been a stream of diverse theoretical developments that are usually placed under the rubric of deconstruction. Influenced by the writings of Foucault, Lacan, and especially Jacques Derrida, "the most far-reaching consequence of a deconstructive perspective on film concerns the act of interpretation."[11] According to film theorist Peter Brunette: "Ultimately deconstruction shows that it is, strictly speaking, impossible to specify what a 'valid' interpretation would look like. In this sense, it might be said that deconstruction's most important work has been the investigation of the institutions that allow or restrict reading, or meaning-making of any sort."[12]

What deconstructionists questioned were all claims to universal truth—seeing them "as self-serving deceptions perpetrated by wielders of power."[13] And most deconstructionists repudiated the idea that a work of art conveys "meaning, beauty, and authorship"[14]—sometimes ending with an extreme skeptical perspective where any critical interpretation could be seen as equally valid.

Though our book does not embrace semiological, structuralist, and deconstructionist theoretical perspectives, we are aware that they have at times given us new ways of seeing the underlying cultural codes inherent in film. For example, the idea of the camera's gaze, in classic Hollywood films, as a male one—that sees women as objects of voyeuristic pleasure (modified since then by its author, Laura Mulvey)—alters one's way of thinking about familiar films. If, on one hand, modernist and post-modernist theories lead to fresh insights into the role culture plays in shaping films, on the other hand, it remains abstracted from the particularity of the individual film and its historical context. In their attempt to get the respect of the hard sciences, the post-modernist theorists have constructed a specialized and obfuscating vocabulary of their own (e.g., words like "valorizing" and "multivalent"). Also, in their contempt for subjectivity (despite their deriding any claims to objective knowledge), the contemporary theorists often tend to be removed from the concrete act of viewing a film—an emotional experience which makes one see how often the complex texture of a film undermines those structures and theories that have become the lifeblood and ultimate trap of academic film study.

In writing this book, however, we have been influenced by genre, auteur, feminist, psychoanalytic, Marxist, structuralist, multicultural, post-structuralist and other critical perspectives, but not wedded to any singular critical system. Our aim is to depict and evaluate, both politically and aesthetically, the way American films convey their social and cultural values and commitments. Given our belief in film's historical and social significance, it is the particular purpose of this study to look at American films from 1945 to the present and analyze how they perceived and cor ured up the American social and cultural landscape. In addition, we have included a brief rendering of some of the major political events and social and cultural trends that dominated a decade and left a mark on its films.

To accomplish this our method is simple. For one, since American screens and a large percentage of foreign ones are dominated by Hollywood films, we have treated Hollywood and American film as being synonymous. And for the purpose of this study we have left out avant-garde and most documentary films. We are also aware of the hazards of adopting a decade-by-decade approach, for clearly the culture and politics of the sixties did not end on December 31, 1969—and the Cold War and the anticommunist crusade were not limited to one decade. The general tone, concerns, and values of one decade often overlap with the following one. Despite the somewhat arbitrary nature of our book's structure, it has the advantage of convenience and popular acceptance—references to decades like the fifties and sixties continue to denote a particular set of social and cultural norms and patterns.

One serious difficulty in writing the book was making a selection of films that best illuminated these trends. In order to accomplish this we have relied in the main on a large body of films that could be called "public classics"[15]—films whose box office grosses, awards, and critical reputation (which have either stood the test of time or grown with it) indicate by their broad acceptance that these films have a connection with the popular consciousness. Undoubtedly, there are many other films that might point in different directions, deal with the themes we have analyzed in a clearer, sharper manner, or were perhaps visionary in their ability to herald future trends and themes. Nevertheless, it does seem to us that some degree of consensus exists about the importance of specific films and their relation to the society of their times—for example, films like *The Best Years of Our Lives* and the forties, *Rebel Without a Cause* and the fifties, *Bonnie and Clyde* and *Easy Rider* and the sixties, *Nashville* and the seventies, *Do the Right Thing* and the eighties, and *Philadelphia* and the nineties. We have included in our study a number of films of this type. Also, since this book was intended as both an introduction and a guide to American film and culture for students, we have tried to include films that are accessible to them through video rental services and stores and available archives, although this was by no means the decisive factor in our choices.

Finally, as far as the theme of this study goes, it is important to return for a moment to *Let There Be Light*. When that film is placed alongside some films of the seventies dealing with similar problems and themes, like *The Deer Hunter* and *Coming Home* (1978), and a documentary like *Hearts and Minds* (1974), one cannot help but see what a different portrait the seventies' films provide of American life and how that image has radically changed over time. In *Let There Be Light*, for example, the officer informs (without irony) the just-discharged patients that: "On your shoulders falls much of the responsibility for the post-war world." It is the sort of uplifting sentiment that traumatized Vietnam war veterans, like Nicky (*The Deer Hunter*) and Bob (*Coming Home*), would greet with the stony stare of suicidal despair. Throughout the book we have attempted to show how American films moved from the relatively self-confident affirmation of the American Dream in the late forties (Hollywood at its zenith) to the films of the sixties and seventies, and even the politically retrograde and nostalgic Reagan eighties, where despite the continued emphasis on big budgets, stars, and genre formulae the films in general grew increasingly more anxious, alienated, and nihilistic. (One trend that makes one feel hopeful is that, by the end of the nineties, despite all the high concept, big budget films like *Independence Day* and the *Mission Impossibles*, there seemed to be a great deal more room in theaters for low budget and idiosyncratic films.) In constructing this pattern we have tried to avoid subsuming the contested meanings of individual films and the often contradictory history of cinematic cultural trends under reductive and rigid sociological categories. We have been conscious of the feelings of doubt and loss that began to appear beneath the buoyant surface of forties' films, and the preservation of American Dream imagery in the darker, more pessimistic work of the sixties, seventies, eighties, and nineties.

Ultimately, what we have written is only one more step in the ongoing and complex study of the multiple and diverse interactions of culture and society, and more specifically, film and society. We have not conceived this book as a definitive work, but as one among a number of possible ways, which help illuminate the nature of American society and culture. The book is based on the anachronistic idea that a passion for and a personal commitment to the imaginative life of films can be an integral part of the critical process, and the critique can be conveyed in a language that any intelligent person who cares about film can understand. It is best summed up in the humanist perspective of Raymond Williams, which holds that art is a means to "learn, describe, to understand, to educate"[16]—a way of heightening one's perception of self, others, the larger world, and the human condition itself. To that list we would add that the capacity of film to grant aesthetic pleasure in the contemplation of camera movement, composition, color and other formal elements is as significant as any other end. We finally believe, as did James Agee on writing his first film review in *The Nation*, that the final function of any review or critical study is to aid those "who watch any given screen, where the proof is caught irrelevant to excuse, and available in proportion to the eye which sees it, and the mind which uses it."[17]

NOTES

1. Andrew Sarris, "Hobgoblins of Reality," *The Village Voice* (January 21–27, 1981), p. 45.

2. Erwin Panovsky, "Style and Medium in the Motion Pictures," in G. Mast and M. Cohen (eds.), *Film Theory and Criticism* (New York: Oxford University Press, 1974), p. 152.

3. Ibid.

4. John E. O'Connor and Martin A. Jackson (eds), *American History/American Film: Interpreting the Hollywood Image* (New York: Frederick Ungar, 1979), p. x.

5. Thomas Schatz, *The Genius of the System: Hollywood Filmmaking in the Studio Era* (New York: Pantheon, 1988), pp. 3–12.

6. Robert Warshow, *The Immediate Experience* (Garden City, NY: Anchor, 1964).

7. Tim Bywater and Thomas Sobchack, *Film Criticism: Major Critical Approaches to Narrative Film* (White Plains, NY: Longman, 1989), p. 121.

8. Siegfried Kracauer, *From Caligari to Hitler: A Psychological History of the German Film*, 3rd ed. (Princeton, NJ: Princeton University Press, 1970), p. 6.

9. Stuart Hall and Paddy Whannel, *The Popular Arts* (New York: Pantheon, 1965), p. 28.

10. Bywater and Sobchack, *Film Criticism*, p. 175.

11. Peter Brunette, "Post-Structuralism and Deconstruction," *Film Studies: Critical Approaches* (Oxford: Oxford University Press, 2000), p. 92.

12. Ibid., pp. 92–93.

13. Andrew Delbanco, "The Decline and Fall of Literature," *The New York Review of Books* (November 4, 1999), p. 36.

14. Ibid., p. 36.

15. Michael Wood, *America in the Movies: or, "Santa Maria, It Had Slipped My Mind!"* (New York: Basic Books, 1975), p. 11.

16. Raymond Williams, *Communications*, 3rd ed. (London: Pelican, 1976), p. 11.

17. James Agee, *Agee on Film: Reviews and Comments* (Boston: Beacon Press, 1966), p. 23.

2

THE FORTIES

In 1936 President Franklin D. Roosevelt announced that Americans had a "rendezvous with destiny." The war years turned that prophecy into a reality as America emerged from its traditional isolationism and became an imperialist, interventionist nation—the most powerful nation in the world. The political energy that had once gone into the struggle against the Depression was now concentrated on the war effort. And that undertaking granted to many people on the home-front a sense of purpose, exhilaration and community that was rare in American history.[1]

The same energy and optimism that helped bring about victory carried over into the postwar years. However, this optimism had more to do with people's material well-being (in the 1940s the average American enjoyed an income fifteen times greater than the average foreigner)[2] and national pride than with any new political and social commitments. In fact, most Americans had become weary of the long years of economic depression and foreign wars and, in general, bored with politics. Constricted by the enforced savings of the Second World War, Americans wanted to enjoy their new-found prosperity and victory. A new era seemed about to open, offering ordinary Americans not only increased income, but a chance for education and greater social and economic status.

One of the driving forces behind this new mood was the GI Bill of Rights which became law in 1944, helping returning veterans to borrow money to set up businesses and attend universities which they had once viewed as preserves of the upper middle class. In addition, a baby boom gave evidence that Americans felt freed from the social anguish of the past decade and a half, and had begun to feel that the future held infinite promise.[3]

Another key factor in this changing climate was the accession to the presidency, upon the death of FDR in 1945, of Vice President Harry S. Truman, who was a moderate, Democratic party organization stalwart from Missouri. At first, Truman's presidency suffered by comparison with the charismatic Roosevelt. In addition, he was beset by a resurgent conservative congressional coalition of Southern Democrats (Dixiecrats) and Republicans, who frustrated his attempts to extend the New Deal, and forced him to watch helplessly as they overrode his veto of the anti-labor Taft-Hartley bill in 1947. However, even when he came into his own, after a startling come-from-behind victory in the presidential campaign of 1948, he merely introduced a Fair Deal program that was only a pale copy and codification of the New Deal. Thus, despite his political triumph, the Truman era was dominated by the profits and developing prestige and power of the corporations rather than by the forces of social reform.[4]

Nevertheless, although feelings of both material abundance and the irrelevance of social conflict were prime cultural themes of the forties, there were darker signs. A crippling strike wave, culminating in a coal strike led by FDR's nemesis John L. Lewis, served notice that labor was no longer willing to continue its rather unequal collaboration with business and wanted a larger share of the wealth generated by the war. The labor insurgency coupled with high inflation caused ripples of anxiety in the economy. Equally significant, though largely beneath the surface, were a pair of major demographic changes. One was the great migration of poor blacks to the North to work in defense plants during World War II where they exchanged the certainties and oppression of Southern rural life for the anxieties and higher wages of the Northern cities. Paralleling this black migration was the movement of whites (aided by low-interest Federal Housing Administration and Veterans' Administration loans) to the suburbs. Hand in hand, the twin migrations would alter the entire social fabric of America.[5]

However severe these labor problems and demographic changes were, they were merely minor irritants compared to the turmoil caused by foreign affairs. Long used to neglecting foreign relationships, the Americans were thrust by the war into a leading international position. It also moved the United States into an alliance with the Soviet Union—a nation considered in some prewar American circles as a greater menace than Germany, Italy, or Japan. Nonetheless, most Americans were little disturbed by the wartime alliance with the Soviet Union. In fact, many liberals saw that alliance (with the Soviet Union as the junior partner) as the basis of an enduring peace where postwar social reforms would become the prime commitment of both nations. Yet among conservatives there were always undercurrents of suspicion of the Soviet Union and the U.S.-Soviet Alliance. And when Stalin, in quest of greater security, broke the 1945 Yalta agreements, conservative unease and anger toward the Soviet Union increased, a wariness which many liberals soon began to share.[6]

During the next few years, despite the dream of a new international order embodied in the United Nations, the Cold War (as it came to be known) escalated and relations between the United States and the Soviet Union were permeated with fear, suspicion, and distrust. As a result, the two ideologically expansionist powers, their wartime co-operation seemingly forgotten, confronted each other with neither side genuinely seeking peace or rapprochement. On their side the Americans continually evoked images of an "iron curtain" and the threat of Soviet expansion, while the Russians talked of "American imperialism" and the constant threat to their borders and security.[7]

The conflict was not solely confined to rhetoric. In 1947, breaking with a long-standing American tradition against peacetime military and political alliances, President Truman gained congressional approval for $400 million in military and economic aid to Greece and Turkey to help them in their struggle against communist guerrillas. This action, soon to be dubbed the Truman Doctrine, had broader implications—including the seeds for later American interventions—for in the words of Truman, America was now committed "to support free people who are resisting attempted subjugation by armed minorities or by outside pressure."[8]

The crisis between the two former allies deepened as a Soviet-sponsored coup in Czechoslovakia in 1948 eliminated the last vestiges of democracy in eastern and central Europe, and the Marshall Plan and the North Atlantic Treaty Organization established an American-backed cordon sanitaire in western Europe. The cordon sanitaire was worked out by diplomat-scholar George F. Kennan and his State Department policy planning group and given political sponsorship by Secretary of State George C. Marshall, reasoning that an anti-communist foreign policy was not enough to impede the spread of communism in Europe. They believed that it was only with the recovery of the European economy (one that would also provide markets for the United States) that the Soviet threat could be thwarted. Indeed with the passage of the Marshall Plan in 1948 western Europe took a giant step toward economic recovery and enhanced its capacity to resist communism.[9]

However, even with western Europe stabilized by 1949, American anxieties about communism hardly lessened. The fear of communist aggression from abroad was soon replaced by terror over a native communist fifth column whose task was seemingly to ferret out military secrets as they subverted America's will to resist. These feelings were reinforced by a successsion of spy ring revelations—Igor Gouzenko, Judith Coplon, Elizabeth Bentley, and Whittaker Chambers. The explosion of a Soviet A-bomb coupled with the fall of mainland China to the communists transformed these fears into a full-fledged anti-communist hysteria. Angered by their sense of a growing visible and invisible communist menace and becoming anxious over their own survival, Americans sought facile explanations for what they saw as an imminent threat. Rather than confront the long-term economic and social causes that produced both wars of "national liberation" and communist takeovers (at the time they were neatly equated) Americans found the reasons for the success of the left in a supposed international communist conspiracy.[10]

In the vanguard of this search for traitors was the House Un-American Activities Committee (HUAC). Dormant during the war years, the committee saw its chance to regain the limelight in 1947 when it held hearings investigating communist influence in the motion picture industry. Drawn by the prestige and glamor of the film industry, the committee was more interested in the political affiliations of its ten "unfriendly" witnesses—some of whom were the most talented and politically active writers and directors in Hollywood (for example Dalton Trumbo, Albert Maltz, Ring Lardner Jr.)—than in the supposedly subversive content of their films.[11]

At first the moguls and liberals in the industry protested about the committee's actions, but seeing the witnesses take the first amendment regarding their politics they quickly succumbed to expediency, fearing their profits and careers might be threatened. In a meeting at the Waldorf-Astoria Hotel soon after the "ten" appeared before the committee the moguls issued their craven Waldorf Statement which was in essence a tacit agreement to establish a blacklist refusing to either re-employ the "Hollywood Ten" or other members of the Communist Party.[12]

Of course the HUAC investigations of Hollywood were just one element of the growing fear of and attack on the presumed communist conspiracy. In 1949 the leaders of the U.S. Communist Party were convicted under the Smith Act for conspiracy and sent to prison. More significantly, the deeply symbolic Hiss-Chambers affair, which saw the former high level New Deal bureaucrat Alger Hiss accused of espionage and convicted of perjury, brought the New Deal under attack for being soft on communism. The forties concluded with a portion of the American public, dominated by mid-Westerners, recent immigrants, and Catholics, holding that New Deal liberalism and communism were one and the same thing.[13]

Nevertheless, despite the growing fear of the "red menace," the forties were still essentially a time of optimism and consensus, and nowhere was this more evident than in American film. For although they had a dark side touched with pessimism and self-doubt, the movies basically endorsed and reflected a feeling of national triumph. Moreover, for the industry itself the postwar era was a bloom time. From 1942–44 Hollywood produced about 440 films a year, and 1946 was the most commercially successful year in its history. The forties were a time of big stars and big audiences where the studios, with their armies of talented technicians and performers, reigned supreme. The last years of the decade did see Hollywood beset by labor troubles, adverse Supreme Court decisions (the Paramount case), and the after-effects of the HUAC hearings—leading to the blacklisting of a large number of major creative contributors to the industry. But the forties were still "the last great show of confidence and skill" by Hollywood before it became paralyzed by competition from television and the death of the studio system.[14]

Nowhere was this optimism more evident than in the war films that the studios churned out through the war years. The overriding purpose of these films was patriotic uplift, and despite the fact that an occasional hero lapsed into *Casablanca* (1942)-like cynicism or malaise, they were all eventually aroused to a commitment to the collective struggle against fascism. With Hollywood helping to shoulder the wartime burden of maintaining morale, there were few films that dealt with the reality rather than the romance of combat, or with the psychological effects of the war. Those that did, like John Huston's pacifistic documentary, *Battle of San Pietro* (1945), which evoked haunting and harrowing images of the war with great immediacy and intensity, were prevented by the Pentagon from reaching the public. Neither the Pentagon nor Hollywood wanted films which filled the screens with images of exhausted soldiers, cemeteries of dog tags, and terrified peasants. They desired war films which exulted in America by creating mythical—ethnically, regionally, and occupationally heterogeneous—platoons, to personify American democracy.

By the end of the war, however, with victory clearly in sight, self-righteous propagandistic films like *God Is My Co-Pilot* (1943) and *The Purple Heart* (1944) were replaced by more sophisticated and realistic films. Among the first of these was Lewis Milestone's *A Walk in the Sun* (1945) which provides a realistic treatment, through its subtle and moving use of close ups, and light and shadow, of an infantry unit's battle fear and anxiety. The soldiers are fallible human beings, not Hollywood heroes, though the film still contains the usual sentimentalized melting pot of "dogfaces" who engage in tiresome, colloquial banter, and even go in for self-conscious interior monologues. But if *Walk in the Sun* indulges in anti-fascist and pseudo-democratic (Popular Front) clichés and rhetoric about the "mighty Joes" and the people's folksy wisdom and capacity for artistic feeling, its images of long lines of soldiers walking in the darkness are vivid and poignant. And its generally unromantic treatment of a war where men become frightened and die placed it far above the run-of-the-mill-war films with their bloodthirsty and barbaric "Nips" and "Krauts" being put to route by the derring-do of an Errol Flynn or John Wayne.

William Wellman's *The Story of G.I. Joe* (1945) was a much leaner and more solemn film than *A Walk in the Sun*. Based on Ernie Pyle's Pulizer Prize-winning dispatches, this dry, understated, quasi-documentary work avoids almost all the inflated political rhetoric, histrionics, and stereotyping that characterized most other World War II films. The film is constructed, without a driving narrative to propel it, as a series of abruptly terminated scenes that powerfully capture the pathos and tragedy of the war. Wellman's infantrymen are not clean shaven or well fed, and the war takes a palpable toll—all the men are exhausted by the day to day slogging and fighting, a tough sergeant, obsessed with home and his son's voice has a breakdown, and the strong, quietly dignified captain of the platoon, Bill Walker (Robert Mitchum), who is a towering figure, dies. Watching this film James Agee was sufficiently moved to compare it, especially its final, sombre, dark moments, to a Whitmanesque war poem.[15]

In a far different mode was John Ford's romantic and leisurely *They Were Expendable* (1945). Ford's film displayed little interest in the psychology or sociology of his PT boat officers and crew, but was deeply committed to paying homage to a community of men who were portrayed as gallant and heroic in defeat. The film was filled with epic long shots of almost painterly sea battles, and of the men's ritualistic arrivals from and departures into battle. Ford believed in the virtues of the military, conceiving it as a community built on a hierarchic code of power, self-sacrifice, responsibility, and obligation. The film's officers are viewed as heroes, men free of any fear or anxiety about the war, best illustrated by the impetuous, tough Captain Rusty Ryan (John Wayne) who is unwilling to allow mere wounds to prevent him from going into battle. They also understand that leadership demands that they subordinate individual desires for the good of the squadron—to become "team players."

Ford's film was a celebration, not a critical portrait of the American war effort. *They Were Expendable* is filled with patriotic and elegaic sentiments—a soundtrack playing "The Battle Hymn of the Republic" and "Red River Valley," an affecting montage of wounded men—one of them who is blind, smoking a cigarette with trembling hands—and a melancholy full shot of exhausted, courageous nurses seen in silhouette walking through a hospital corridor. Consequently, it should come as no surprise, from such a paean to the military that the film's apotheosis is the appearance of an actor embodying Ford's personal deity, General MacArthur, accompanied by a series of reaction shots of sailors with glowing faces standing in awe of this American icon.

In the hands of another director without the pictorial or narrative gifts of Ford these rituals and stereotypes might have become mere historical tableaux. However, Ford's treatment of military rituals and codes is so profoundly felt, and his images so grand and stately that the conventional and sentimental emotions and characters are transformed into archetypes, and the clichés into myths.

No less important in raising morale and maintaining commitment to the war effort than some of the flag-waving combat films were the home-front melodramas. In fact, a film such as David O. Selznick's *Since You Went Away* (1944) actually opened with the announcement: "This is the story of an unconquerable fortress, the American home, 1943." What followed was Hollywood's sanitized version of American women's commitment to the war effort. The plot has a typical suburban housewife, played by a miscast Claudette

Colbert, leaving her comfortable home for a job in a welding factory. There she becomes a mentor in Americanization for the immigrant women who work beside her, who see her as the embodiment of the American dream. It's not only the immigrant women who view her in this manner, for the film itself idealizes Colbert's family and friends, portraying their world as clean, unruffled and innocent. The dream is made complete by a black mammy cook (Hattie McDaniel) who, though the family can no longer afford her, returns each night after a full day's work to provide free housework, comic relief, and consolation. It's an image of racial unity that provides a fitting capstone to this relentless celebration of home-front USA.

Nevertheless, despite its sacccharine, wish fantasy quality, *Since You Went Away* did touch on one very important home-front reality, the new role for women as workers in defense industries. There were over four million in 1943, with many more working in other industries. Mass circulation magazines reacted to this new development by creating the symbol of "Rosie the Riveter," and Hollywood responded by having its female stars play women who go to work (for example, Lucille Ball as a defense plant worker in *Meet the People*, 1944). Hollywood's casting its stars as workers beautifully encapsulated the fact that everything shot in Hollywood during the years 1942–45, be it combat films such as Walsh's *Objective Burma* (1945), the Tarzan series, or Donald Duck cartoons, reflected or was actively committed to the war effort.

However, as the war came to a close, Hollywood began to turn from making films about the war to those that would help ease the transition from war to peace. Here it was the symbol of the returned veteran who became the embodiment of those issues. As a matter of fact, as Dr. Franklin Fearing wrote in the first issue of the *Hollywood Quarterly* (predecessor of the present *Film Quarterly*):

"When Johnny Comes Marching Home" is not only the title of a popular Civil War song, it is a symbol and a situation. It is a symbol with curiously ambivalent meanings, it signifies the return of heroes, or wars ended, of happy reunions after hardwon but glorious victories, and of peace after battle. It is also a sign of dissension, of nervous uncertainty lest, in truth, we have not prepared a 'land fit for heroes,' of anxiety regarding possible capacity to adjust and even curiously of fear and hostility. The laughter and tears which welcome Johnny home reflect honest joy and relief, but there is an undertone of nervous tension. Has he changed? How much have I changed? Can we get along together? What is ahead?[16]

It was this type of anxiety that a film such as *Pride of the Marines* (1945) was intended to assuage. The film itself was taken from the real life experiences of marine hero Al Schmid (John Garfield), who was blinded at Guadalcanal. After detailing Al's early life and his being wounded, the film presents his subsequent withdrawal into a shell of rage and resentment. In the hospital ward other veterans with problems like Al's overcome them by believing that the country will take care of them with the GI Bill, or that just standing up for your rights will get you heard. Al however, remains unconvinced that there is a place for him in civilian society, and it's made clear that it's his personal problem, not America's. With the issue defined in psychological terms and society absolved, the conventional Hollywood solution is easily achieved. His fiancée confronts his self-pity and tells Al she needs him, predictably his neurosis (as does our concern about the fate of the returned veteran) then quickly dissolves.

The same theme of postwar adjustment was taken up by *Till the End of Time* (1946) where the crippled veteran has no girlfriend, but a mother and a friendly army officer who rouse him from his anger and withdrawal to enter the world again. These films paled by comparison with Samuel Goldwyn and William Wyler's *The Best Years of Our Lives* (1946) which dealt with the return home of three World War II veterans from different social backgrounds, and the psychological, economic, and physical problems of readjustment they confronted.

The Best Years of Our Lives swept the Academy Awards, was the top box office attraction of 1947, and garnered great critical praise. James Agee, for one, wrote that it was "one of the very few American studio made movies in years that seem to me profoundly pleasing, moving and encouraging."[17] The Marxist, and soon to be blacklisted writer-director Abraham Polonsky, wrote that "the era of human character which *The Best Years* makes available to its audience is a landmark in the fog of escapism, meretricious violence and the gimmick plot attitude of the usual movie."[18]

Praise like this catapulted the film into the realm of an instant masterpiece. And though that judgment was probably inflated, for the film tended to take few intellectual risks and be somewhat sentimental, *The Best Years* still contained more truth and insight about the readjustment of veterans to peacetime than any other forties' film. Moreover, its subtle and eloquent use of deep focus, flowing camera movements, and moving reaction shots that caught the emotional nuances of the characters' behavior, made it an unself-consciously beautiful and lyrical film as well.

The Best Years was an intelligent, humane, deeply felt attempt to deal with the problem of the readjustment of veterans in postwar American society. At the same time, it was a stately, carefully balanced, and shrewdly manipulated tribute to the American way of life. It paid homage to American institutions like the small town (the camera lovingly providing a montage of American icons like hot dog stands, ball parks, and Woolworth's), the family, and to Hollywood's own belief in the redemptive power of love. And the film tended to obfuscate social issues—dismissing class as a factor in American life by constructing a world where the comradeship of veterans, who run the gamut from bank officers to soda jerks, could unself-consciously carry over into civilian life. It also personalized social problems such as the difficulties that GI's without capital had when they wanted to own a business or some land. Of course, the answer the film offers is not built on any institutional or structural reform. In the Capra tradition (e.g., *American Madness*), it's politically sufficient that the film's liberal banker, Al Stephenson (Frederic March), grant small loans without any collateral to respectable and hard-working veterans. Implicit in that act is the film's belief that the system can be made to work by good-natured, "regular guy" bankers (Al tells a nervous applicant for a loan, "Don't sir me—I'm just a sergeant"), and that in America anybody with enough drive can make it.

In the same fashion as the other veterans films, the family and a woman's love help Al adjust to civilian life. Al comes home to his comfortable apartment and to the warm embrace of an urbane, supportive wife, Millie (Myrna Loy), and two almost grown children who now have lives of their own. However, he feels generally uneasy about his familial role and sexually tense, drinking and bantering compulsively to avoid confronting his feelings of alienation from both family and job. Al's behavior suggests more complex and tortured emotions about job, family, marriage, and self than the film is willing to explore (feelings that can't have all been caused by his war experience). By the film's conclusion, it is all neatly righted, and though Al may still drink too much and have some genuine discontent with the way his life has evolved, the domestic warmth and love of his family will ease his return without too much difficulty.

What is true for Al holds true for both the other veterans, Fred and Homer. Fred Derry (Dana Andrews) returns home a war hero with ribbons, citations, and nightmares from living so close to death. He also comes back without any qualifications for a decent job (the ribbons doing nothing to help him) except for the soda jerk position he had left and feels degraded working at. Fred is sharp, cynical, tough, and filled with middle-class ambitions, but the good jobs don't seem available to him. He also carries the added burden of marriage to a brassy, sexy blonde, who is that particular symbol of anxiety that bedeviled so many GI's—the unfaithful wife. Too narcissistic and independent, Marie (Virginia Mayo) cannot offer Fred any support and only makes him feel worse about himself. However, a good woman's love ultimately suffices to rescue Fred from despair, as Al's pert and sensitive daughter Peggy (Theresa Wright) offers him female understanding and support.

Although Fred's rescue by Peggy and the offer of a job recycling old bombers into pre-fab housing is rather contrived, the subplot provides one of the best reasons why *The Best Years* has been assigned a niche in the pantheon of American films. In one of the film's most formally dazzling and powerful scenes, Fred walks into an airplane graveyard overrun with weeds, which contains rows of bombers that are going to be turned into scrap (a metaphor for the now obsolete Fred), and climbs into one of the cobwebbed planes. Camera movement, sound, and editing then work together to reconstruct the sensation of take-off and flight. There is a close-up of a sweating, feverish Fred, the sound of engines on the sound track, and a nightmarish shot of Fred through the blurred glass of the cockpit. It's a sequence which provides a profound insight into Fred's relationship to a war that gave him both a sense of power, self-esteem, and pain. By reliving the war in this one scene, both Fred and the movie audience get a chance to exorcise the war experience.

The postwar adjustment of the third veteran, the inarticulate, vulnerable Homer (Harold Russell), is sensitively and honestly rendered. The poignancy of his story is heightened by the fact that Homer is played by a real amputee (an example of the care that Wyler took in casting the film), who exudes great naturalness in the role. Homer's problem is not his handicap—he has already achieved a great deal of good-humored self-sufficiency using his hooks, but the unwarrented fear that his passive, loving fiancée, Wilma (Cathy O'Donnell), will be unable to deal with him. Homer does not want to be pitied or treated as a freak; in turn, he rejects Wilma and, as a result, begins to feel isolated and angry. Of course, in the context of the film, all he needs to be happy is to be willing to accept Wilma's love. However, before this foreseeable conclusion is reached, there are tender, understated scenes where Homer's father undresses him and takes off his hooks; and one where Homer sitting somberly in the shadows puts Wilma to the test by removing his hooks and describing how helpless he is: of course, maternal, caring Wilma comes through.

Despite its limitations, *The Best Years*'s emotionally moving scenes, its formal luminosity, and its well-defined characters did provide a genuine glimpse of postwar American life. And though it ultimately allowed each of its characters a graceful, albeit predictable, re-entry into postwar American society, it suggested there were genuinely real and traumatic problems inherent in returning home from the war. There were also hints that underneath the film's essentially optimistic surface there existed some feelings of doubt about America's future. (The film's brief portraits of the civilians who stayed home and prospered during the war are so repellent, one begins to wonder about how benign American society could be, if it was populated by people of this type.)

This anxiety about America was not merely confined to the returned veteran, it also extended to other areas of American life. The traces of it could even be found in the work of that apostle of Hollywood optimism, Frank Capra. In Capra's very first postwar film, *It's a Wonderful Life* (1946), he began to modify his normal optimism and belief in the "little people" with a vision of a nightmare world. Capra's usual mythic, tranquil, small town, Bedford Falls, is destroyed by selfish materialism and turned into a raw, industrial, neon-lit Pottersville (a fantasy possibly inspired by the squalid boom towns that grew up across America in the wake of the wartime industrial explosion). Even his archetypical common man, George Bailey (James Stewart), is beset with feelings of self-doubt and resentment. Nevertheless, Capracorn and the spirit of

Christmas eventually do triumph, the whole cast of characters ultimately singing in unison "Auld Lang Syne," and the significance of each man's life, no matter how ordinary, reaffirmed. In this Capra film the act of affirmation becomes more difficult, and Capra must contrive the deus ex machina of a cute, folksy angel, Clarence (Henry Travers), to bring this film to its benign and joyous conclusion.

It's a Wonderful Life (1946) was Frank Capra's favorite film and probably his most personal.[19] Its hero, George Bailey, is the most individualized and psychologically complex of Capra's heroic everyman. George is decent, intelligent, caring, and doomed to living a life he finds constricting, devoid of adventure or great success. In fact, despite the good he does in town (he builds a subdivision of clean, inexpensive new homes) George sees himself as having no real identity, a failure.

Unlike some of Capra's earlier films, especially his populist trilogy (Mr. Deeds Goes to Town, Mr. Smith Goes to Washington, and Meet John Doe) this film is more meditative, less dependent on montage and more on lengthy close ups of George Bailey isolated within a frame. Previously, Capra had questioned the value of his form of populist political vision in Meet John Doe (1941) and there were moments of anguish in his other films, but in It's a Wonderful Life, the despair becomes more personal and deeply felt. And in the style of forties' films, the doubts expressed deal more with the nature of identity and self than with social or political abuses. As a result, there is no steely-eyed Edward Arnold to play a corrupt political boss or a forbidding fascist tycoon who in the film can ominously threaten Bailey and Capra's ethics and politics. Instead, there is only Mr. Potter (Lionel Barrymore), the "meanest man in town," a solitary, Scrooge-type who owns slum tenements. Potter is a Dickensian cartoon, a small-town tyrant in a wheel chair whose threats cannot really be taken too seriously. George's nightmare, though supposedly brought on by Potter's villainous machinations, comes from inside himself, carrying the sort of intense rage which has him cry out to his cloyingly sweet wife Mary (Donna Reed), "Why do we need all these kids!" George's anger is finally defused, but it takes all of Capra's genius at manipulating an audience to achieve it and a trace of his anguish cannot be fully erased.

What is more, Capra's nightmare sequence, filled with flashing neon lights, gin mills, harsh, pained characters, and a dark shadowy ambiance, contained most of the elements that characterized a whole genre of forties' films. For many of Hollywood's films, especially those dealing with contemporary American life, conveyed, through their somber black and white photography, a tone of claustrophobia and entrapment. Obviously some of this dark, oppressive mood derived from the budgetary limits placed on wartime film-making, where lighting had to be cut down and sets substituted for location shooting. Nevertheless, the eerie menace inherent in the films' look was more than an adjustment to industry economics. It was a conscious choice made by the films' directors, many of them expatriates who had been at Germany's UFA (the largest single pre-World War II European studio) and received basic training in the German Expressionism of the twenties, with its emphasis on the visual evocation of emotional and intellectual states (e.g., *The Cabinet of Dr. Caligari, Nosferatu*). Other significant influences were the murky atmospherics of French prewar poetic realist films (e.g., *Port of Shadows*), the Warner gangster films of the thirties, and a strain of nineteenth-century romanticism.

Some leading figures among these expatriate directors were Billy Wilder (*Double Indemnity*, 1944), Otto Preminger (*Laura*, 1945), Robert Siodmak (*The Killers*, 1945 and *Cry of the City*, 1948) and Fritz Lang (*Scarlet Street*, 1945, and *Woman in the Window*, 1945). They made films which tended to, in stylistic terms, deliberately disquieting editing, low-key lighting, night for night shooting, subjective view shots, voice over and flashback, and oblique camera set-ups. Their films were also characterized by images of rainswept, foggy-night streets, shadowy figures, seedy bars, flickering street lamps, isolated coast roads and rooms dominated by mirrors. Postwar French critics identified the films containing many of these elements as a genre, which they dubbed film noir.[20]

Many of these film noir works constructed worlds where paranoia was the dominant feeling, and almost nobody could be trusted. It was a world where women, often in the central role, were glamorous and dangerous—seductive sirens whose every action was marked by duplicity and aimed at satisfying a desire for wealth and power—while the male protagonists were frequently weak, confused and morally equivocal, susceptible to temptation, and incapable of acting heroically. In turn, the villains were often superficially sympathetic figures whose charm masked malevolence and perversity, and on occasion operated as alter egos or doubles for the films' heroes. Film noir also contained bizarre and seedy minor characters, ritualized violence, sado-masochistic behavior, sexual alienation, and a general sense of the perverse, and when the good triumphed at the film's climax (for the genre was still dominated by Hollywood conventions), its triumph was usually ambiguous.[21]

The film noir style encompassed a wide range of works of varying quality. For example, there were films like Fritz Lang's visually powerful *Woman in the Window* (1944) and *Scarlet Street* (1945) where a lonely, repressed, conflicted male (Edward G. Robinson) is victimized by a beautiful, temptress (Joan Bennett), who is also a victim. Both films were especially striking in their elegant mise-en-scène—more interested in the precise projection of a pessimistic world view through high overhead shots, low-key lighting, and emotionally charged objects than in an evocation of beauty. Lang's cold, nightmarish films envisioned a corrupt world where people are trapped by abstract forces—fate, instincts, society—and nobody really escapes punishment. The films also had a special gift for both imagining sado-masochistic encounters, and creating vicious, insidious villains like those played by Dan Duryea in the two films.

There were also less successful films like Robert Siodmak's *Cry of the City* (1948) which had a pungent, quasi-documentary feeling for low-life locales: perennially wet streets, neon lights reflected in windows, sinister cocktail lounges, and decaying tenements. It also contained some imaginatively constructed noirish set pieces: a gross six-foot masseuse (Hope Emerson) seen both in close-up devouring her breakfast, or through a glass door, in full shot, ominously striding through a house switching on the lights in room after room; a police interview of a group of emigré abortionists, which is enveloped in squalor and pathos; and a meticulously executed escape scene, accompanied by a swelling drumbeat on the soundtrack, as the film's corrupt and charming villain slips right past the police. However, the film turns out to be no more than the sum of its carefully constructed and calculated tensions, a work of strong surface effects and style based on a banal, cliché-ridden script, and dominated by characters devoid of internality or genuine interest.

Much of the same film noir style also dominates Michael Curtiz's *Mildred Pierce* (1945), adapted from a novel by James Cain. *Mildred Pierce* charts the rise, through hard work, of a housewife, Mildred (Joan Crawford), from a waitress to becoming the wealthy owner of a chain of restaurants in southern California. Elements of film noir—stylish low-key lighting, seedy, smoke-filled police stations, pools of shadows, and avaricious, venal characters permeate the film. *Mildred Pierce* could also be seen as a women's picture, romantic films designed to offer women, especially housewives, a cathartic experience. Glamorous Hollywood stars like Bette Davis (*Deception*, 1946) and Joan Crawford (*Possessed*, 1948) portrayed women who had to lie, scheme, even murder to get what they wanted from life. The films gave expression to both alluring wish fantasies about love and luxury and to the frustrations of housewives by dealing with women who led self-sacrificial lives, had ungrateful children, or had to deal with chronic and terminal illnesses. Though often hopelessly soap-operatic and melodramatic, the women's films often featured strong women fighting for their own identities in a world controlled by men.[22]

In many ways, *Mildred Pierce* fit the women's films pattern. It carried a predictable narrative about a mother's self-destructive love for her daughter, tended towards overstatement and hysteria, and contained major characters who lacked even a hint of psychological nuance. A prime example was Zachary Scott's cardboard cutout Monte—an aristocratic, decadent, heel recycled from innumerable Hollywood melodramas. For all its lack of subtlety, however, *Mildred Pierce* was a work which resonated culturally and socially beyond its conventional narrative.

Crawford's Mildred is supposedly an ordinary, lower-middle class housewife (though Crawford can never quite convince audiences that she is anything but tough-minded and glamorous) who escapes household drudgery and an ener-vated husband to become a successful entrepreneur. Warned early that the pur-suit of success (it would have been interesting if the film had really begun to question the whole American obsession with success) and the abdication of her maternal role will prove destructive, she is punished by seeing her sweet, perky, younger daughter die of pneumonia, and by having a relationship with the feckless, parasitical Monte, who is unfaithful and lives off her money.

But her ultimate punishment for being a strong, independent women is to be treated with contempt and betrayed by her monstrous, eldest daughter Veda (Ann Blyth). Mildred has spoiled Veda, compulsively sacrificing herself so that Veda can be raised to become a lady. In fact, Veda becomes so absurdly pre-tentious that despite Mildred's success she continues to treat her as if her own life has been irrevocably tainted by Mildred's having to work for a living. And Veda's contempt for Mildred's being merely a waitress, and in turn Mildred's own embarrassment about her job, feels emotionally true, and conveys some insight into the sort of status and class anxiety that the usual Hollywood my-thology of a classless America rarely would recognize or deal with.

On another level, as mentioned before, the film's treatment of career women is the most powerfully suggestive aspect of the work. Hollywood films usually treated career women (especially in the post-World War II era) as peo-ple who had to be domesticated and made to see the error of their ways when they competed with men. Even Katherine Hepburn, Hollywood's most noted feminist, had to accept ritualistic degradation and defeat (*Adam's Rib*, 1949) in her classic bouts with Spencer Tracy.[23] In a similar fashion, Joan Crawford's Mildred is clearly superior to the men who surround her, but is still supposedly enough of a traditional woman to allow herself to be manipulated by these same callow males. Nor does the film even allow Mildred to pursue a career for profit, power, or a sense of self—it is conceived of as merely a means to acquire and hold Veda's love. And Veda's behavior itself can possibly be viewed as an extension of Mildred's success drive, or a demonic variation on it.

At the film's conclusion there is a tacked-on happy ending with Mildred now bravely facing the future with her passive, dull, chauvinistic husband, who looks even more inadequate when forced to stand next to her. But given Hollywood conventions, he is there to save her from being a single woman. To underline this chauvinistic point, the film allows Ida (Eve Arden), Mildred's handsome, sarcastically witty friend and workmate, to be treated by men as if she were not a "real woman." The moral being that aggressive, intelligent ca-reer women are usually doomed to lonely and asexual lives, and in Ida's case would trade all their independence for the right man.

Obviously, Joan Crawford's career woman owed more to the conventions of the women's pictures than to film noir, but in both genres women often en-joyed a great deal of power over the imagination and will of men. There were a number of possible reasons for the diverse and powerful images of female menace, power, and maternal patience and sacrifice that pervaded these films. For one thing, female stars had a great deal of prestige in Hollywood of the forties, and the films reflected that fact. Another explanation for their taking on the image of murderous wives and lovers may have partially derived from the American soldiers' nightmare of infidelity at home during World War II. Of course, the narrative, no matter how much the camera focused on the predatory sexuality or the psychological strength of the female, always restored male dominance by the film's climax.[24]

It was Rita Hayworth, a pin-up favorite of American males in the forties and Columbia Pictures' only major film star and sex symbol, who became the apotheosis of these dangerous females. In fact, the effect of her role as the sensual, nightclub singer in Gilda (1946) was so strong that it inspired the U.S. Air Force to place Gilda's name on the atomic bomb dropped on Bikini. That role was shortly followed by her playing the character of a mysterious, seductive Circe, Elsa, in the intricately murderous plot of The Lady from Shanghai (1947).

The Lady from Shanghai, directed by her then-husband Orson Welles, is a virtuoso piece of baroque filmmaking filled with striking and bizarre aural and visual images and metaphors (for example, the symbolic intercutting between the film's characters and flamingos, crocodiles, and snakes), unusual camera angles, and the rich use of depth of focus. The world it depicts was an embodiment of film noir, a dark, nihilistic universe of men and women who deceive and destroy each other. This time, in exotic settings such as the Caribbean and Acapulco. Although there are moments when the film seems like nothing more than stylish nonsense—all windy rhetoric and meaningless confusion—the bewitching Elsa's manipulation of Michael O'Hara (Welles himself), a romantic innocent and aspiring novelist, is touched with interesting ambiguities. Elsa is motivated by both greed and a feeling of being utterly adrift in the world, and while caring for Michael, she is also willing to use and destroy him.

Throughout the film, Welles takes pleasure in his cinematic virtuosity, and creates original images and sequences to evoke Elsa's lethal charm. For example, there is an overhead shot of Elsa languidly lying down and singing on the deck of the yacht, luring O'Hara from the bowels of the boat. And an aquarium scene where her face is juxtaposed with an octopus, a metaphor for her predatoriness. For a grand finale, Welles constructs a playland sequence with grotesque laughing dolls, chutes, masks, and a house of mirrors—a labyrinth of refracted and reflected multiple selves. Elsa is the incarnation of film noir's femme fatale whose snares are difficult to escape. And although her image is figuratively and literally destroyed, Michael, although escaping her trap into the light of day, we know, as in many other forties' films, is bound to her image for life. As he states: "Maybe I'll live so long that I'll forget her. Maybe I'll die trying."

O'Hara's final lines were characteristic of the romantic despair and angst that was so much a part of film noir. The films projected a world which was almost universally corrupt and morally chaotic, but gave little sense of how particular social values and institutions helped shape or contribute to this vision (though there were exceptions like Abe Polonsky's *Force of Evil*, 1948). Corruption was defined primarily in metaphysical—and, at moments, psychological—terms, though the monstrosity of characters, like Veda in *Mildred Pierce*, was too outsized for the film's psychological explanations. Many characters in film noir were impotent and helpless in the face of evil, bending to its force, which seemed to reside in an inalterable human nature. Others struggled against it, but in the process were tainted by evil even when they achieved a victory. And there were still other characters who acted as if they were the personification of that corruption.

Though a writer like Barbara Deming could still suggest in her book *Running Away From Myself: A Dream Portrait of Americans Drawn From Film of the 40's*, that forties' films (not only film noir) revealed a crisis of public faith: "A vision of hell in which we are bound."[25] Of course, she qualified that perception by stating that the theme and the audience's response to it were mainly unconscious. Other critics speculated that the bleak mood of film noir derived from the cumulative anxieties of the Depression, World War II, and the Cold War, though it was difficult to see, by a close analysis of these films, how public events may have directly influenced or shaped the perspective.

If we took a critical leap and suggested that these films may, on some level, been a revelation of an unconscious public despair, they could just as easily be seen as works which were mere derivations from other popular arts such as the successful hard-boiled detective novels of Hammett (*Maltese Falcon*, 1941), Cain (*The Postman Always Rings Twice*, 1946), and Chandler (*The Big Sleep*, 1946). On yet another level, like many Hollywood film trends, they could be viewed as a popular genre, which since it made a profit at the box office, was adopted by the industry. And though a number of film noir works may have expressed a genuine directorial sensibility, the look of them—lighting, sets, and camera angles—often seemed more significant than their perspective on the world. In fact, many of these films were potboilers who seemingly did no more than adopt a successful set of formal and narrative codes.

Even more interesting and ironic is that the existence of film noir served only to highlight the essential optimism of the 1940s. Despite the hopelessness, cynicism, and sense of universal decay that film noir projected, both the filmmakers and the audience were readily prepared, even desirous of, avoiding their implications. As a result, even though the logic of the film's imagery demanded an opposite conclusion, the simple solution—the happy ending and even justice—often triumphed. Of course, much of this had to do with Hollywood's system of self-censorship and genre conventions. On the other hand, it was possible to conclude the films in this manner because of the audience's willingness and desire to suspend belief—an attitude that was probably aided by the war-inspired conviction that sufficient energy and good will existed in society to solve any problem and triumph over any evil. In fact film noir's evocation of evil may have served only as a delicious contrast, making the victory of goodness that much more grand and satisfying. Consequently, though film noir portrayed the darker side of human nature, it was one based as much on cinematic form and style than on the expression of a genuine moral or personal vision, and the films and the audience's response to them hardly affected the basic self-confidence of the era.[26]

Nowhere is the era's basic optimism better illustrated than in some of the forties' films that dealt with social problems, particularly discrimination and racism. In the postwar years a number of Hollywood producers, directors, and writers were determined to extend the democratic ideals which ostensibly underlied the war effort into an examination and attack on racism and bigotry in America. Films like *Crossfire* (1947) and *Gentleman's Agreement* (1947) were probably two of the first Hollywood studio products to confront anti-Semitism as a serious social problem. For although almost all of the Hollywood moguls were Jewish, they were Jews who craved assimilation and made films which "reinvented the country"[27]—creating their own myth of America. Except for films like *The Jazz Singer* (1927), Jews were usually seen as secondary characters—often comic ethnic types in films usually dominated by the moguls' upper-middle-class WASP ideal. (Though Warner Brothers thirties films had many ethnic, working class, but not Jewish, protagonists.) So even when films like *Crossfire* and *Gentleman's Agreement* proved profitable, no other films dealing with the subject followed.

Crossfire was an edgy thriller, whose visual texture—its mise-en-scène—was much stronger than its script. The film is filled with film noir shadows, razors so gleamingly polished that characters can be reflected in them, and a number of ominous low-angle and overhead shots. There is also a psychopathic villain, Montgomery (Robert Ryan), who is a deceptively soft-spoken sadist, seething with feelings of inferiority, resentment, and anti-Semitism—"Jewish people live off the fat of the land."

The power of the film lies in Ryan's performance and in its gift for evoking a tense, seedy night world of smoky bars, all-night movie theaters, and cheap apartments inhabited by characters such as Gloria Grahame's Ginny, a tough, exhausted woman, and her odd, pathological-liar boyfriend. The bitterness and venom that is exchanged between the two of them, and the feeling that most of the characters are living near the precipice, is much more striking than the film's attack on anti-Semitism.

Crossfire's social vision is timid and evasive. The anti-Semite is conceived as an uneducated psychopath, distancing the situation from the audience's own experience and values and absolving them of any guilt. The Jewish victim, Samuels (Sam Levene), is a war hero and an empathetic good guy, the film seeming to suggest that an ordinary Jewish scapegoat would be unable to elicit audience sympathy, only the extraordinary Jew being capable of eliciting moral or social concern. And by turning the homosexual victim of the novel into a Jew the film demonstrated Hollywood's timidity and fear during this period (homosexuals could not be dealt with in a sympathetic light in films of the 1940s). Finally, in its implicit belief that all problems of prejudice and racism are interchangeable, Hollywood manifested an unwillingness to deal with the particular historical and social experiences of different groups. The films expressed a faith that tolerance—a decent, liberal principle—was sufficient to encompass and solve a variety of complex social problems. Both compounding and illustrating this mixture of intellectual and political timorousness and vaguenesss was Crossfire's tendency to be awkwardly and superficially didactic. Its liberal spokesman, pipe-smoking police Lieutenant Finley (Robert Young), stops the action and provides a vaporous sermon about standing up to prejudice. It's an editorial which safely invokes nineteenth-century discrimination against the Irish, as a historical parallel to anti-Semitism, rather than the more charged and contemporary issue of race.

In contrast to Crossfire, Elia Kazan's Gentleman's Agreement (which won the Oscar for Best Picture in 1947), though lacking the former's visual style and texture, examined and dramatized facets of anti-Semitism which Crossfire never touched on. In the film a WASP magazine writer, Phil Green (Gregory Peck), pretends to be a Jew for two months so he can write an exposé of bigotry. In pursuit of his story a gallery of anti-Semites make their appearance, running the gamut from raging bigots to genteel WASPs ("nice people"), who indulge in polite prejudice, and to self-hating Jews who object to Jews who are too ethnic ("kikey").

Despite Gentleman's Agreement's more complex perspective on anti-Semitism, it is characterized by the same political superficiality endemic to social-problem films. Its use of a Gentile journalist to confront anti-Semitism evaded the whole issue. It made it seem that the distinct social and cultural history and ethnic characteristics which distinguished Gentile from Jew never existed. And a Gentile being the victim gave the audience the chance to express anger without having to confront the moral wrongness of prejudice. They now could get upset because an innocent man—a non-Jew—has by mistake become a victim of prejudice.

It was not only Jews who got a touch of liberal optimism from Hollywood in the forties. Blacks, from Birth of a Nation (1915), had usually been seen by Hollywood either as brutal, savage bucks, or good toms and mammies. In thirties' films two new black stereotypes began to appear, sympathetic victims who were symbols of general rather than racial oppression (the black janitor who is brutally questioned by the police in *They Won't Forget*, 1937) and "tragic mulattoes" (e.g., *Imitation of Life*, 1934) whose skin color allowed them to pass into white society. However, until the 1940s problem, films' blacks were mainly confined to minor roles, and racism was never explored as an issue.

By the end of the decade Hollywood began to deal with the issue and a number of films dealing with race prejudice were released. In one of these, *Home of the Brave* (1949), an educated, emotionally disturbed black GI, Peter Moss (James Edwards), is cured of a trauma (psychosomatic paralysis) by a white psychiatrist. Moss's character is in the tradition of the noble martyr (though the film deals directly with racism, not generalized oppression), a passive, self-effacing figure who embodies white values. He is the perfect black to exemplify the liberal ideals of the film, since he is a war hero and a successful professional. He is a man who can be viewed by the white audience as someone whose character and life style are no different than any white's. Just as in *Gentleman's Agreement*, Hollywood again affirmed tolerance and integration, provided it was for blacks and Jews who behaved like or really were WASPs. *Home of the Brave* defined racism as a psychological problem—racists being pathological and blacks being oversensitive to prejudice. For forties' Hollywood there was no such thing as institutional racism—where racist practice permeated, consciously and especially unconsciously, the dominant political and economic institutions of the society. And almost no sense of how profound a role racism played in the daily life of both the whole society and blacks. It was conceived of as a problem that neurotic individuals suffer from, which could be simply resolved with a dose of shared sympathy and understanding between whites and blacks.

In films like *Lost Boundaries* (1949) and *Pinky* (1949) a somewhat similar social perspective was communicated. *Lost Boundaries* was produced by documentary filmmaker Louis de Rochemont (creator of the *March of Time* newsreels), and shot on location in New Hampshire and Maine, using a largely nonprofessional cast. Based on a true story, the film deals with a dedicated black doctor, Dr. Scott Carter, and his family, who in the tradition of Hollywood's tragic mulattoes, pass for white in an idyllic New England town. The only seeming legacy of Dr. Carter's racial past is his children's gift for music (the "natural rhythm" of blacks)—though he still guiltily goes to Boston once a week to practice at a ghetto clinic. Ultimately the family secret is revealed when Dr. Carter is rejected for a naval commission because he is black, and the family is forced to deal with the mild social prejudices of the town, and more importantly, their sensitive son's confusion (the children were never told) over his racial identity.

Lost Boundaries is a well-intentioned film, but it is limited by a neat Hollywood formula which turns the problem of racism into a peripheral racial problem and totally blurs even that issue by having the black Carters played by white actors (Mel Ferrer and Beatrice Pearson) in the Hollywood tradition of *Showboat* and *Imitation of Life*. For Hollywood was unwilling to take the risk that audience sympathy could be elicited for black actors passing for white, so it made it easy for them. It gave them white actors, playing characters, who by some unperceptible accident of fate may have some black blood.

The film concludes with the town's Episcopal minister giving a sermon affirming Christian principles ("I am my brother's keeper") and announcing that the navy has seen the light and has begun to grant officers' commissions to all people of all races. The sermon has a magical effect, moving a number of townspeople to apologetically welcome the Carters back into the community. Liberal optimism triumphs, and though black social and economic conditions are alluded to in some affecting documentary footage of Harlem squalor and violence and there is a self-conscious speech by a black police officer of the pernicious effect of an impoverished environment on black lives, it is in no way the core or prime concern of the film. The political essence and hope of the film lies in the acceptance of one upper-middle-class, church-going, white-black family by white society.

In a similar fashion, Elia Kazan's *Pinky* (1949) also focused on a tragic mulatto passing for white (again played by a white actress, Jeanne Crain) but the film lacks even the surface realism of *Lost Boundaries*. *Pinky* takes place in a studio-set southern town, all wisteria and willows, and trades in racial stereotypes and clichés: an irascible but just and independent white matriarch (Ethel Barrymore); a traditional, strong, wise nanny (Ethel Waters); a hypocritical, fat clubwoman bigot; white trash rapists; and a lazy, no account black with his razor-carrying wife. At the film's conclusion Pinky has refused to pass for white any longer, and affirmed her racial identity by starting a nursery-hospital for blacks. In rediscovering her black roots, Pinky's triumph is a personal rather than social one. Its victory is achieved with the assistance of paternalistic whites, and gives no sign that the South's repressive and segregated order will ever be confronted, much less changed.

Other social-problem films during the period dealt with subjects like mental illness—for instance, Anatol Litvak's *The Snake Pit* (1948) which did bring about reform of some state mental hospitals, and juvenile delinquency, Nicholas Ray's *Knock on Any Door* (1949). But none of them really broke from the Hollywood norm.

In retrospect, the intellectual faintheartedness of these forties' social-problem films seems even more blatant. Of course, the films were, as always, constrained politically by the industry's prime commitment to making a profit. These films, however, were not only pallid, evasive, and sentimental in their handling of social issues, but most of them also had little cinematic energy, style, or dramatic life of their own. The characters inhabiting these works were usually impersonal figures, lacking a semblance of internality or psychological nuance, and operating as mere representations or symbols of social problems. The films conceived of their characters' behavior as being shaped by external forces or problems, rather than being people with genuine inner lives who reacted to charged social situations. The result being that the characters' existential or political choices never seemed to stem from their own reflections or feelings.

All the same, despite their shallowness these films must be seen and evaluated within the context of their own times. For one thing they strongly suggest how deeply a politically committed culture of liberalism had taken root in historically conservative Hollywood since the thirties (one shortly to be decimated by HUAC and the blacklist). They also attest to the economic security enjoyed by the industry which enabled it to feel confident enough to touch on previously taboo themes. Indeed the very existence of these social-problem films testifies to a shift away from the conventional Hollywood wisdom about social issues, which was, "if you want to send a message use Western Union," to an equally crude belief in the power of the image and a vague form of liberalism to produce instant social change. In fact the lack of subtlety and complexity in these films can in some ways be seen as yet another sign of the overwhelming optimism of the era—a sanguine belief that no problem was insoluble.[28]

A few films departed from this facile optimism. *Force of Evil* (1948), written and directed by Abraham Polonsky (who was soon to be a victim of the blacklist), was a sharp contrast to films like *Lost Boundaries* and *Gentleman's Agreement*. On the surface *Force of Evil* was a formula melodrama about the numbers racket—complete with a head racketeer and his femme fatale wife—whose violent confrontations were awkwardly edited and devoid of dramatic tension. However, there was much more to the film than the predictable tale of a bad-good guy lawyer, Joe Morse (John Garfield), who is ready to go straight at the film's climax. Polonsky crafted an ambiguous and imaginative work that uses Hollywood conventions to evoke on one level a portrait of American society dominated by greed and acquisitiveness; on another level, it's the story of a passionate, guilt-ridden, love-hate relationship between Joe and his older brother, Leo (Thomas Gomez), who had given up going to college to send Joe to law school. The brothers share both a profound resentment of and love for each other.

Though Polonsky's characters are all caught in the coils of the social system and its pernicious values, they are not simply symbols of a corrupt society. They have inner lives which are both shaped by and independent of social forces. The characters being people who choose the direction of their life. In this small, poetic, near-masterpiece, Polonsky has successfully fused Marxist and Freudian strains. The film's protagonist, Joe Morse (John Garfield), is a tough, perceptive lawyer who is aware of his inability to resist being part of the rackets and becoming corrupt. But Joe is adept at rationalizing his choices by asserting that everybody is guilty—that they all hunger for "the ruby." And in *Force of Evil* all the characters, including sweating, apoplectic, self-righteous Leo and even Leo's naive, dreamy stenographer, Doris, are tainted by the seductions of money and success.

Polonsky's direction is characterized by extremely long overheads of minute, isolated figures dwarfed by Wall Street buildings (seemingly based on a Paul Strand photo)—a metaphor for monolithic and alienating capitalist power—and by the film noir images of seedy numbers parlors, opulent winding staircases, and shadows augering doom. Much more original than the film's imagery is Polonsky's use of language—both dialogue and narration—which he aims to make play an equal, sometimes dialectical, relationship with the visual images. And though at moments the words become overly literary and self-conscious, its Joycean repetitions, city argot and inflection and metaphors (e.g., "money spread over the city like perfume") convey a genuine street poetry and set the film apart from almost all other forties' films.

Force of Evil concludes with Joe Morse descending on a grey morning to the "bottom of the world" to discover Leo's dead body left looking like an "old dirty rag." Polonsky does not have Joe indulge in grand, heroic gestures nor does he insert polemics for radical change. There is only a solitary Joe, willing to make his own understated moral stand, ready to help if he can. Polonsky's film offers no easy solutions. It knows how powerful the capitalist ethos is. Polonsky holds that it is not only Wall Street that pursues a capitalist-gangster ethic, but that the consciousness of most Americans is suffused with capitalist dreams.

Besides *Force of Evil*, other films that dealt with some insight and intelligence about political and social themes were Robert Rossen's *All the King's Men* (he had directed a boxing film *Body and Soul*, 1947, with a script written by Abraham Polonsky) and Billy Wilder's *A Foreign Affair* (1948). *All the King's Men* was based on a novel by Robert Penn Warren dealing with the career of populist demagogue and Louisiana governor Huey Long, here called Willie Stark (Broderick Crawford in a flamboyant, forceful, Academy Award performance). Stark begins his political career as a man of the people but, thwarted by the political machine, he adopts its corrupt tactics to achieve and sustain his power.

All the King's Men is an intellectually ambitious but clumsy film. Stark's transformation into a power-mad megalomaniac is too abrupt and extreme, the reasons for the alcoholic, drifting journalist-narrator, Jack Burden's (John Ireland) continuing loyalty to Stark are never really illuminated, and the script tends to telegraph its point of view. But despite the melodramatic turns and the choppy continuity, the film trenchantly captures the perniciousness of political power, and how the use of corrupt means in pursuit of social change can ultimately become an end in itself.

In *A Foreign Affair* Wilder displayed a talent for mordant, cynical comedy satirizing the foolishness and naivete of an American congressional committee investigating the morale of American troops (who are entwined in black market dealings and affairs with German women) in postwar occupied Germany. Wilder is particularly nasty about American provincialism and ethnocentrism, and shows how easily the committee's self-righteousness is subverted when confronted by European cynicism and sophistication. Although the portrait of the Germans, who are interested only in self-preservation—personified by a ruthless, sensual, ex-Nazi collaborator played by Marlene Dietrich—is not a sympathetic one. However, as is Wilder's wont, by the climax he has thoroughly softened the film's bite, endorsing the American values he, at first, so savagely poked fun at.

Clearly, the compromises inherent in *A Foreign Affair* were the Hollywood norm, since the industry rarely had the courage or the imagination to deal truly with controversial political and social themes. It was much easier for Hollywood to work in genres which provided comforting fantasy images, such as the musical—a genre which ever since its "All Talkin,' All Dancin,' All Singin" days of the late twenties and early thirties had become one of Hollywood's glories. During the late thirties various studios vied for the honor of producing the best musicals, but by the forties the undisputed leadership in the genre had fallen to MGM. There the Arthur Freed unit, with talents like Gene Kelly, Judy Garland, Fred Astaire, Vincente Minnelli, and others, turned out hit after hit.[29]

Though often considered the most escapist of the Hollywood genres the musical nevertheless succeeded in striking emotional chords that few other films could match. Its tunes became the hallmark of particular eras. For example, Judy Garland's *Wizard of Oz* (1939) rendition of "Over the Rainbow" became a world-wide hymn of a hoped-for postwar world of peace and prosperity. The same film's "We're Off to See the Wizard" became the anthem of the British Army as it chased Rommel across the sands of North Africa, and "Ding Dong the Witch is Dead" was danced the world over on VE day.

On another level, the film's singing and dancing intimated that a great deal of energy lurked beneath the everyday surface and seemed ready to burst forth at any moment. During the war years that energy seemed to nestle softly in a nostalgic evocation of a turn-of-the-century America; an idealized world that was perhaps never better realized than in Vincente Minnelli's vividly colored and stylized *Meet Me in St. Louis* (1944). Except for the momentary anxiety over the family's possible uprooting because of the father's new job in New York, some nervousness about whether or not the boy next door, John Truett (Tom Drake), loves Esther Smith (Judy Garland) and the strikingly visualized Halloween night terrors of little "Tootie" (Margaret O'Brien), the Smith family lived on the surface a warm, almost idyllic existence. The film constructed an Edenic past centering on home and family, and topped off by a vision of an ever-progressing future embodied in the 1903 St. Louis World's Fair.

This version of a bright, promising new world was fully realized in Gene Kelly and Stanley Donen's MGM film *On the Town* (1949). The tale of three sailors on a three-day pass in New York, the film uses real locations—the Brooklyn Bridge, the Statue of Liberty, and Washington Square—and artfully designed sets to turn the city into a magical place where all of one's dreams can be fulfilled.

The film begins serenely with a long crane shot of a longshoreman lazily on his way to work at dawn, singing "I feel like I'm not out of bed yet," and then cuts to three animated sailors (Kelly, Sinatra, and Jules Munshin) bounding off their ship ready to take on New York. The sailors are "ordinary Joes"—innocents filled with a sense of wonder and exhileration as they move naturally from everyday speech to sing "New York, New York, it's a wonderful town." There is nothing serene or simple about the city they're hungry to experience. But they are filled with confidence that all of New York can be absorbed, the camera tracking after them as they sing "We're really living, we're going on the town." Their energy is so infectious that it allows them to liberate three young women—an overworked taxi-driver (Betty Garrett), an oversexed socialite (Anne Miller) (class differences are no obstacle), and a pert ballerina reduced for financial reasons to kootch dancing at Coney Island (Vera Ellen). As they romp through New York, the city becomes a metropolis of grandeur, romance, vitality, and sentiment (even the cops are soft-hearted), the exhuberant center of an even more buoyant America.[30]

It is this inexhaustible sense of energy, joy and confidence that more than anything else characterizes the forties and their films. Certainly there were dark clouds looming, such as HUAC threat to sap Hollywood's vitality. In addition, film noir had raised the curtain on a darker side of the American psyche and character. Nevertheless, for most Americans the forties—particularly the late forties—were the first relatively unruffled period of peace and prosperity that they had enjoyed in almost two decades. Despite the fact that there were fears of Russia and a native communist fifth column there was also the faith that America had both the material and the moral capacity to deal with the "red menace" and any other problem it confronted. For example, films like Howard Hawks's epic western about the first cattle drive up the Chisholm Trail, *Red River* (1948), conveyed great confidence in the strength of the American character. The film's monomaniacal, forbidding hero, Tom Dunson (John Wayne), easily masters the land, cattle stampedes and Indian attacks. And this exemplar of American individualism can even learn to temper his rigidity and rage, and reconcile himself with his more flexible, feelingful (but still tough) stepson, Matt Garth (Monty Clift).

Hollywood had emerged from the war with its coffers, audience, and prestige at an all-time peak. As a result, the forties' films were perhaps the last time that Hollywood had sufficient self-confidence to create an insulated coherent world, which could unself-consciously endorse the American dream. For most Americans and for Hollywood the forties were truly "The Best Years of Our Lives."

NOTES

1. Godfrey Hodgson, *America in Our Time: From World War II to Nixon, What Happened and Why* (New York: Vintage Books, 1978), pp. 17–64.

2. Ibid., p. 20.

3. Ibid., p. 54.

4. Eric F. Goldman, *The Crucial Decade—and after, America, 1945–1960* (New York: Vintage Books, 1960).

5. Ibid., pp. 46–70.

6. Stephen E. Ambrose, *Rise to Globalism: American Foreign Policy 1938–1970* (Baltimore, MD: Penguin Books, 1971), pp. 102–35.

7. Ibid., pp. 136–66.

8. Dean Acheson, *Present at the Creation* (New York: W. W. Norton, 1969), p. 297.

9. Ambrose, *Rise to Globalism*, pp. 136–66.

10. Alistair Cooke, *A Generation on Trial* (Baltimore, MD: Penguin Books, 1952).

11. Walter Goodman, *The Committee: The Extraordinary Career of the House Committee on Un-American Activities* (Baltimore, MD: Penguin Books, 1969), pp. 207–25.

12. Ibid., p. 300.

13. Cooke, *A Generation on Trial*, pp. 337–41.

14. Charles Higham and Joel Greenberg, *Hollywood in the Forties* (New York: Paperback Library, 1970), p. 18.

15. James Agee, *Agee on Film: Reviews and Comments* (Boston: Beacon Press, 1966), p. 173.

16. Franklin Fearing, "Warriors Return: Norman or Neurotic," *Hollywood Quarterly* (October, 1945), pp. 91–109.

17. Agee, *Agee on Film*, p. 229.

18. Abe Polonsky, "The Best Years of Our Lives: A Review," *Hollywood Quarterly* (April 1947), pp. 91–92.

19. Frank Capra, *The Name Above the Title* (New York: Bantam, 1972), pp. 418–26.

20. Higham and Greenberg, *Hollywood in the Forties*, pp. 19–39.

21. Ibid.

22. Molly Haskell, *From Reverence to Rape: The Treatment of Women in the Movies* (Baltimore, MD: Penguin Books, 1974), pp. 153–88.

23. Ibid., pp. 189–230.

24. Ibid.

25. Barbara Deming, *Running Away From Myself: A Dream Portrait of American Drawn From the Films of the Forties* (New York: Grossman Publishers, 1969), p. 6.

26. Joseph G. Goulden, *The Best Years, 1945–1950* (New York: Atheneum, 1976).

27. Neal Gabler, *An Empire of Their Own: How the Jews Invented Hollywood* (New York: Crown, 1988), p. 7.

28. Peter Roffman and Jim Purdy, *The Hollywood Social Problem Film* (Bloomington: Indiana University Press, 1981).

29. Hugh Fordin, *The World of Entertainment! Hollywood's Greatest Musicals* (Garden City, NY: Doubleday, 1975).

30. Richard Dyer, "Entertainment and Utopia," in R. Altman (ed.), *Genre: The Musical* (London: Routledge & Kegan Paul, 1981), pp. 175–89.

3

THE FIFTIES

The fifties began on an ominous note with the United States, as part of a nominally UN force, becoming involved in a war in Korea, and the repressive and paranoid investigations of Senator McCarthy and company in full throttle. The decade, however, ultimately evolved into one permeated by a broad political and cultural consensus.[1]

The first years of the decade were dominated by the stalemated Korean War, where the Truman administration was willing to eschew military victory for a limited war and a negotiated settlement. Truman's military policies were challenged by World War II hero General Douglas MacArthur, who was then commander of the United Nations forces. Cloaking himself in his own sense of omniscience and his nineteenth-century patriotic pieties, MacArthur saw Truman's policies as the appeasement of communism and committed himself to total victory in Korea. Truman, in turn, responded by firing MacArthur for insubordination, and subsequently discovered himself the object of intense public rage.[2]

That rage soon found a home in the McCarthy, HUAC and Senate Internal Security Subcommittee investigations of a domestic communist conspiracy. This conspiracy was seen as a threat to take over a number of American institutions like the church, universities, private industry, and Hollywood. During the fifties the anticommunist crusade elicited the involvement either out of fear, political self-interest or conviction of a number of liberal groups and individuals. It included the American Civil Liberties Union, who from 1953–59 refused to defend communists who were under attack or lost jobs and Hubert Humphrey, who as a Senator proposed a bill to outlaw the Communist Party.[3]

Interestingly enough, many liberal intellectuals placed the blame for men like McCarthy on the actions of the left rather than on the right, at times even supporting the general public's view that the rights of communists and communist sympathizers should be denied.

The leading and most brazen figure in the anti-communist crusade was Senator Joseph McCarthy, a crude, Wisconsin Republican who opportunistically manipulated the issue to promote his own power and career. For four years he successfully used smears, innuendoes, and lies to trample on individual rights and helped create a climate of political fear and conformity, which even had establishment institutions on the defensive. But in 1954, when McCarthy went after the army and even dropped hints that President Eisenhower was soft on communism, he overreached himself and initiated his own rapid fall from power and celebrity. McCarthy's decline did not signify a turn to the left. There was no sudden opening of public discussion on such issues as the admission of China to the United Nations or talk about a social commitment to the poor, but it did mean a moderation of the repressive and divisive impulses that dominated the early fifties.[4]

The prime American political symbol of the fifties, however, was not Joe McCarthy but General Dwight Eisenhower, from 1952 to 1960 the Republican President. Ike was a Second World War military hero, whose calm, avuncular, optimistic public presence helped create a non-ideological political mood which muted controversy and offered something both to liberals and to conservatives. Though disliking the welfare state, Ike accepted the reforms of the New Deal without extending them and was prepared to use fiscal and monetary measures to maintain full employment. Despite believing in the Cold War, and unable to see the difference between communist and nationalist revolutions (e.g., CIA interventions in Iran and Guatemala occurred during his administration), he believed in a nuclear truce, refusing to engage in an arms race with the Soviets and studiously avoided getting the United States involved in a war.[5]

Eisenhower was a cautious president, who, though unsympathetic to the growing Civil Rights Movement, reluctantly sent troops to Little Rock to ensure school desegregation in 1957, and in crisis after crisis kept political tensions beneath the surface. By dint of his confident cautiousness and political skills, Eisenhower was able to preside over a national political consensus which excluded only paranoid right elements, Southern reactionaries, segments of the old left, and the few independent radicals who were still functioning as critics.[6]

This political consensus was built on and reinforced by an intellectual consensus shared by most American intellectuals. Some like John Kenneth Galbraith believed in a theory of "countervailing power" where big business power would be balanced off by the power of big labor and government.[7] Others held that the age of ideology was over (e.g., Daniel Bell, *The End of Ideology*) and in its place substituted an optimistic faith in capitalism, political pluralism, and the uniqueness and perfectibility of American society. These tough-minded anti-ideologues had constructed their own ideology—building it on a belief that economic growth and the practical application of social science principles would provide social justice and solve social problems. In this social vision there would be no need for economic redistribution (many of them were ex-radicals and leftists who out of a complex of motives rejected their own political past), for the American people were supposedly becoming more economically equal. And poverty, during the rare times it was acknowledged to exist, was seen as gradually disappearing. In turn they also read the idea of class conflict, and even the significance of class, out of American social and political landscape, promoting their own liberal mythology that in a totally middle-class society everybody had an equal opportunity to succeed. The other prime element of this ideological consensus was the aforementoned rise of liberal anti-communism (e.g., *The Partisan Review*, once a critical, sophisticated, Marxist journal became an avid defender of the West) which viewed Cold War politics as far more significant than domestic affairs. This commitment was so potent that even the newly merged American Federation of Labor and Congress of Industrial Organizations gave more attention to the anti-communist struggle than to organizing the mass of workers who remained outside the unions.[8]

However, though most intellectuals were either utterly at home with the direction of American politics or turned to contemplating existential and religious questions emphasizing the limitations of human nature and simply ceased to be political dissenters and critics, there were still a number of intellectuals who preserved their critical skills by analyzing and attacking the character of American mass culture. In the fifties the economy of abundance helped create a powerful suburban and consumer culture where the pursuit of success and an emphasis on social conformity became the dominant values of the era. As novelist Edmund White wrote about growing up in the Midwest in the fifties: "That was a time and place where there was little consumption of culture and no dissent. . . . It felt, at least to me, like a big gray country of families on drowsy holiday, all stuffed in one oversized car and discussing the mileage they were getting. . . "[9]

College students were in harmony with this mood and were for the most part apolitical ("a silent generation")—interested in a fraternity-sorority-based social life and in preparing for future careers. The Reverend Norman Vincent Peale, with his message of "positive thinking," became the country's most popular moralist and preacher, and the country's growing religious interest seemed built on sociability rather than spirituality.

The mass media of the fifties reflected and reinforced these values. Television was dominated by entertainers like the droning, folksy Arthur Godfrey, who became one of its most powerful personalities, by the skilled slapstick of *I Love Lucy* and the naked greed of quiz shows such as *Twenty-one*. And though there were imaginative comedy programs like *Your Show Of Shows* and original television drama on *Playhouse 90*, the most popular programs were often built on the most inane premises and on the marketing of personal comfort and instant gratification. One interesting statistic that conveyed something of the anti-intellectual taste of the times was that "about four times the expenditures on public libraries were paid out for comic books."[10]

In books like William H. Whyte's *The Organization Man* (1956) and David Riesman's more scholarly and complex *The Lonely Crowd* (1950), American middle-class life was criticized for its penchant for uniformity, social role-playing, and privatism. Other critics, both liberal and conservative, poked fun at the mass media, advertising, the automobile culture, and the anxiety-laden drive for social status and material goods. However, though the banality and tastelessness of much of what appeared on television and the blandness of suburban life were criticized, there was no attempt by these critics to break from the political and social consensus of the fifties. For the most part, they accepted the political and social system that helped shape the culture, and most of the targets they attacked were not particularly controversial ones.[11]

Nevertheless, despite the serene and confident veneer of the Eisenhower years, there were subversive currents, that though sometimes unrecognized co-existed with the dominant mood of stability and complacency. The threat of nuclear war shadowed the period, creating among a number of people a sense of fatalism and despair, and leading to protests in the late fifties against the civil defense program. The program was seen as treating nuclear war as an acceptable military alternative which people had to prepare themselves to survive.

The fifties also saw the Civil Rights movement begin to take shape. Whites may have been content with the political and social world of the fifties, but black needs and problems were clearly left unmet by an indifferent Republican administration and a Congress paralyzed by the southern Democratic bloc. The only arm of government responsive to black grievances was the Supreme Court led by Chief Justice Earl Warren. In 1954 the Court came to a monumental decision. In *Brown v. Board of Education of Topeka* it outlawed segregation in the public schools. There were violent reactions in the South, but de jure segregation of the schools (de facto segregation is a continuing and deepening reality) was at the beginning of its end.

The Court decision led to the 1955 Montgomery bus boycot—a grass-roots black protest against segregation in public transportation. The boycott was followed by protest movements in other Southern cities, and, most importantly, marked the ascent to national black leadership of Martin Luther King Jr.

The movement to the suburbs by urban whites also carried a critical, even dark, undercurrent. For though it was viewed either satirically—as a flight to a sterile, tedious, and vulgar world—or sympathetically—as ordinary Americans achieving their small portion of the American Dream—the radical consequences (by 1950, forty to fifty million Americans lived in the suburbs) of this flight for the inner cities of the 1960s and 1970s were not foreseen. The departure of the white middle- and lower-middle-class from the cities and their replacement by black and Hispanic poor led in the following decades to the erosion of the urban tax base (built on the sales and property taxes of its inhabitants), the escalation of often insoluble urban problems, and even greater residential segregation than existed in the past.[12]

There were also other fifties' currents that indicated resistance to the conservatism of the decade. The Beat movement, which was an attack on the middle-class conformity, the hypocrisy of the Eisenhower years, and the elite literary culture of the universities, came of age in the 1950s. Led by serious poets like Alan Ginsberg and Gregory Corso and novelists like Jack Kerouac (*On the Road*), the Beats modeled their writing on poets like Walt Whitman and novelists like Henry Miller and on the improvisation of jazz musicians like Charlie Parker. In their writing and lives they emphasized spontaneity, personal freedom, contempt for authority, and spiritual exploration. The Beat movement did not consist only of artists. There were other young people—Beatniks—who taking their lead from the Kerouacs and Ginsbergs, adopted or mimicked a more natural, anti-bourgeois (i.e., some pot, jazz, and freer sex) lifestyle. And though the Beats were never a part of a political or social movement, their writings rejected racism and the nuclear arms race and treated homosexuality without contempt or condescension.[13]

The fifties also saw the development of a distinctive youth culture accompanied by a new (though derived from black rhythm and blues music) form of music—rock and roll. For many older Americans rock music was too loud and overtly sexual, and sounded to them like aimless noise. However, at its best and most innovative (e.g., the rock of Chuck Berry and Elvis Presley), the music had an energy, freedom, and earthiness that offered the possibility of an undefined, new lifestyle, which strongly contrasted with 1950s conventionality. Of course, by the late 1950s much of rock music's class and regional identity had been bleached out and transformed into the mass-produced, soporific sound of Frankie Avalon and his clones.[14]

Clearly these deviant currents and dark strains were not the preeminent ones in fifties' America. It is important, however, to recognize that the era was more complex than the usual images and descriptive phrases evoking a time supposedly dominated by a passive "silent generation."

Similarly, the films produced in Hollywood also defied facile labels and categories. In the early 1950s, as they did in the late 1940s, HUAC garnered publicity by investigating the film industry. Its hearings helped buttress the already powerful blacklist of actors, writers, and directors, and created in its wake a "clearance"[15] industry which passed on the political purity and future employ-ment of the people worked in Hollywood. And just as in the late 1940s (*I Married a Communist*, 1949) cheap genre films were produced to purge the Hollywood image of any taint of radicalism. A film like *Big Jim McLain* (1952) used a documentary style including an authoritative narrator to exult the FBI and HUAC while condemning communists more for their character traits (they were either criminals, idealistic dupes, nymphomaniacs, or disturbed fa-natics) than for their ideology. In fact, the ideology was never defined or ex-plored. Communists were reduced to caricatures who saw human life as dispensable, had no room for private feelings, and were even in opposition to God and motherhood.

The most hysterical of these films, and probably the one least bound by genre conventions was *My Son John* (1952). Its director was Leo McCarey (e.g., *The Awful Truth*, 1937) who had distinguished himself during the 1947 HUAC hearing by replying to a question about why the Russians had banned his last film (*Going My Way*, 1944): "Because it had God in it." In addition, in 1950 he joined Cecil B. deMille in urging all members of the Directors' Guild to take a loyalty oath. *My Son John* differed from other anti-communist films by focusing on the conflict between father and son rather than the usual exposé of communist crimes and conspiracies. The film operated most powerfully on a barely acknowledged Oedipal level where both father and son struggle for the wife-mother's time and respect. However, it is clear that what McCarey tried to do in *My Son John* was to pit the all-American "Jefferson" family's communist son John, an unathletic, sexually ambiguous intellectual, played in his insidi-ous, contemptuous *Strangers on a Train* (1951) style by Robert Walker, against his modest, down-to-earth parents (Helen Hayes and Dean Jagger) who be-lieve in football, the Bible, the American nation, and the flag.

It is obviously an unequal struggle since the sullen, slick John is seen by McCarey as a monster and though the overpossessive mother is a mass of neu-rotic tics—rolling eyes, tense smile, and flapping hands—and the father is a rigid, banal legionnaire, they are totally vindicated at the film's conclusion. In an unbelievable final scene, the dead John (killed by communist agents) leaves a tape-recording of a commencement speech, which enveloped in almost di-vine light, plays from the lectern to his former university's graduating class. The tape affirms his faith in his father and mother, and informs the students how the communist serpent numbed his brain and led him to become a traitor.

In McCarey's feverish world, being an intellectual was clearly a dangerous, un-American vocation, and redemption could be found only in the moralisms of John's elementary school principal father and the hysterical religiosity of his mother. For McCarey it is the heart and emotions, no matter how pathological, that won't lie or lead you astray. But the intellect is dangerous—it makes you question and doubt and leaves you open to subversive ideas and the rejection of commonsense wisdom.

Nor was McCarey alone in this view of the perfidy of the intellectual. It was a perspective that was shared, albeit with greater subtlety and complexity, by Elia Kazan, who also played a leading role before HUAC. Kazan had joined the Communist Party in the 1930s, but resigned feeling intense bitterness and hostility towards it. However, he continued to see himself as a man of the left.[16] And in 1951, at the height of the Cold War, and close to the time he delivered his infamous cooperative testimony before HUAC, he made Viva Zapata, a film dealing with the heroic leader of the Mexican revolution. It was Kazan's first truly personal and structurally cinematic work—an intense film characterized by highly stylized and powerful imagery and lighting and a political perspective open to a variety of conflicting interpretations. That was a sign either of its profound ambiguity or its intellectual confusion.

Nevertheless, at the HUAC hearings Viva Zapata was viewed as a sustained anti-communist film, and Kazan himself promoted it as an anti-communist work. What could be considered anticommunist in the film was evoked most vividly by the character of Fernando (Joseph Wiseman), a Machiavellian, professional revolutionary, and intellectual. Kazan conceived him as a sterile, cold man—an anti-life force—dangerous not only because of his political opportunism, but because of his lack of capacity for human connection. In fact, Fernando is portrayed as a revolutionary devoid of any political ideology excepting a commitment to power—a common stereotype that Hollywood used to provide a negative portrait for revolutionaries. He is willing to shift from the political left to the right without a moment's hesitation or reflection. It is clear that Kazan wanted Fernando to be seen, despite the vagueness of his ideology, as the apotheosis of the Communist Party commissar—a man who could use and betray both the people's demands and his personal relationships and loyalties to achieve power.

Kazan's evocation of the intellectual's power hunger is, however, only one example of the film's prime theme: the oppressiveness and meaninglessness of political power. For example, in a key scene Zapata (Marlon Brando) is depicted occupying the Presidential palace, and continuing both to temporize and to intimidate the peasants as the tyrant Diaz had done before him. Obviously, in this somewhat abstract, schematic sequence, Kazan wished to demonstrate to the audience that power corrupts and that revolutionary regimes have sustained the tyrannical patterns of their right-wing predecessors.

However, Viva Zapata cannot be reduced to an anticommunist polemic on the lines of My Son John, since it is filled with diverse (sometimes half-developed) strains which lead to often contradictory interpretations. Given this fact, it is understandable that the Daily Worker would have attacked the film for being Trotskyist,[17] that a number of film critics could condemn it for its Cold War anticommunism, and a great many people in the 1960s New Left could love and embrace it.[18]

Viva Zapata conveyed both populist and anarchist sentiments along with its anticommunism. The film was filled with images of peasants acting heroically and collectively to promote the revolution. For the most part Kazan tended to romanticize them, portraying them in static, archetypal images and in silhouette as models of innocence and solemn dignity. But Kazan's populism also had an underside in the person of Eufemio (Anthony Quinn), Zapata's brother, who is a barbarian desiring the fruits of the revolution—booty, women and the land—without any other commitment beyond self-gratification. And the power of the people is often undermined by the charismatic figure of Zapata. Though Zapata is able to inform the people that "there is no leader but yourselves" he is depicted as a mythic figure whose instinctive nobility and life energy dwarfs the noble peasants that surround and follow him. The mixture of Brando's larger than life performance, and Kazan's conception of Zapata make it difficult to believe that with Zapata's death the peasants have become a populist force—the "strong people that don't need a strong man."

If Kazan's populism is bound by contradictions, his anarchism exists much more as a personal response, a belief in acting spontaneously and passionately rather than a politically coherent idea of state and society. There are no hints of Kropotkin, Bakunin, or some form of anarcho-syndicalism inherent in the film. There is just Kazan's personal disdain for bourgeois repression and respectability and his ambivalence about the quest for middle class success. And if in Viva Zapata there exists a genuine antagonism to political structures and hierarchies, it is more out of a commitment to the revolutionary image and emotion than to the political and social ends of revolution. Kazan is finally more interested in heroic myth (Zapata heroically astride his white horse) and the act of rebellion than in history or politics.

Clearly, Viva Zapata was not the unequivocal anticommunist polemic some critics perceived it to be. But Kazan did pay his dues to HUAC with his next film, Man on a Tight Rope (1953). The film was neither a commercial success nor a personal favorite of Kazan's. Filled with Cold War speeches and stereotyped characters it deals with a Czech circus fleeing to the West. It pits communist thugs and bureaucrats against the cosmopolitan life force and artistry of the circus performers. The communists are seen as stupid, petty, and anti-intellectual, committed to stifling all individuality and shaping it to fit the party line. Man on a Tight Rope was a conventional melodrama, devoid of real people, whose main aim was to propagate an anticommunist line and help Kazan escape the committee's hook.

In 1954, however, Kazan's craft revived with his Academy Award-winning direction of On the Waterfront—on one level an emotionally charged and moving melodrama dealing with both one man's personal redemption and the nature of union corruption on the New York waterfront. On another level, Kazan used the film to justify being an informer before HUAC with his protagonist, Terry Malloy (Marlon Brando), acting as a heroic stand-in for himself. Malloy becomes an informer in a extremely difficult situation—where he could be dubbed a Judas for breaking the neighborhood code of silence. But it is also a situation where the decent and virtuous characters (along with the audience) would view his unwillingness to talk as an act of moral cowardice. In fact, Kazan stated: "Terry Malloy felt as I did. He felt ashamed and proud of himself at the same time. . . . He felt it was a necessary act."[19] In addition, Kazan partially sanitized the HUAC investigations by having their film counterpart, the crime commission, represent all that was benign and honest in governmental action.

However, in *On the Waterfront* the parallels to Kazan's experience with HUAC and the social significance of the film are overshadowed by the powerful and complex portrait of Terry Malloy that Brando and Kazan created. Malloy is a mumbling, shoulder-shrugging, boy-man who raises pigeons, pals around with adolescents who worship him, and survives as the condescended-to pet of the egotistical and vicious union boss Johnny Friendly (played in a roaring, larger than life style by Lee J. Cobb) on the periphery of the longshoremen's community. He is also a gum chewing, alienated, tough, urban wise guy with scar tissue over his eyes from his earlier stint as a prizefighter, who masks his vulnerability by upholding a code which is based on the notion that the world is a jungle where your first obligation is to look out for yourself.

As the film evolves, Kazan turns Terry from a comic-reading bum into a moral and social hero. It's a change seen most poignantly and concretely in his relationships with the fragile, protected, "good girl" Edie (Eva Marie Saint), the morally tough Father Barry (Karl Malden) and his opportunistic, shyster, brother Charlie (Rod Steiger). Terry is barely articulate, but Brando is able to totally inhabit the role, and with every gesture and word grants the character a complex inner life. Malloy is composed of a variety of parts: a profound sense of personal failure and lost dignity; a powerful loyalty to his brother and corrupt union boss; and a mixture of tenderness and brutality in his character. It all comes together in such a manner that the change in Terry is utterly believable.

On the Waterfront is also a film which deals with the world of the longshoremen and their corrupt union. The film's cinematography, though self-consciously pictorial, does evoke the physical surface of a world of heavy mist, haunting boat whistles, seedy pocket parks, garbage-ridden backyards, tenements covered with clotheslines, television antennae, pigeon coops and an omnipresent river filled with boats. There are also painful glimpses of longshoremen rituals such as the soul-destroying shape up, where the men scramble on the ground for tokens which provide them a day's work. But it is all more an expression of Kazan's sharp eye for dramatic detail than his interest in the so-cial texture and dynamics of the docks. Kazan's longshoremen are never really particularized, they are "more social masks than people."[20] They are seen as a mass, first intimidated and submerged by the union boss and his goons, and by the film's conclusion, following a bruised and martyred (though Kazan denies it there is more than a hint of Christian symbolism in the film) Malloy back to work.

Aside from trying to vindicate the role of the informer, On the Waterfront is a much less political film than Viva Zapata. Kazan is not really interested in ex-ploring the politics of one type of American unionism. The relationship of the longshoremen's union to the shipping interests and the political machine is barely touched on. The populist strain that is found in Zapata doesn't exist here. The workers are cowed by the union and docile—incapable of generating any collective political action on their own. It's the character and redemption of Terry Malloy that is the film's centerpiece; and although, in the film's oper-atic climax, Malloy leads the workers against Johnny Friendly, there is no po-litical dimension to his victory. (There is even a note of warning about the nature of the triumph inserted, with a beaten but still defiant Johnny Friendly screaming "I'll be back." And in the real world, his counterparts still control the docks.)

The heroic attack against corrupt power and repression of Zapata has be-come a purely personal and moral act. There is no suggestion that Malloy has developed a political and social vision like Zapata's; he is merely a more alien-ated and resentful version of that classic American hero, the courageous indi-vidual who stands up for the good against those who would degrade and threaten our lives. Though this time there is an upright government to be of some help to the hero.

On the Waterfront can be seen as a conventional Hollywood film, filled with stock villains, overly-theatrical sequences (e.g., Father Barry's speech in the hold attacking the mob) and a manipulative and intrusive score. However, a listing of the film's weaknesses does not convey Kazan's characteristically driv-ing energy and passion. And in Brando's Malloy, the film successfully brought to life one of the most striking manifestations of an anti-hero, who began to ap-pear frequently in the films of the 1950s.

Kazan was hardly alone among fifties' directors that either dealt directly with communism or indirectly with the ideology and psychology surrounding the anticommunist crusade. Even Alfred Hitchcock in his commercially suc-cessful, charming, chase film North by Northwest (1959) added a Cold War spy story to its stylish mix of romance, wit and suspense.

Early in the decade, with the advent of the Korean War, Samuel Fuller made The Steel Helmet (1951), a crude, earnest, low-budget film, which on one level seemed determined to be second to none in its portrayal of communists as the last word in bestiality and savagery. Fuller has the North Koreans leaving booby-trapped corpses of dead GIs around, killing innocent children and indulging in human-wave attacks which give clear evidence of their contempt for the value of human life. Nonetheless, Fuller, in his primitive anarchic fashion, gave ample hints that he was wary of all ideologies: finding fault with his American GIs' racial and cultural blindness; depicting his alienated hero Sergeant Zack (Gene Evans) as a cynical, sadistic, cigar-chomping figure, interested only in survival and untouched by the slightest hint of humanitarian impulse (except for his love for his South Korean ward). *The Steel Helmet*, despite its tabloid script and cartoon-like characters, had a great deal of bite and reality. It also gave evidence that the war film could simultaneously mouth and subvert patriotic platitudes, and convey that the anti-communist side was no community of saints.[21]

To a degree, this flexibility allowed some directors and writers to use genres as a means of commenting on American politics. In 1952 director Fred Zinnemann (*The Search* 1948, *From Here to Eternity* 1953) and scriptwriter Carl Foreman (who had been cited by HUAC in 1951, refused to cooperate and was subsequently blacklisted) made *High Noon*, a popular western which was clearly a left-liberal parable about HUAC's attack on Hollywood. *High Noon* was a "mature western" about an aging, weary Marshal (Gary Cooper in an Academy Award-winning performance) who has a deeply lined face, sagging flesh and admits to being scared. Uncharacteristically for a western hero, he asks for the assistance of the townspeople, but is deserted by them and left alone to confront a murderous psychopath and his henchman. The craven townspeople find a variety of reasons why they cannot stand up to this threat to law and liberty: the parson cannot commit himself to killing; the old sheriff is paralyzed by despair; the judge is a smooth careerist whose only loyalty is to self-preservation; and others of them just hide or flee from the confrontation. We are left with the lone American hero who must face and, of course (for some of the genre conventions are maintained), defeat the villains.

High Noon is a skillfully directed, gripping, and intelligent film which uses incisive cross-cutting and an exciting sound track—an Academy Award-winning score by Dimitri Tiomkin—and the rhythmic ticking of a clock (the film's running time runs parallel to this time of crisis in the marshal's life) to successfully build narrative tension. However, it is a film whose images are merely functional, and whose characters are intelligently conceived types without any genuine individuality. The film's moral heroism does not quite translate into political terms, for the hero has no politics and the villains have no institutional connections. Nevertheless, in its commitment to individual moral responsibility and courage, the film did convey to a portion of its audience that evils such as McCarthyism could no longer be rationalized or evaded and must be resisted.

Given the political mood of the period, *High Noon* was a bold film, but its use of metaphor and allegory and its emphasis on moral rather than political courage, made it a relatively oblique one.[22] A film that dared to criticize American capitalism directly stood the risk of having its production disrupted by vigilantes and even if completed would find few distributors or theaters willing to exhibit it. Such a film was *Salt of the Earth* (1954) which was independently made by blacklisted writers Herbert Biberman (who also directed it), Michael Wilson, and Paul Jarrico, and sponsored by the Mine, Mill, and Smelter Workers, a union that had been expelled from the CIO in 1950 for its communist ties. The film focuses around the strike of a group of primarily Mexican-American zinc miners against a racist, exploitative, and repressive mining company. There are moments that the film was crudely polemical and stilted, more socialist than social realism, particularly in its use of militant music, heavy-handed cross-cutting, and stereotyped villains; a clownishly crude and violent sheriff and his deputies; a callous pipe-smoking superintendent; and a company president who goes on African safaris. Of course, the Mexican workers are seen as spontaneous, brave, and and the film's heroine Esperanza (Rosaura Revueltas, who was deported three times during the film's shooting) is a shy, glowing beauty who conveys great warmth and courage.

On the other hand, *Salt of the Earth* projects a feminist consciousness unique either for the left or the right during the fifties. For the film centers on the conflict between the sexes on the workers' side, as well as with class oppression. The miners have never thought about the feelings and lives of their wives, who are taken for granted, traditionally bound to home and children. But as the strike develops, the women, who are forced to take the men's place on the picket line, assert themselves, asking to be treated as equals. The men's pride and machismo is hurt, but eventually they begin to accept the change in traditional patterns, and not only do they win the strike but they transcend their chauvenist notions of sexual identity. It is a pat conclusion, but the images of women gathering on a hill to join the picket line, and some men struggling with the laundry are moving ones and pre-date anything Hollywood was to conjure up until the feminist-conscious 1970s and 1980s.[23]

With its unabashed left perspective *Salt of the Earth* was an aberration in the fifties. A film more in tune with the spirit of the decade was Don Siegel's *Invasion of the Body Snatchers* (1956), a low-budget, witty, science fiction film dealing with the subject of alien infiltration and mind control that pervaded so many of the science fiction films of the decade.

In *The Thing* (1951) a U.S. scientific expedition is threatened by a ferocious monster they thaw out of a spaceship. In William Cameron Menzies' *Invaders from Mars* (1951) a small boy is unable to convince adults that Martians are kidnapping important figures, and placing crystals in their brains which will force them to commit brutal acts. Of all these films, however, *Invasion of the*

Body Snatchers was the most subtle. Its most distinctive quality stems from its director Don Siegel's matter-of-fact, realistic style which eschews violence for still, silent, ominous images. The film projects a world where ordinary objects are strangely illuminated and people's faces remain unlit, where light signifies safety and hope, and darkness and shadows mean danger. The paranoid plot focuses on an invasion of alien pods (a product of atomic mutation) of a small, neighborly town where everybody knows each other's first name. As the pods possess the people in the town, they turn them not into violent monsters but into bland, expressionless vegetables, who are incapable of love, rage, pleasure, or pain.

It is the depiction of the pods that opens *Invasion of the Body Snatchers* to a variety of interpretations. In one interpretation the pods can be seen as a symbol of a society where alienated people flee their individuality and seek refuge in mindless mass conformity—an exaggerated version of Riesman's "Lonely Crowd." In another, more probable interpretation, the pods could be seen as communists, the omnipresent aliens of the fifties, who are everywhere conspiring to turn people into robots. Of course, it is doubtful if *Invasion of the Body Snatchers* was perceived by its audience as anything more than a conventional entertainment film. Nonetheless, the anxiety, hysteria, and paranoia it tapped about the threat of communist totalitarianism made it a perfect expression of some of the decade's obsessions.[24]

Undoubtedly, a direct or even an oblique commitment to dealing with political issues was far from the dominant force in the Hollywood of the fifties. Given the competition from television, and decreasing movie theater attendance, Hollywood gave a great deal of thought to recapturing its audience. Using color more heavily and then seeking out new technological processes, the studios attempted by overwhelming the viewer to attract him back to movie-going. Processes such as Cinemascope, Vista-Vision, Cinerama, and 3-D were introduced, exploiting the size of the film image and experimenting (unsuccessfully) with the creation of the illusion of depth.[25]

Ultimately, the wide-screen processes led to a number of expensive, lengthy blockbuster films like *The Robe* (1953), *The Ten Commandments*—which cost thirteen and a half million dollars to make (1956)—and *Ben Hur* (1959). These epics were on one level part of the religious revival of the fifties—cartoons of religious piety—and, more important, with their color, crowds, chariot races, and crucifixions they were the last great flings of studio excess (where "only too much is really sufficient")[26] which allowed these films to fully exploit the vastness of the new screen.

The new Hollywood could be glimpsed in Billy Wilder's smart *Sunset Boulevard* (1950). The plot centers on an aging, once famous and glamorous silent screen actress, Norma Desmond (Gloria Swanson), who lives in a decaying mansion as if time has stood still. She fantasizes about making a comeback film with the aid of a decent, weary, and hungry screenwriter, Joe Gillis (William Holden) who becomes first her collaborator, then her lover and kept man. *Sunset Boulevard* follows a number of the conventions of film noir, using voice-over narration and flashback and centering on a possessive, hysterical, sexually devouring heroine and a morally ambiguous hero. However, the film's prime focus is not on the corruption of Joe Gillis but on the contrast between the old Hollywood and the new—not necessarily to the latter's advantage.

Though Billy Wilder and his co-writer Charles Bracket depict Norma Desmond as something of a wild-eyed, campy grotesque, the film is still an idiosyncratic homage to the absurdity, excesss, and graciousness of the flamboyant, old Hollywood. Luminaries of the old Hollywood like Buster Keaton, Cecil B. deMille and Erich von Stroheim (who plays Max, Norma's first-director, ex-husband, and present-day protector and servant) are treated sympathetically, while in the plainer, sharp-tongued, grasping new Hollywood producers dismiss the "message kids," want to make Betty Hutton musicals out of baseball stories, and have no time for truth or art. For Wilder, the old Hollywood, if nothing else, had style which made the more pragmatic, businesslike Hollywood of the fifties (which he was an integral part of) pale in comparison.

Contrary to *Sunset Boulevard*'s sour view of the contemporary Hollywood scene, many producers still felt optimism about the future. Some of that hopefulness was based on the success of big-screen musical comedies, particularly adaptations of Broadway hits like *Oklahoma* (1955) and *Guys and Dolls* (1955).[27] However, these musicals, though commercially successful, suffered from ponderous and inflated production values. It also began to seem ridiculous for characters to break into song and dance at the slightest provocation. The best musicals of the decade appeared in the early fifties and came from the illustrious Freed unit at MGM. These medium-budget original musicals included Vincente Minnelli's decorative and stylized *An American in Paris* (1951) with an athletic Gene Kelly; his sombre and witty *The Bandwagon* (1953) with the elegant and feathery Fred Astaire; and Stanley Donen and Gene Kelly's classic show-business musical *Singin' in the Rain* (1952).

Singin' in the Rain is a breezy, good-natured satire of Hollywood's Busby Berkeley musicals, film premieres, star biographies, and the introduction of sound, written by the urbane Betty Comden and Adolph Green and starring Gene Kelly, as an earthy, dynamic, ordinary American Hollywood star, Don Lockwood. Kelly is as always, brashly self-confident and jaunty, and in the film's stirring title number, he wistfully stamps around in rain puddles, and holding his sole prop, an umbrella, he exultingly embraces the studio rain. With its pastel colors, cheerful songs ("Good Morning"), and acrobatic pratfalls (Donald O'Connor energetically dancing through cardboard sets), *Singin' in the Rain* created a world where any action can spontaneously, calmly, and naturally be turned into music and dance. It was a world where despair and doubt do not exist and where the happy ending continues to survive. And if *Singin' in the Rain's* plot about the transition to sound is a metaphor of the challenge that Hollywood faced from TV, it is also an indicator of just how much carefully honed optimism still dominated the studio product.[28]

A few years later, a much more melancholy and despairing note was conveyed in Donen and Kelly's final collaboration, *It's Always Fair Weather* (1955). In many ways a successor to *On the Town*, its three GI buddies (Dan Dailey and Michael Kidd recreating the Jules Munshin, Frank Sinatra roles) decide to get together ten years after the war is over. It is a measure of the sour mood of the film that the three find they have very little in common and do not really like one another. Although both Dailey and Kidd are better dancers than Munshin and Sinatra there is very little chemistry between the three—even their bravura garbage-can dance together, though clever, has none of the inspired warmth of the numbers in *On the Town*. Indicative also of the darkening Hollywood mood is the film's negative response to the world of media and TV. It takes satiric pot shots at advertising—Dan Dailey as an ad executive singing the drunken "Situationwise"—and at TV shows like *This Is Your Life*.[29]

Even if *It's Always Fair Weather* did sound a despondent chord and few fifties' films had *Singin' in the Rain's* charming airiness, and feeling of being at home in the world, the era still contained many genre films that upheld traditional virtues and values and were commercially successful. In George Stevens' carefully composed, beautiful *Shane* (1955) a blond, mysterious stranger in white named Shane (Alan Ladd) is befriended by a group of homesteaders and protects them in turn from a predatory rancher and his psychopathic, hired killer dressed in black (Jack Palance). In a sense *Shane* is no ordinary western. It is a self-conscious attempt to create a mythic West populated by archetypes—with the enigmatic, perfect-featured, sententious Shane seen continually from the perspective of a hero-worshipping young boy (Brandon de Wilde).[30] However, despite its portentousness, it was a more conventional film (for all his grandiosity, Shane is not that much different from the more pedestrian radio and TV hero, the Lone Ranger) than the 1950s westerns of Anthony Mann (*The Naked Spur*, 1953), austere, bleak films built around a revenge motif or John Ford's epic western *The Searchers* (1956) with John Wayne as the most ambiguous of Fordian heroes.

Ford's later films like *The Searchers* depicted a darker, less morally defined world than earlier works like *Stagecoach* (1939) and *My Darling Clementine* (1946). The plot of *The Searchers* revolves around a driven, ex-Confederate soldier Ethan Edwards (Wayne) who searches for years for his niece Debbie (Natalie Wood). Debbie has been kidnapped by Indians—who for the most part are treated here as savages or childlike, comic foils—whose way of life she's adopted. Edwards still has enough left of the character of the old Wayne-Ford

hero to display indomitable courage, rescuing Debbie from the Indians he passionately hates, and returning her to Ford's ideal world of family and community—the garden in the wilderness.

But nothing is quite the same in Ford's world in this film. Everything has become grimmer: the landscape is more threatening; Ford's beloved cavalry both
less noble and more absurd; and his sullen, violent hero consumed by murderous rage and racist feelings. Ford's heroes can usually reconcile their individuality with community—nature with civilization. But Ethan is the "man who
wanders," and is unable to enter the door of the hearth again. The stirring long
shot of his riding away, framed by the doorway of the house, is not an affirmation of the romance and freedom of a Shane-like hero who can never be domesticated, but is a tragic, desolate image of a man doomed to solitude. (In the
1980s *The Searchers* became a model for films like *Rambo: First Blood Part II*,
where the freeing of MIAs from the barbaric captivity of the North Vietnamese followed the pattern of Ethan's quest to free Debbie from the Indians.)

Despite the sense of unease that began to creep into fifties' films, neither
Hollywood nor the public were particularly open to films which took formal or
intellectual risks. Exemplifying this attitude was the popular comedy team of
the fifties, Martin and Lewis (*Artists and Models*, 1955), whose slapstick routines and Jerry Lewis's twitchy, idiotic, victim's persona did not differ much
from the style of earlier B-film comic teams like Abbott and Costello.

Just as indicative of the basic conservatism of popular taste and values were
films dealing with woman's consciousness and identity. During the decade
there were not only fewer films about independent women than in the thirties
or forties, but there were fewer films dealing with women at all. In the literate,
epigrammatic Academy Award-winning *All About Eve* (1950), a temperamen-
tal, sarcastic, ambitious star of the theatre, Margo Channing (Bette Davis) is
also a vulnerable, insecure woman underneath all her wit and drive. She ultimately sees her career as insufficient, as something separate from being a real
woman, and opts for marriage, children, and retirement. And her mousy and
devoted protege Eve (Anne Baxter), turns out to be a predatory and manipulative actress who wants to be a star and is willing to use any means to supplant
Margo. In *All About Eve* successful women are either unhappy or so distorted
by their ambition that they lose their humanity in the process.

In a minor role in the same film, Marilyn Monroe, the sex symbol of the fifties, plays another of her dumb blondes, a woman-object, whose sexuality is
unthreatening, guileless, and childlike. Toward the end of the decade, in films
such as Billy Wilder's frenetically paced, transvestite sex farce, *Some Like It Hot*
(1959), she added vulnerability to her victim's persona.

While Monroe was more a male fantasy figure than a woman that other
women could identify with, the freckled, eternally sunny Doris Day was one female star who was capable of eliciting both male and female sympathy. In a pe-

riod where being popular had become a prime cultural value, Day's persona in battle-of-the-sexes comedies, such as *Pillow Talk* (1958) with Rock Hudson, conveyed a super-hygienic, wholesome cheerfulness. However, though these comedies were built on an extremely puritanical, timorous form of sexiness, with Day remaining always the virgin, her supposed sexual innocence was less significant than her drive, ambition, and spunkiness. In fact, so potent were those qualities that as a tailored-suited journalism professor in *Teacher's Pet* (1958) she is tough enough to even put to rout Hollywood studs (albeit he had begun to age) like Clark Gable. Despite Day's girl-next-door looks and behavior, her characters often had jobs and projected a tougher, more independent persona than most of the other major female stars (e.g., Grace Kelly, Audrey Hepburn) of the decade.[31]

But though the characters Doris Day played may have held down jobs, most women in the 1950s' films were housewives or women seeking to avoid spinsterhood, who found salvation in marriage. In one traditional genre, however—the soap opera—German-born, director Douglas Sirk made films which used the genre's conventions to make oblique criticisms of traditional female roles and middle-class conformity.

Backed by one of the most commercial Hollywood producers, Ross Hunter, *All That Heaven Allows* (1955) was characterized by artificial studio landscapes and townscapes, melodramatic, fortuitous accidents, a saccharine score, and a predictable, neat conclusion. Despite the clichés that permeated the film, Sirk was a consummate stylist who could use color, light, clothes, and furniture to express his sensibility—thru capturing his heroine's state of mind. Throughout the film Sirk uses both reflections on TV screens, mirrors, and piano tops and ubiquitous screens and doors both to evoke a middle-class world dominated by gleaming surfaces and appearances, and to catch the heroine's feelings of imprisonment. It's an eloquent use of cinematic form to comment on content,[32] and, at moments, transcends the lack of subtlety and soap operatic quality of the script.

The film presents the world from the point of view of an older heroine, Carrie (Jane Wyman)—an upper-middle class widow with few interests, little emotional connection between herself and her unpleasant, grownup children, and a number of acceptable men desiring to marry her. She breaks from the mores of her country club set and the disapproval of her children, becoming involved with a young, passive, handsome hero Ron Kirby (Rock Hudson). He is not only much younger than her, but he is also a landscaper who lives a comfortably bohemian life that is dimly committed to simplicity, a love of nature, an uncompromising belief in being autonomous, and a disdain for snobbery and status-seeking. But he's college educated and refined and his home and friends look more like models for a Norman Rockwell magazine cover—cute and unnaturally wholesome—than some bohemian enclave.

For all that, Kirby is not the usual alternative for heroines in fifties' and women's pictures. Carrie chooses to fulfill her own emotional and sexual needs, and not only rejects her friends but decides she won't be a Stella Dallas (heroine in Vidor's film of same name in 1937) or Mildred Pierce and sacrifice her life for her children. Sirk's film, however, was clearly no feminist work. Carrie's choice of a new way of life is predicated on the existence of a man to provide her with an alternate set of values and a refuge in marriage; in terms of the narrative, it is a very safe sort of rebellion. But its criticism of middle-class materialism, hypocrisy, and emptiness (more telling in the film's mise-en-scène than its narrative) was symptomatic of much less oblique works which rebelled against the complacency and conformity of Eisenhower America. In these films, male stars such as the aforementioned virile, angry Brando (*On the Waterfront*), the brooding, vulnerable Monty Clift (*A Place in the Sun*, 1951; *From Here to Eternity*, 1953) and James Dean (Kazan's *East of Eden*, 1955) played antiheroic heroes who in different ways were at odds with the prevailing social order.

In *A Place in the Sun* (1951) Clift plays a haunted, sensitive outsider in a dark, romantic version—all dramatic tight close-ups, shadows, superimpositions and dissolves—of Dreiser's naturalistic novel *American Tragedy*. George Eastman (Clift) is a quietly ambitious, uneducated young man who wants to escape his street missionary boyhood and enter the world of his wealthy relatives. However, the film's emphasis is much less on the nature of social class and the hunger for success in America than on Eastman's doomed relationships with a clinging, drab, working class woman (given texture and poignance in Shelly Winters' performance) and with Angela Vickers (Elizabeth Taylor) who is the embodiment of glamor and wealth. In the Oscar-winning *From Here to Eternity* (1953) Clift played another vulnerable, doomed outsider (Prewitt), brutalized by a corrupt army on the eve of Pearl Harbor. Prewitt is a man of courage and integrity who is unwilling to bend to the dictates of an institution he loves.

The rebellion expressed by three actors, was, however, neither political nor social in nature, nor were the characters they played artists, beats or bohemians. They were just sensitive, sensual, and often anguished young men seeking to discover and define their identities. In the process they raised doubts about the values and behavior that dominated American culture and society and indirectly conveyed some of the undercurrent of dissatisfaction that existed during the decade.

Of the three stars, James Dean had the most profound effect on the consciousness of the young in the fifties. Dean had an aura—a mythic presence—and with his abrupt and tragic death in a car crash in 1955 generated a cult and became a legend. His film career was a brief one, but in Nicholas Ray's extremely popular *Rebel Without a Cause* (1955) he left his unique mark on the fifties.

Rebel Without a Cause was less about rebellion than about the anger of Jim Stark (James Dean) toward his middle-class parents and the world. Jim is a brooding, suffering, isolated, high-school student who hates his apron-wearing father's (Jim Backus) flaccid amiability and weak submission to his self-involved, backbiting wife. Mumbling, slouching, hunching his shoulders, curling up in a fetal position, with a cigarette dangling from his mouth, the tormented Jim is like a coiled spring ready to cry and rage. Surrounding Jim are two other pained, rejected adolescents, Judy (Natalie Wood), stunned and emotionally thrown by her father's sudden rejection, and Plato (Sal Mineo), a morbid, friendless boy who lives alone with a black maid because his divorced parents have deserted him.

Rebel Without a Cause's uniqueness rests more in its cinematic style and Dean's performance than in its script. Ray uses a variety of camera angles, a dislocated mise-en-scène, tight close-ups, point-of-view shots, intense color, and rapid, turbulent cutting to successfully project the tension, anger, and sense of almost metaphysical alienation that permeates the film. There are also luminous, metaphoric sequences like: the "chicken run," with a pinkish-white specter, Judy, signaling the beginning of the race in the center of a pitch-black runway lit by car headlights—an initiation rite or journey confronting death; and the scene shot in the vastness of the planetarium (which is located on a precipice) with its apocalyptic, end-of-the-world images of the galaxy exploding—as the three alienated kids sit alone in th dark watching—provides a powerful metaphor for the insecurity and isolation of adolescence.

Rebel Without a Cause's dialogue and narrative are much more pedestrian than its imagery. In terms of the narrative, the film sees the causes of adolescent turmoil as solely psychological—caused by both the instability and conflict within families and their failure to communicate and provide understanding. There is an implicit critique of upper-middle-class status striving and conformity, but the script's emphasis is not on social or class reality. In fact, the film even introduces an understanding detective who acts as a social worker (the helping professions, such as psychologists, social workers, etc., became commonplace in fifties' films) and surrogate father to Jim.

The film's conclusion is both clichéd and sexist: the submerged father taking off his apron, asserting his authority and embracing Jim, and reconciliation and love triumphing over fragmentation. However, what is most memorable is not Jim's opting for a 1950s affirmation of domesticity—shedding his asocial self for a responsible familial one—but those powerful existential images of lostness, of being a romantic outcast and alone in the world.[33]

Dean departed from this image in his third and last film, George Stevens' *Giant* (1956) which was adapted from Edna Ferber's novel. He plays Jett Rink, a sullen, inarticulate ranch-hand who becomes an oil millionaire. Rink is the only character in the film with the suggestion of an internal life—a tribute to Dean's gift for giving nuance and complexity to even this most seemingly stereotypical of characters. Although in *Giant* Dean continued to mumble and slouch, he is transformed from a hostile, arrogant outsider, filled with resentment of those who have power, to a wealthy but pathetic power-wielder consumed by alcoholic self-pity, racism, and the resentments of youth. Dean's Jett is not a particularly sympathetic figure, but the tension and energy he conveys in the role is one of the few vital elements in this inflated and trite epic about Texas culture and society.

However, in contrast to Dean's earlier films, *Giant* does make some interesting social points, albeit they are built on a sentimental, liberal point of view characteristic of the Hollywood social films of the mid-1950s. For *Giant* is both a ponderous soap-operatic chronicle about a wealthy ranching family and a critique and a bit of a satire of Texas materialism, anti-intellectualism, machismo, and racism. Unfortunately, the critique is subverted both by the long shots exalting an almost-mythic Texas landscape and by the beautiful and somewhat progressive, Eastern heroine, Leslie's (Elizabeth Taylor) ultimate embrace of Texas and its ethos. And her acceptance of that world after years of ambivalence only occurs when her stolid rancher husband Vic (Rock Hudson) displays his humanness and manliness by brawling for the rights of his half-Mexican grandchild. *Giant* contains no real political critique. Leslie does not want to give up her privileges or make changes in the political and economic structure, for she merely wants the elite to be more paternalistic (to sustain the values of her Maryland adolescence), and demonstrate some kindness to the poor Mexicans who work for them. However, she is bold enough to accept intermarriage and the film clumsily suggests, through its final shots of Leslie's and Vic's white and copper-skinned grandchildren sitting together in their playpen, that the answer to racism may lie in the coupling of the races. The traditional Hollywood embrace of personal rather than political solutions.

Richard Brooks' *Blackboard Jungle* (1955) was a fifties film carrying more social bite and tension than *Rebel Without a Cause* or *Giant*, and dealing with similar issues—delinquency and racism. In fact, when the film was screened at the Venice Film Festival it elicited a diplomatic protest from Claire Booth Luce (ambassador to the Vatican) because she felt it exported a squalid, unfavorable image of American life. [34]

Blackboard Jungle centers around a tough, crew-cut idealistic teacher, Mr. Dadier (Glenn Ford) who believes in education and democracy and must tame a group of violent young hoods. In true 1950s style the actions of the hoods are given no social roots or explanation, merely psychological chatter about permissive child-rearing. Nevertheless, these hoods are no Bowery Boy cream puffs, but are alienated, resentful, and vicious—especially their leader, West (played with an imitation Brando-Dean posture by Vic Morrow). *Blackboard Jungle* is a perfect example of what in Hollywood passes for social realism and social exposé. New York is reduced to a studio set devoid of any sense of texture or place and the teachers in the main are stereotypes, ranging from Murdoch (Louis Calhern), a cynic who calls the school a "garbage can," to the frustrated Miss Hammond, who wears tight, sexy clothes and is almost raped by one of the students. The plot is also built on a series of contrived, mechanical twists, featuring sudden shifts of destructive or cynical characters to the side of virtue, and of course offering Hollywood's usual solution to complex social problems: the concern and commitment of one courageous, caring individual—Dadier.

Despite these discordant elements, the film was still capable of capturing some of the difficulties involved in teaching tough, disruptive adolescents (it uses the dissonant sounds of a machine shop class and the passing elevated subway train to help evoke feelings of oppression). The potent use of one of the first rock hits "Rock Around the Clock" conveys a strong feeling of the unbridled energy and antagonism of 1950s youth culture. The issue of racism is also raised with the introduction of the character of Miller (Sidney Poitier in one of his early, more complex roles). Miller is a sensitive, strong, intelligent underachiever, who at first is angry and resentful of what he perceives to be a white-dominated education system, baits and torments Dadier. But by the film's climax he turns into a noble hero joining Dadier against West and his brutish allies.

Blackboard Jungle is filled with embarrassing clichés about the promises of equal opportunity in America—Dadier attempts to get Miller to continue to go to school by invoking the successful careers of black stars Joe Louis and Ralph Bunche. Nevertheless, the film does touch on the reality of black anger, and that is a positive step in a decade where, excepting *No Way Out* (1950)—Poitier as a middle-class doctor—there were no other films dealing with black consciousness and problems until Martin Ritt's *Edge of the City* (1957). However, in *Edge of the City*, Poitier plays a longshoreman-saint who sacrifices his life for a confused, neurotic, white friend, played by John Cassavetes, and no real feelings of black life or problems are conveyed.

In Stanley Kramer's *The Defiant Ones* (1958) Poitier plays an escaped convict (Cullen) in the South whose character is given enough pungency and reality to directly express his anger at Southern racism. Being a symbol of virtue, Poitier's rage is balanced by qualities like intelligence, tenderness, loyalty, and courage. *The Defiant Ones* is a conventional, contrived work of liberal poster art whose key image—a close-up of two hands, black and white, manacled together—is an obvious metaphor for Kramer's view that blacks and whites are inescapably linked to each other in America. Cullen has escaped chained to a white convict, Jackson (Tony Curtis), who is morally and physically much weaker than him. Jackson is an insecure, petty criminal, who dreams of big money and lives by the Southern racist code. But it is predictable from the very beginning that Jackson will be transformed and the hate between him and Cullen will be turned into concern and love.

The Defiant Ones, like *Blackboard Jungle*, has a great deal of surface excitement and even some dramatic punch—the cross-cutting between the convicts on the run and the liberal sheriff (Theodore Bikel) in pursuit is especially effective. However, like *Jungle* it offers a simplistic social answer—the achievement of racial solidarity through the commitment of individual blacks and whites to each other. And there is no attempt in the film to depict or even suggest the complex economic, political, and cultural dimensions of the race problem. Of course, integration is made easy for whites because the black character is Sidney Poitier, a charismatic, seductive, and superior presence, who at the film's climax even sacrifices his freedom for his white friend (invoking jeers from the blacks in the audience). Indeed it was this dignity and transcendent humanness, which made Poitier the one black star who was consistently successful and acceptable to white audiences. Poitier never bowed or scraped to whites, but he was so reasonable and humane that the white audience knew that his anger would always stay within acceptable bounds, and that there was nothing to fear from the characters he portrayed. They were men who could arouse the hatred or abuse of only the most ignorant or reactionary of whites.

Later on, during the more militant sixties, blacks often put down Poitier's persona as middle-class, masochistic, and liberal.[35] Nevertheless, he was one black actor who no longer had to sing, dance, and roll his eyes to have his image appear on the screen. And though Hollywood's handling of the race problem was neither bold nor imaginative, given the conformist political tenor of the time, the emergence of a token black star could still be viewed as a minor triumph.

Ultimately it was this lack of political and artistic ferment or originality in 1950s' Hollywood that allowed an opening for a group of independently produced films such as the Academy Award-winning *Marty* (1955). Ironically, it was Hollywood's bête noir, TV, that was the inspiration of *Marty* and other films of this type. For along with the hours of dross that dominated 1950s' TV there were some moments that broke the mold. Under the inspiration of innovative spirits such as NBC's Sylvester "Pat" Weaver, new forms like the magazine concept show ("Today"), talk shows ("Tonight") and spectaculars ("Peter Pan") were produced on TV. Producers such as Fred Coe and Worthington Minor created original live drama shows such as Studio One and Philco Playhouse featuring the talents of new writers (Paddy Chayevsky, Rod Serling, Horton Foote), directors (Sidney Lumet, John Frankenheimer) and actors (Paul Newman, Kim Stanley, Rod Steiger).

Marty was the first and most commercially successful of these films adapted from live television. Written by Paddy Chayevsky and made on location in the

East Bronx in low-budget black and white, it dealt with the daily lives of ordinary people. Marty's major achievement was in evoking the tedium and loneliness that permeates the life of an unattractive Bronx butcher (Ernest Borgnine), who ultimately finds happiness by going out with a shy, homely teacher.[36] Although Chayevsky claimed that his work opened up the "marvellous world of the ordinary," Marty was a dialogue-bound, formally inexpressive film, whose camera did not probe deeply into the faces and behavior of lower-middle class life. It was merely a quietly sentimental story, characterized by a fine ear for Bronx dialogue and syntax—answering a question with a question (e.g., "What do you feel like doing tonight? I dunno, what do you feel like doing?"). And offering Hollywood's predictable, all-purpose solution—love—to give Marty's life some purpose.

It was Marty's commercial success that led to other small films, the most distinctive being Sidney Lumet's Twelve Angry Men (1957) adapted from a television play be Reginald Rose. Twelve Angry Men is an account of a jury's deliberations over a murder case where the defendant is a Puerto Rican boy. Using a single set of a New York City jury room on the hottest day of the year, Lumet succeeded in adapting most of the conventions of the television play—tight close-ups, medium group shots, panning, and fluid and precise cutting from sweating face to face to build a dramatically effective film. He was especially gifted directing actors, and a cast which included a combination of New York character actors (Lee J. Cobb, Jack Klugman, E. G. Marshall) and a Hollywood star, Henry Fonda, as the jury gave a seamless illustration of ensemble playing.

Twelve Angry Men was a socially committed work which raised questions about the nature of the jury system, and by extension the nature of American democracy itself. The jury was a gallery of social types: bigots, a shallow, spineless advertising man, a decent working man, an immigrant deeply committed to the democratic process, a cold, logical stockbroker, and the hero, an intelligent, decent, liberal architect (Henry Fonda) who must convince the rest of the jury members that what seems like an open-and-shut case is liable to reasonable doubt. He is a resolute man with a soft, cultivated voice, who ingeniously and logically succeeds in convincing the other jury members that the prosecution's case has holes. Despite the doubts the film raises about a system where bigotry, complacency and convenience (one juror wants to resolve the case quickly so he can get to a Yankee game) become the sole basis for deciding the guilt or innocence of a defendant, the film ends on a positive note, with the defendant allowed to go free and the American system of justice affirmed.

Twelve Angry Men's strength lies in its dramatic fireworks and its well-drawn social types rather than in the depth of its social critique or the psychological complexity of its characters. It is a film where the villains sweat, rage, and bellow a great deal, and the hero is a totally admirable and reasonable man. Every scene in the film is neatly choreographed and calculated for dramatic impact, with each of the characters given a single note—the old man on the jury is observant and notices details—to define themselves, and a significant moment where they shift their vote. And though the film does not gloss over the fact of how ambiguous and complex the meting out of guilt and innocence in a criminal case can be, it still holds that for our institutions to be just they merely need one good person who will tap the basic virtues of other ordinary Americans. It is the type of Hollywood political fantasy that such vastly different directorial sensibilities as Frank Capra and Sidney Lumet could share.

Besides *Marty* and *Twelve Angry Men* there were other small films that elicited critical attention during the late fifties, such as Richard Brooks' *Catered Affair* (1956) and Delbert Mann's *Middle of the Night* (1959). One of the most striking was Alexander Mackendrick's hard-boiled, atmospheric, bracingly colloquial (script by Clifford Odets) *Sweet Smell of Success* (1957) depicting the relationship between a vicious, megalomaniacal Broadway gossip columnist (Burt Lancaster playing a version of Walter Winchell) and Tony Curtis as a slimy, hungry, publicity man who obsequiously serves and is victimized by him.

However, the production of these small films began to decrease at the same time as live drama was replaced on television by filmed series. And although good, small, realistic films were still produced during the next three decades—*The Luck of Ginger Coffey* (1964), *Hester Street* (1974), *El Norte* (1984)—after the fifties there never again was a time where the small film seemed capable of becoming one of the dominant cinematic forms in Hollywood.

The small, realistic films did not attempt either to subvert Hollywood conventions or the dominant political and cultural values of the fifties. However, in the late fifties two films were made which were critical of the military mind and of the development of nuclear weapons—*Paths of Glory* (1957) and *On the Beach* (1959).

Of the two, the more formally distinctive and politically subversive was Stanley Kubrick's independently produced *Paths of Glory*. Despite the fact that the film takes place within the confines of the French Army of World War I rather than in the more charged and contemporary setting of the U.S. Army of the Korean War, *Paths of Glory* trenchantly conveys the cynicism, hypocrisy, and careerism of the French officer class and provides a powerful indictment of war.

In what was to become his characteristically cool, dazzling, and original style, Kubrick evokes an unjust and death-saturated world through sound (drum beats, whistles), camera movement, lighting, and vivid imagery rather than through antiwar sermonizing. The two prime villains of the film are the calculating, subtle, and insidious General Broulard (Adolph Menjou) and the neurotic, murderously ambitious General Mireau (George Macready) who live in opulent chateaux and hold glittering formal dress balls. They are totally contemptuous of their men treating them like chess pieces to be manipulated or ants to be casually slaughtered—"scum" who can be sacrificed to their own career ambitions. Mireau watches the battle through binoculars (one of Kubrick's many devices conveying war as a voyeur's sport of the officer class) and hysterically rages at the soldiers' retreat.

Though the film puts greater emphasis on the class structure and inequity of the war machine than on the horrors of the war, Kubrick still evokes the advance and retreat of the soldiers in nightmarish, richly textured battlefield scenes. The battlefield is a lunar landscape of craters, mud, and puddles, littered with bodies, barbed wire, and the wreckage of a plane, punctuated by whistling shells and enveloped by a flare-lit sky. The camera relentlessly tracks the men as they scramble to their anonymous deaths through the debris and smoke.

The hero of *Paths of Glory* is the granite-faced, courageous, and compassionate Colonel Dax (Kirk Douglas), who is at one with the men. Dax is an uncomplicated idealist who can openly say to Mireau that "patriotism is the last refuge of scoundrels." He also defends three innocent, court-martialled soldiers—he is a defense lawyer in civilian life—who have been chosen arbitrarily from the mass of soldiers to be punished for their supposed cowardice (in reality to cover the general's mistakes) in battle. Though Dax is a jut-jawed hero and idealist, the three soldiers are fallible, frightened men who cry and rage, and whose death is absolutely barbaric and meaningless. Kubrick concludes the film without a glimmer of hope—Dax not only failing to prevent their deaths, but almost immediately after the court martial, is forced to lead the exhausted troops, who are longing for home, back to the murderous trenches. The system has him in its hands, and there is no escape.

Stanley Kubrick went on to make much more mordant and outrageous films, where strong, noble figures like Dax not only rarely appear but would be parodied and undermined if they did (e.g., *Dr. Strangelove*, 1963, *Clockwork Orange*, 1971). For the smug fifties, a film which portrayed the military hierarchy as moral monsters, and maintained such a bleak view of the human condition was a radical work and, of course, doomed to commercial failure. *Paths of Glory* did not offer the facile, personal, and liberal solutions of *Blackboard Jungle* and the *Defiant Ones* or the leftist optimism of *Salt of the Earth*. It was a profoundly pessimistic work which offered only contempt for the conduct of war and the corruptions of power and privilege, and nothing more.[37]

In contrast, Stanley Kramer's disaster movie, *On the Beach* (1959), although it is built around the notion that the world is on the verge of extinction by nuclear war, ends on a curious note of hope. Based on Australian novelist Nevil Shute's best-selling book, the film was seen in some ways as a small step toward the easing of Cold War tensions by being screened almost simultaneously in

Moscow and Washington. But despite its political pretensions, this tale about the aftermath of the Third World War and a last surviving American submarine arriving in Australia just ahead of a post-nuclear exterminating cloud, seems nothing more than a backdrop for a doomed love affair between Ava Gardner, an alcoholic war widow, and Gregory Peck, the submarine commander.

Stanley Kramer's aim to make a star-laden film (Fred Astaire also had a role in the film), which would act as a warning about the consequences of the nuclear arms race had good intentions. In fact, few people could take exception to the film's decent instincts, but only in Hollywood would bromides like the need to preserve the wonder of life be seen as socially significant. There is also something bland and antiseptic about the images of the nuclear holocaust that the film projects. However, there are moments when the film captures the kind of despair that might become an integral part of the lives of the doomed survivors, particularly in a car race in which the drivers drive with a consciously suicidal recklessness and abandon. These scenes are rare, and On the Beach's real purpose is revealed in its final image of a Salvation Army banner proclaiming the message that "there is still time, brother!"[38]

Though intended as a cautionary message about the apocalyptic consequences of the arms race and nuclear war, the implications of this message might also serve as a convenient summary of Hollywood's passage from the optimism of the forties to the anxiety of the sixties. On the one hand it evokes the complacency of an industry that despite economic decline and political problems still went on churning out the same films built on the ersatz emotions, melodramatic conventions, and evasive political and social formulae of previous decades. On the other hand, however, a number of these films managed to contain a deeper sense of uneasiness, an urgency, and a greater sense of the imperfections of American society than in the past. Of course, the fifties ended with Eisenhower in the White House and Doris Day starring in Pillow Talk (1958), but inherent in all that manufactured calm and good cheer was a sense of disquiet, perhaps even of time running out on a period of stability and consensus.

NOTES

1. Eric F. Goldman, The Crucial Decade—And After, America 1945–1960 (New York: Vintage, 1960).

2. Ibid., pp. 292–311.

3. Richard Rovere, Senator Joseph McCarthy, rev. ed. (New York: Harper and Row, 1973).

4. Ibid.

5. Ronald Steel, "Two Cheers for Ike," The New York Review of Books (September 24, 1981), pp. 10–12.

6. Richard Rovere, "Eisenhower Over the Shoulder," *The American Scholar* XXI (Spring 1962), pp. 34–44.

7. Frederick F. Siegel, *Troubled Journey: From Pearl Harbor to Ronald Reagan* (New York: Hill and Wang, 1984), p. 99.

8. William L. O'Niell, *Coming Apart: An Informal History of America in the 1960s* (New York: Quadrangle, 1971), pp. 3–24.

9. Edmund White, *The Beautiful Room Is Empty* (New York: Ballantine, 1988), pp. 7–8.

10. Eric Goldmen, *The Crucial Decade*, p. 291.

11. O'Neill, *Coming Apart*, p. 4.

12. Godfrey Hodgson, *America in Our Time: From World War II to Nixon, What Happened and Why* (New York: Vintage, 1978), pp. 54–64.

13. Morris Dickstein, *Gates of Eden: American Culture in the Sixties* (New York: Basic Books, 1977), pp. 3–12.

14. Charlie Gillet, *The Sound of the City: The Rise of Rock and Roll*, rev. ed. (New York: Pantheon, 1984).

15. Victor S. Navasky, *Naming Names* (New York: Viking, 1980).

16. Michel Ciment, *Kazan on Kazan* (New York: Viking, 1973), p. 94.

17. Ibid., p. 94.

18. Peter Biskind and Don Georgakas, "An Exchange on Viva Zapata," *Cineaste* VII, 2 (Spring 1976), pp. 10–17.

19. Ciment, *Kazan on Kazan*, p. 110.

20. Ciment, *Kazan on Kazan*, p. 108.

21. Nicholas Garnham, *Samuel Fuller* (New York: Viking, 1971).

22. Nora Sayre, *Running Time: Films of the Cold War* (New York: Dial Press, 1982), p. 176.

23. Deborah Silverton Rosenfelt (ed.), *Salt of the Earth* (Old Westbury, NY: Feminst Press, 1978).

24. Stuart Samuels, "The Age of Conspiracy and Conformity: Invasion of the Body Snatchers," in John E. O'Connor and Martin A. Jackson (eds.), *American History/American Film* (New York: Frederick Ungar, 1979), pp. 203–17.

25. Pauline Kael, *Kiss, Kiss, Bang, Bang* (New York: Bantam, 1969), pp. 446–47.

26. Michael Wood, *America in the Movies: or, "Santa Maria, It Had Slipped My Mind!"* (New York: Basic Books, 1975), pp. 180–81.

27. Robert Sklar, *Movie Made America: A Cultural History of American Movies* (New York: Vintage, 1975), pp. 283–84.

28. Wood, *America in the Movies*, pp. 146–64.

29. Ibid.

30. Phillip French, *Westerns* (New York: Oxford University Press, 1977), p. 70.

31. Molly Haskell, *From Reverence to Rape: The Treatment of Women in the Movies* (Baltimore, MD: Penguin, 1974), pp. 231–76.

32. Jon Halliday, *Sirk on Sirk* (New York: Viking, 1972), pp. 97–98.

33. Venable Herndon, *James Dean: A Short Life* (New York: Signet, 1974).

34. Garth Jowett, *Film: The Democratic Art* (Boston: Little, Brown, 1976), p. 385.

35. Sidney Poitier, *This Life* (New York: Ballantine, 1980), pp. 331–41.

36. Eric Barnouw, *Tube of Plenty: The Evolution of American Television* (New York: Oxford University Press, 1977), pp. 154–65.

37. Norman Kagan, *The Cinema of Stanley Kubrick* (New York: Grove Press, 1972), pp. 47–67.

38. Donald Spoto, *Stanley Kramer: Filmmaker* (New York: G. P. Putnam's Sons, 1978), pp. 207–15.

The Best Years of Our Lives (William Wyler, 1945). *Courtesy of the Museum of Modern Art.*

Rebel Without a Cause (Nicholas Ray, 1955). *Courtesy of the Museum of Modern Art.*

Easy Rider (Dennis Hopper, 1969). *Courtesy of the Museum of Modern Art.*

The Godfather II (Francis Ford Coppola, 1974). *Courtesy of the Museum of Modern Art.*

Platoon (Oliver Stone, 1986). *Coursesy of the Museum of Modern Art.*

4

THE SIXTIES

In 1848 revolutions broke out almost simultaneously in Paris, Berlin, Vienna, and Milan which toppled long-established reactionary regimes and attempted to institute political and social reforms. Historians referring to this period call it the "springtime of the nations." These revolutions were ultimately crushed or gave way to even more sophisticated autocratic governments which were in many ways more repressive than the ones they replaced. Nevertheless, in their brief moment of triumph these revolutions exposed some of the most glaring contradictions of their societies—most notably the growing, almost unbridgeable, gulf between the bourgeoisie and the newly emergent industrial working class—laying to rest the myth that Europe was moving toward a harmonious era of the golden mean.[1]

If the events of 1848 sound familiar to modern ears, it is because a somewhat similar pattern of events took place during and after 1968. That year saw concurrent riots, insurrections, and near-rebellions in the streets of New York, Chicago, Detroit, Paris, Mexico City, and Prague. This " '68 Spring" was also crushed in successive waves of assassinations, Russian tank invasions, police and army tear gas and bullets. However, like their 1848 predecessors these revolts also exposed a number of the contradictions inherent in their societies.[2]

In America, 1968 was merely the most apocalyptic year of a momentous decade. During that period the myths underlying the foreign policy of containment, the belief that domestic affluence ensured social peace, and the basic optimism that dominated American life and spirit since the Second World War were buried forever. For many Americans their image of themselves, their society, and their place in the world underwent a painful transformation. Despite the fact that it ultimately ushered in a period of intense social and political conservatism (whose force and grip on power has still clearly not abated) it left hope that this was no permanent state of things—that some form of social and cultural rebellion could arise again.[3]

The decade was ushered in with a growing sense of possibility for political change. Symbolic of that hope was the presidency of the handsome, youthful John F. Kennedy. He projected an image of energy and eloquence which veiled his militant Cold War postures and other political assumptions he shared with his Republican opponent in the 1960 election, Richard Nixon. Kennedy was elected on his promise to "get the country moving again" and his vision of a "New Frontier." The public had become a bit tired of the malaise and apathy of the last years of the Eisenhower administration: the constant economic dislocations (recessions and unemployment); foreign policy disarray (U-2 incident, Japanese student riots, Cuban revolution); and missile gap myths. Still, the reaction to the cool, stylish Senator from Massachusetts wasn't overwhelming—he won the presidency with the slim mandate of only 118,000 votes.[4]

In his inaugural address, Kennedy neglected to mention domestic issues but promised a renewed dedication to world leadership and proceeded to convert his mandate into a foreign policy of constant challenge to the Soviet Union and its allies. Kennedy and his crisis-management teams ranged worldwide confronting the communists in Laos, Berlin, and Cuba until they almost brought the world to the brink of nuclear disaster with the 1962 Cuban missile crisis.

Sobered by this flirtation with the apocalypse, Kennedy negotiated a long-awaited nuclear test ban treaty and raised hopes for further detente with a thoughtful foreign policy address at the American University in Washington, D.C. in June 1963. His assassination, however, tragically cut short more concerted attempts to bring about disarmament and disengagement.[5]

Kennedy's capacity for exciting the public's expectation of a breakthrough in the Cold War was paralleled by his seeming encouragement of black American hopes for some form of civil rights legislation. Hardly a radical on the issue during his senatorial career, and barely mentioning it in his Churchillian inaugural address (one brief sentence), race was initially not a major Kennedy concern. However, equality for black Americans was "an idea," in the words of Victor Hugo, "whose time had come."[6]

Ever since the forties, blacks had almost imperceptibly made significant social and economic gains, and become more critical of racist and discriminatory policies and practices. Their migration to the urban North led them to become one of the mainstays of the Democratic Party's political coalition and provided the margin of victory for both Truman and Kennedy. In the 1950s, the NAACP, which had diligently struggled in the courts against segregation and discrimination in education and voting, won the aforementioned landmark decision in the Supreme Court against segregation in the schools (1954 Brown decision) and established racial equality as one of the prime and unavoidable political and moral issues facing the United States.[7]

What is more, the black community had produced leaders in the 1950s and 1960s such as Martin Luther King Jr., James Farmer, Roy Wilkins, Whitney Young Jr., Bayard Rustin, and the younger "new abolitionists" of the Student Non-Violent Co-ordinating Committee (SNCC). Beginning with the successful Montgomery bus boycott, through sit-ins, freedom rides, and voter registration drives, blacks made clear their demand for integration and equal rights. It was a demand which peaked during the Kennedy administration in the 1963 "March on Washington," where blacks made a highly visible, well-organized, and disciplined bid for their demands to be heard, culminating in Martin Luther King's eloquent and evangelical speech, "I have a dream."

Though the March was probably the apotheosis of liberal optimism and self-confidence, in its midst there were the seeds of discord symptomatic of tactical, ideological, and programmatic differences within the black leadership and community. The most fully reported of these episodes was the radical speech attacking the Democratic Party leadership that John Lewis, executive secretary of SNCC, intended to make, which was so objectionable to other members of the March coalition that it almost caused their withdrawal.[8]

However, even if the March maintained its facade of harmony, it did not prevent a northern black leader, scornfully dismissing the March's goals of civil rights legislation, from commenting: "What difference does it make if you can sit at a lunch counter with whites if you didn't have the money to order a hamburger?" This remark neatly summarized the feelings of many northern blacks who for years had de jure civil rights but were deprived of jobs, adequate education, housing, and imprisoned in a psychology and ethos shaped by racism, that no amount of civil rights could allay or transform.[9]

It was this oppressive and alienating situation which propelled blacks into a series of violent ghetto riots that engulfed numerous major cities in the 1960s. The riots resulted in a diminution of white liberal support for (and in some cases a backlash against) the Civil Rights Movement--edging the movement further away from its integrationist philosophy. The move away from both non-violent resistance and a commitment to integration had already begun to take place. Continued violent Southern resistance—the murder of three civil rights workers in Mississippi in 1964—and a feeling that institutions such as the Democratic Party and the labor unions were hesitant about dedicating themselves to social change helped bring about this shift. There emerged a number of militant, angry black leaders like Malcolm X and Stokely Carmichael who repudiated acceptance by and integration into white America for an ideology of black nationalism and separatism.[10]

The task of Kennedy's successor, Lyndon B. Johnson, was to respond to demands that went beyond mere civil rights. Johnson was a complex man of immense energy, virtuoso political skills, and genuine compassion whose crudely manipulative and abrasive personality and ideology of globalism were ill-suited to the demands of the time. A southern moderate, who in his senatorial career had been more conservative than Kennedy, he nonetheless fully committed himself to the task of civil rights legislation. He succeeded in winning the passage of laws, like the Voting Rights Act, that assured blacks of their rights as no other political figure, including Kennedy, could have accomplished. In an attempt also to deal with black as well as white economic and social deprivation he updated the New Deal and fashioned a program (e.g., community-action groups, aid to minority businesses, etc.) which he called the "War on Poverty," intended to be a link in creating for all Americans what he dreamed would be a "Great Society."[11]

Unfortunately, from its inception Johnson's war fell victim to underfunding, administrative chaos, ripoffs, and an insufficient understanding of how complex and profound were many of the social problems confronting the poverty war. The program also caused resentment and anger among white working-class and lower-middle-class people who felt that the government was neglecting their needs in favor of blacks—a problem that still confronts almost any social program that seems exclusively aimed at helping minorities. This set of circumstances ultimately became terminal as the United States became more and more enmeshed in a futile ten-year war to stop "communist aggression" in South Vietnam, and the poverty program in turn began to lose both funding and the President's attention and commitment.[12]

The Vietnam War dominated political debate and policy making during the second half of the sixties, and the assumptions that guided this struggle were the same as those that had directed American policy in Europe since 1945. We continued to believe that Soviet Russian-controlled communist movements were seeking to expand at the expense of weak liberal-democratic regimes, and must be contained by the military and economic power of the United States. The corollary of that notion was that if one nation fell, all would collapse—the "domino effect."

However, the principles of containment did not apply to Southeast Asia and particularly South Vietnam. Here the communist monolith had long been stalled on the shoals of divergent Moscow-Peking versions of communism, ancient distrusts, and even ethnic and racial hostility. There was no evidence that Ho Chi Minh had any desire to do more than create a unified Vietnam. And the governments that the United States tried to support were never democratic and hardly liberal. Finally, the war was also not quite a naked communist power grab, but at first largely the result of indigenous communists and nationalists attempting to wrest power from the hands of increasingly isolated, dictatorial, and corrupt neo-colonialists.[13]

Instead of confronting communist expansionism the United States self-destructively thrust itself into a civil war. This meant little to the policy planners of the State Department and the Pentagon, who saw the war as both a way of extending the Pax Americana to Asia, and testing their new military tactics against the post-World War II "wars of national liberation."[14]

To accomplish this policy the government had to hide its purposes behind carefully built up subterfuges such as claiming that the United States was helping the Vietnamese to help themselves, and by instigating provocations that inflamed American patriotic feeling (the Tonkir Gulf and Pleiku incidents) as a pretext for a military buildup. Indeed, as a consequence of this policy the government had over 500,000 troops in South Vietnam by 1968, and was spending upwards of $27 billion a year on the war.

The inconsistencies and contradictions of this well-orchestrated escalation were not lost on a growing number of middle-class, white, American youth whose commitment to activism and social change had been inspired by the early idealism evoked by the rhetoric and style of the Kennedy administration and the actions of the Civil Rights Movement. In the early sixties a group of college students formed Students for a Democratic Society (SDS) and elaborated and attempted to implement a program of political and social reform based at first on non-violence and participatory democracy. This "New Left," as it was called, took the lead in recruiting and politicizing an effective and dynamic antiwar movement numbering thousands of Americans (most of whom were far from being new leftists) repelled by the U.S. conduct of the war, the growing number of American casualties, and the rising draft calls.[15]

The New Left was the most politically conscious section of a larger movement of students, young and not-so-young men and women, who were not only estranged by the war but were also alienated from what they perceived as American culture's spiritual emptiness and puritanical repressiveness. A product of the baby boom of the postwar era, the expansion of education, and the growing suburban affluence of American life, the "hippies" or "flower children" (most accurately the counter or adversary culture, since most of its most influential spokesmen were well over the dread age of thirty) gained intellectual awareness and legitimacy from the writings of 1950s intellectual radicals such as Norman Mailer, Paul Goodman, C. Wright Mills, and the novelists and poets of the "beat generation." Nonetheless, the basis of the counterculture's ethos was not intellectual (indeed, many were aggressively anti-intellectual) but the shared experience of drugs like marijuana and LSD; personal style—long hair, army cast-off clothes; folk and rock music—the Beatles, Bob Dylan, The Rolling Stones; and a burgeoning, assertive underground press—*Los Angeles Free Press, Berkeley Barb,* and *East Village Other.*[16]

Though there were stylistic and intellectual differences between the amorphous counterculture and the chaotic but more self-conscious and organized New Left, they existed in uneasy coalition with each other. The coalition reached its apogee of political power and influence when their shared antagonism to the war helped lead to Johnson's dropping out of the 1968 presidential race. They were also able to join together in the demonstrations and riots that engulfed Columbia University in the spring of that year and the Democratic Convention in Chicago that summer. A similar public expression of the communal spirit of the sixties, though much more affected by the values of the counterculture, was the Woodstock Music Festival in the summer of 1969.[17]

However, both the New Left and the counterculture quickly splintered as Martin Luther King Jr. and Robert Kennedy were assassinated and demonstrations did not bring the instant collapse of the Pentagon or the war effort. Revolution-intoxicated leaders turned from community building and constructing a resistance to the war to nihilistic terrorism or sterile neo-Stalinist and Maoist dogmatism. At the same time, the counterculture found itself usurped by hip capitalists and a sensation-hungry media, who marketed and trivialized some of its more innovative and original elements. And the simplistic counterculture ethic of "doing your thing" was used by criminal elements to penetrate the milieu and exploit its ingenuousness. In addition, the anti-work, anti-family, anti-patriotic, and anti-white working-class rhetoric and image of the "New Left" and the counterculture aroused an aggressive backlash which first manifested itself in the populist racism of the Wallace movement and then became an integral part of the conservative coalition that elected Richard Nixon to the presidency in 1968.[18]

The last years of the decade saw what was left of these movements destroy themselves and most of their appeal in a paroxysm of violent "Weatherman" demonstrations, the bloody Rolling Stones concert at Altamont, and the paranoid and murderous destruction of the Manson family (which could be seen as a pathological parody of the counterculture). Helping to also bring it to the ground were the cunning policies of the Nixon administration. Nixon manipulated Vietnam troop withdrawals and began to end the draft, while at the same time intensifying the air war in Vietnam and expanding the ground war into Laos and Cambodia. It was all done to give the public the impression that the war was gradually winding down, and lead to its removal as a prime element in the national consciousness.[19]

Despite ending on such discordant notes, the 1960s nevertheless had positive results. Among the most permanent of these was a revisionist impulse which stimulated many Americans to look critically at themselves, their history, and social and political ideas and institutions. Of course this did not guarantee that real change would come about, but it did make political and social nonconformity more difficult to repress and the simplistic pieties of the past harder to sustain.

Nowhere was this tendency to ignore reality or bend it to its will more firmly entrenched than in Hollywood at the beginning of the sixties. Nonetheless, even in Hollywood the 1960s was a force for renewal and transformation. The spirit of optimism may have marked the opening of the decade for the rest of the country, but the film industry was at its nadir. The most startling victim of that decline was the vaunted studio system, whose final demise was symbolized in the 1970 MGM auction of artifacts like Judy Garland's *Wizard of Oz* ruby slippers.

Taken over by financier Kirk Kerkorian in 1969, the studio (which once boasted "more stars than in heaven") was promptly turned into a hotel-gambling enterprise with only incidental filmmaking interests. MGM was only one (albeit the most prominent) of a number of studios that went completely out of the filmmaking business (RKO), or became part of the leisure-time divisions of conglomerates like Gulf and Western (Paramount), Transamerican (United Artists), MCA (Universal), Warner Communications (Warner Brothers).

Gone forever were the dream factories with their armies of contract actors and actresses, writers, directors, craftspeople, technicians, and publicists. Instead the new studio head, who operated under the logo of the old studio, was likely to be a former talent agent (Ted Ashley, Barry Diller) who could put together talented packages of super-star actors, actresses, and directors. By the end of the decade the studios were no longer interested in making films, they had assumed merely the marketing and financial end of the process.[20]

Nevertheless, not every change during the sixties was an unmitigated disaster. Indeed, as a result of relaxing societal sexual standards and court rulings overturning rigid obscenity laws, the sexual taboos long governing Hollywood began to fall by the wayside. Gone were the twin beds and in to replace them came full-frontal nudity. Though this freedom was used by some filmmakers as an excuse for sexual titillation, and spawned a successful independent cottage industry of hard and soft-core film pornography, it did permit a widening of the range of permissible film topics. American films now had a greater chance to convey aspects of human relationships that they previously had little freedom to depict.[21]

In addition to sex other Hollywood blind spots were breached by the protest movements of the 1960s. Blacks could no longer be either totally ignored or merely cast in subservient and stereotypical roles—though no great breakthrough for films dealing with black life took place. And the deviant lifestyles and political ideas of the young, though often exploited and adulterated by Hollywood, still had to be dealt with, especially since they had begun to make up the largest portion of the cinema audience.[22]

One of the first intimations of a new mood in Hollywood was Hitchcock's extremely successful *Psycho* (1960). It was a formally dazzling and brilliantly perverse film—oriented to a new generation of filmgoers—more erotic, violent, and macabre than any of Hitchcock's previous work. In this bleak, black and white film, Hitchcock, working with his usual obsessions (i.e., guilt, voyeurism, Oedipal complexes, and misogyny) utilizes the iconography of the horror film—an isolated motel, an old, forbidding Victorian house, a sensational murder sequence (using an Eisenstein-like montage) that arouses feelings of terror, a chilling musical score, and a murderer who is a tranvestite and psychotic. *Psycho* marked the introduction of the formula thriller "which redefined the limits of sex and violence in films,"[23] and would in a decade or more overrun the theatres with mediocre slasher films.

An early sixties' film that both prefigured the style of other films during the decade and had an almost prophetic quality, was John Frankenheimer's *The Manchurian Candidate* (1962). *The Manchurian Candidate* was based on the fifties' liberal conceit which suggested that: "If Joe McCarthy were working for the communists, he couldn't be doing a better job."[24] In a rather intricate, ironic script, adapted by George Axelrod from the novel by Richard Condon, chilling, odious Sergeant Raymond Shaw (Laurence Harvey) comes back from the Korean War a Medal of Honor winner. However, it turns out that the incident for which he was awarded the medal is a fabricated one, and Shaw is really a programmed communist assassin (the brainwashing done in Manchuria by murderous Russian and Chinese Pavlovian psychologists) controlled by his communist agent mother (Angela Lansbury). This monstrous manipulator of a mother turns out to be merely using him as a weapon to put her buffoonish, McCarthy-like senator husband into the White House and acquire absolute power for herself. *The Manchurian Candidate* allows Frankenheimer to succeed in constructing a neat, liberal balancing act, condemning McCarthy while simultaneously invoking the specter of a vicious "red menace" and conspiracy.[25]

Within this inventive but somewhat hysterical thriller framework, Frankenheimer sought to create the ultimate send-up of McCarthy (a bit belated since McCarthy was already dead and his power long since curbed) with war heroes, senators, and even the ne plus ultra of American virtue—Mom—revealed as communist agents. He also succeeded in creating an almost absurdist sense of American politics, where irrationality is the norm, plots abound, mother-dominated sons are turned into robot-like assassins, overwrought liberals denounce right-wingers as "fascists," right-wingers parade around at costume parties in Abraham Lincoln outfits, and most figures of authority and power are never what they seem to be. Frankenheimer may have succeeded beyond his own expectations in creating a film of political prophecy. In it he augured not only the media politics of the 1960s with scene after scene dominated by the almost baleful gleam of the TV screen, but most ominous of all—its political assassinations, particularly the Oedipal and vengeful Madison Square Garden shootings of Raymond's parents, linking private pathology with public and political action.

Unfortunately, Frankenheimer's skillful, flashy, sometimes gratuitous blending of fifties political issues with prefigurings of the late sixties "put on" style—the use of bizzare effects and outrageous overstatement to make a point and get a laugh—did not inspire a host of films which struggled to illuminate American politics. Instead the key issue in films such as Otto Preminger's *Advise and Consent* (1962) and Franklin Schaffner's version of Gore Vidal's cynical, literate novel *The Best Man* (1964), with its political convention-battling between Stevensonian and Nixonian candidates, was homosexuality.

However, there was more to *Advise and Consent* than its melodramatic, prurient treatment of homosexuality. With his cool, objective, and lucid style—characterized by long takes, deep focus and fluid tracks and pans—Preminger was able to successfully evoke the atmosphere of the Senate and its procedures—pages, the gallery, quorum calls, and the workings of the committee system. Preminger endorsed the American system's gift for compromise and flexibility—the film's hero being the honorable, decent Majority Leader, Senator Munson (Walter Pigeon) who is committed to the civilities and rules of "the Club"—the Senate. Munson affirms the system of checks and balances and is repelled by the behavior of the film's villain—a tactless, vile, left-liberal opportunist who respects nothing but his own drive for power. Preminger's idea of a left wing senator is a crude caricature, but the film tries to balance him off with a florid, manipulative, reactionary southern Senator Seab Cooley played with such flair by Charles Laughton that he is able to elicit audience sympathy. However, *Advise and Consent* was not interested in either senator's ideological stance—the film never really explored the rights and wrongs of the issues. Its concern was with honorable behavior, and for Preminger that sort of conduct comes from understanding that the political world is not built on moral purity and pride but on a sense of ambiguity and compromise.

Advise and Consent was a generally intelligent film, which, like many less sophisticated Hollywood products, saw political conflict as primarily a struggle between personalities. However, its personal dynamics were more complex than the usual heroes versus villains. But in its affirmation of political flexibility the film both never questioned the truism that the system serves all segments of the American population, nor asked about the nature of the social ends that the governmental process is geared to. In fact, Preminger's complacency smacked of fifties' consensus thinking about the effectiveness of American democracy.

Nevertheless, Preminger's satisfaction with the workings of the government was supplanted by films dealing with the apocalyptic terror aroused by the possibility of nuclear attack and annihilation. In *Seven Days In May* (1964) a statesmanlike, peace-oriented president (Frederic March) signs a nuclear nonproliferation treaty with the Soviet Union, prompting a group of right-wing generals led by a megalomaniacal, zealot General Scott (Burt Lancaster) to plot a coup. The villains are no longer communist fifth columnists, like in early fifties films, but a charismatic general who believes the country can only be saved from the Russians by a man on a white horse. The coup is predictably subverted by decent men who believe in the democratic process and the Constitution.

Seven Days in May was a much less imaginative work than films made the same year about the actual threat of nuclear destruction. In the words of Susan Sontag, films about nuclear war struck the audience's "imagination of disaster"—their sense of participation—"in the fantasy of living through one's own death and more the death of cities, the destruction of humanity itself,"[26] gained wide popularity. It was a vision of the world that certainly contributed to the success of two films, with radically different styles, Fail Safe (1964) and Dr. Strangelove: Or How I Stopped Worrying and Learned to Love the Bomb (1964).

Unlike Dr. Strangelove, released earlier that year, Fail Safe, adapted from a best-seller by Eugene Burdick and Harvey Wheeler, saw nuclear disaster as resulting from the probable malfunctioning of nuclear weaponry's safe-guarding technology, rather than from the actions of paranoid generals. In Fail Safe it is a technological breakdown which launches American bombers on a full-scale attack of the Soviet Union. Hoping to avert a catastrophe the decent American President (Henry Fonda) negotiates with the Russian Premier over the hot-line. However, the bomber does get through to bomb Moscow, and the American President, to save the world, winds up having to trade the destruction of New York for the obliteration of the Russian capital. Despite this rather far-fetched conclusion, Sidney Lumet's semi-documentary approach and his powerful and horrifying final montage of the destruction of New York and Moscow give the film a chilling measure of reality.

The most compelling moments of the film are the image of Fonda framed in almost total isolation, trying in his characteristic dry, almost laconic, tones to assure the Russians that it was all a mistake; and his shedding a tear after hearing the shrill sound of the telephone that signals the bomb exploding in Moscow. These scenes capture a sense of the unbearable tragedy which hangs in the balance, as men representing very different power structures and interests try, against imponderable odds, to reason with each other about the dire consequences of both nations' nuclear arms policies. An audience viewing these scenes would be hard pressed to avoid feeling how close to the brink we were, and what slender resources there existed to avert such a disaster.

Fail Safe is a cautionary film about an out-of-control technology that makes men its pawns and disciples. It is not particularly subtle, turning most of its characters into ciphers who merely serve its theme. In Walter Matthau's over-stated, Dr. Strangelove-like political science professor (Groteschele) the film has a character who conveys genuine political substance. Matthau represents the 1960s Cold War intellectuals (e.g., Kahn, Teller) who expressed their vision of realpolitik and their machismo fantasies by indulging in "thinking about the unthinkable." These were men who could talk casually and obsessively about building advanced weaponry and the possibilities and necessary risks of nuclear warfare without any moral or humane constraints or qualms about the consequences of these policies.[27]

It is this assault on murderous realpolitik which was one of the prime themes of Stanley Kubrick's sardonic black comedy, *Dr. Strangelove*. The director of one critically acclaimed antiwar film, *Paths of Glory* (1957), Kubrick had long been interested in the problem of nuclear war and its effects. At first, he tried to do a faithful adaptation of Peter George's novel *Red Alert*. However, each time he attempted to write it the whole notion seemed more and more "ridiculous" and he decided to do a black comic film instead.

Kubrick was able to enlist the mimic and comic talents of Peter Sellers, who played three roles (the stiff-upper lipped British Group Captain Mandrake; the balding, literally egg-headed, President Merkin Muffley; and the bizarre, Nazi-refugee scientist Dr. Strangelove). He also blended the talents of George C. Scott as the General Curtis Lemay-like, adolescent, gravelly-voiced, platitude-spouting Air Force Chief-of-Staff, Buck Turgidson, and the dead-pan of Sterling Hayden's mad, grim, General Jack D. Ripper, the man who initiates the unauthorized bomber raid.

Complementing this ensemble acting was Kubrick's genius for creating striking images and settings. This talent is maintained from the opening scene where the B-52 is seen copulating with its refuelling plane (to "Try a Little Tenderness" on the sound track) to the black-comic finale where the doomsday mechanism has exploded and what results is a void with only mushroom clouds filling it, and on the sound track Vera Lynn can be heard singing the World War II favorite, "We'll Meet Again." Kubrick also constructs three imaginative settings, cutting from one to another throughout the film: the extremely realistic and intricate looking technology of the B-52 cockpit; the war room in Washington whose flashing lights, big board, large circular table and vast empty space skirt the line between realism and surrealism; and Burpleson Air Force Base where the psychopathic General Ripper is shot in tight close-up from a low angle, and his troops' violent defense of the base against other American troops is shot with a handheld camera in grainy cinéma vérité style.

These elements came together in a narrative which describes the destruction of the world by a Soviet-constructed doomsday machine ignited by a nuclear attack launched by General Jack D. Ripper. He initiates the attack because he absurdly fears that the nation's sexual potency is on the brink of being undermined by a communist-inspired plot to fluoridate the American water supply. Terry Southern's antic screenplay served Kubrick brilliantly in satirizing a world of well-meaning but ineffectual liberal politicians, war-mongering generals, espionage-obsessed Russian ambassadors, and demonic nuclear-war strategists.

Dr. Strangelove went beyond satire of the foibles of the power structure and its thinking about nuclear war, linking their behavior to the primal instincts of sex and death—eros and thanatos. There are scenes of the president talking over the hot line from his crypt-like war room to a drunken Russian Premier Kissoff who can't comprehend what's being said because he's dallying with his mistress; Turgidson in turn getting calls from his mistress in the midst of a war-room discussion; and Colonel Kong (Slim Pickens) astride the B-52's nuclear bomb (looking like a monstrous phallus) as it descends to penetrate and destroy the Soviet Union and the world.

Of course the humanistic tradition presumes that the forces that kindle these passions can be held in check by reason. However, *Dr. Strangelove's* most caustic barbs are aimed not only at the deadly logic of thinking about the unthinkable, but at sweet, humane reason itself. Time after time, we hear President Muffley's bland, decent conversations with the Russian premier ("Now Dimitri, you know how we've always talked about the possibility of something going wrong with the bomb—the bomb, Dimitri, the hydrogen bomb") or his shouting "you can't fight here, this is the war room" as the Russian ambassador and Air Force chief of staff wrestle on the floor, and we are reminded of the futility and impotence of reason as men try to cope with the enormity of the forces they have unleashed.[28]

Kubrick posits no alternative to an insane world whose leaders are either ineffectual, stupid, infantile, or obsessional personalities. There is no plea for sanity or belief in social change inherent here. There is only the monstrous Dr. Strangelove, who is the personification of scientific reason gone amuck. Strangelove, with his self-propelled Nazi-saluting arm, his belief in the divinity of computers, and his gleeful plans for a postnuclear holocaust society of subterranean polygamy (the ultimate expression of America's obsession with macho potency and power), emerges as a brilliant parody of the worst strains in American politics and culture.

In allowing us to take this black-comic peek at the apocalypse, Kubrick succeeded more in creating an inoculation against the fear of annihilation (laughter providing a means for coping in a world perched on the abyss) than in providing even a hint of some sane strategy for dealing with nuclear weapons. Kubrick's world is a mad, hopeless one, and as Pauline Kael wrote in her review of *Dr. Strangelove*, "What may have been laughed to death was not war, but some action about it."[29]

Despite this sort of criticism, Kubrick's film was able to sum up the anxieties about nuclear disaster which haunted the fifties, and, with the Cuban missile crisis, almost turned into reality in the sixties. And by making both sides responsible for the state of affairs it cut through the Gordian knot of Cold War mythology.[30] As social philosopher Lewis Mumford, writing in the *New York Times* noted, it was "the first break in the cold war trance that has so long held this country in its rigid grip."[31]

Dr. Strangelove's breakthrough may not have changed the nature of nuclear policy, but it allowed film directors to use black comedy and irony to make social and political points. (The use of black humor reflected the influence of savagely satiric novelists like Joseph Heller, Thomas Pynchon, and Kurt Vonnegut.) It gave directors and the industry the opportunity to critically confront controversial issues without alienating an audience.

Besides films like the aforementioned *Manchurian Candidate* there were works like Billy Wilder's Oscar-winning *The Apartment* (1960). It was an acidic serio-comic take on corporate sexual politics and success; the film's central figure, an innocent but ambitious insurance clerk, C. C. Baxter (Jack Lemmon), lends his apartment to his married corporate superiors, so they can have assignations with their mistresses. Nevertheless, though the film concludes sentimentally with a pathetic Baxter both finding true love and finally standing up to his bosses (he refuses to loan his apartment out any longer and gives up his promotion), the film's vision of corporate behavior was an uncompromisingly dark one.

There was also *The Americanization of Emily* (1964) which ironically celebrated cowardice and was a film clearly ahead of its time. The only stir it initially created was by virtue of Julie Andrews's post-Poppins dramatic debut. However, when it appeared again in 1967 its attacks on war and heroism fit nicely into the spirit of the sixties. There was a ready-made audience for its cynical, wheeler-dealer, anti-hero, Naval Lieutenant Commander Charles Madison (James Garner) whose credo was that cowardice does more for humanity than courage.

The film doesn't just pay homage to cowardice, but it takes pot-shots at the madness of war, especially Madison's superior officer who wants the first dead man on Omaha Beach to be a navy man. This sort of satire may not have been profound or radical but it broke from the conventions that dominated films about the military in the preceding decades.

Nevertheless, the industry preferred, in the main, to grind out its usual quota of genre films led by the Cold War-inspired, superspy exploits of James Bond and his imitators like *Our Man Flint* (1966) and the Matt Helm series (*The Silencers*, 1966, *Murderers Row*, 1966, *The Ambushers*, 1967). Occasionally, these films were buttressed by a prestige picture like the anti-Nazi but essentially Grand Hotelish *Ship of Fools* (1965); the theatrical, message-bloated *A Man For All Seasons* (1966); or Sidney Lumet's *The Pawnbroker* (1965), an over-emphatic but moving work that evoked the Holocaust survivor experience in a way that no other Hollywood film has ever done.

The Pawnbroker centers on a haunted, emotionally frozen concentration-camp survivor, Sol Nazerman (Rod Steiger), who owns a pawnshop among the violent, broken, and defeated in New York's East Harlem. The film's emphasis is on the isolated Nazerman's anguish and his catharsis, but there are also some vivid, unsentimental portraits of customers whose lives are also bound by suffering. However, influenced by Alain Resnais' *Hiroshima Mon Amour*, the film indulges in a great deal of parallel cutting from the teeming, inner-city ghetto streets to harrowing memory images of Auschwitz. The film doesn't quite attempt to equate the camps with East Harlem, but the trenchant cutting between the two experiences suggests that the people of East Harlem are on one level prisoners just like Nazerman is, though the streets project a great deal of life energy that co-exists with their oppression.

However, even if *The Pawnbroker*'s prime interest was not in evoking inner city reality, it was one of the few Hollywood films of the 1960s that gave us images of the way those streets (e.g., pool halls, cramped apartments, tenement stoops, nightclubs, indoor markets) looked. Just how far out of step Hollywood was could be seen in the films which focused on black life, for despite the Civil Rights Movement there had been no great surge in the direction of making films about blacks or black life either in the late fifties or early sixties. However, in films like *The Defiant Ones* (1958) and *A Raisin in the Sun* (1962), there was an attempt at least to portray blacks in a positive manner and to wrestle with some social and economic issues (especially in *A Raisin in the Sun*) but all within the context of an optimistic, integrationist philosophy. These were films that suggested that the American Dream was open to blacks if white attitudes shifted and blacks pursued their ambitions more relentlessly.

Despite the fact that the fantasy of equity and integration was being destroyed no further away from Hollywood than the streets of Watts, the film industry still clung tenaciously to its sentimental and reductive vision of black-white relations. In the Oscar-winning crime melodrama *In the Heat of the Night* (1967), a stiff, dignified, black Philadelphia homicide detective Virgil Tibbs (Sidney Poitier) solves a murder case in a Mississippi town and predictably wins the respect of the bigoted, bellowing, lonely police chief (Rod Steiger). Tibbs, of course, is smarter and more professional than any of the local cops—a man toward whom only the most benighted could display any racist feelings. What is distinctive about the film is not the script or performances, but Haskell Wexler's cinematography, which captures the oppressive heat and tension of summer nights in a racist, rural Southern town.

Nowhere was the faith that social change could be brought about through personal understanding and affection between blacks and whites more evident than in Stanley Kramer's *Guess Who's Coming to Dinner* (1967). Kramer's liberal credentials were already well established with his portentous, social-problem productions of the anti-racial prejudice such as *Home of the Brave* (1949), the anti-Nazi *Judgment at Nuremburg* (1961), *On the Beach* and *The Defiant Ones*. In the glossy *Guess Who's Coming to Dinner* Kramer and scriptwriter William Rose decided to tackle the subject of interracial marriage.

However, tackle is hardly the right word since there rarely has been such a field of straw men and women. The black male lead was again Sidney Poitier who had already established himself as a worthy and successful missionary to white folks in a great many films (e.g., *Lilies of the Field*, 1963, *A Patch of Blue*, 1965) and in this film portrays a handsome, chaste, and charming doctor well on his way to someday winning the Nobel prize. In fact, he is too good a catch for the innocent, simpering daughter (Katherine Houghton) of liberal millionaire presslord Matt Drayton (Spencer Tracy) and his feisty, gallery-owning wife, Christina (Katherine Hepburn).

Although there are objections to the marriage, ranging from the bigoted snobbishness of one of Christina's art gallery employees to the comic protests of the Drayton's cute black maid ("civil rights is one thing, but this here's another!"), they are easily brushed aside. More difficult to sweep away are the more serious doubts expressed by Matt Drayton about the social problems the young couple will have to face. However, even his reasonable concerns are effectively bypassed by Beah Richard's (Poitier's mother in the film) suggestion that it is not race that is preventing the marriage, but the fact that he and her husband (who also opposes the match) have forgotten what it was like to be young.

As a result, what ostensibly emerges as a prime issue in *Guess Who's Coming to Dinner* is not race, but the clash of generations. Of course, it's a situation that is immediately rectified in Tracy's valedictory to Christina, about love conquering all, which is as much a commentary on his own twenty-seven-year relationship with Hepburn as it is to his fictional wife, since Tracy was to die within weeks of the conclusion of the film.[2]

And though the issue of the generation gap feels totally bogus, especially in a film ostensibly dealing with the complex issue of intermarriage (not to mention the total blindness and irrelevance of the film's liberal, integrationist impulses to the rage and despair of the black community), it nevertheless superficially touched on something significant, the growing polarization between generations. It was this polarization—resulting from the Vietnam War and the rise of the New Left and counterculture which intensified and helped divide America in the late 1960s.

Already the coming of the young into American politics had been celebrated in the prose of authors such as Norman Mailer who saw them as "those mad middle class children with their lobotomies from sin . . . their innocence, their lust for the apocalypse."[33] However, their image had still not been forged in film, nor would it be until Arthur Penn's *Bonnie and Clyde* (1967).

Bonnie and Clyde not only shifted the focus of film to the young, it also defined a unique sixties' cinema and sensibility in ways that *The Manchurian Candidate* and *Dr. Strangelove* had only hinted at. The best indicator of how far it went in accomplishing this was the vehemence of the attacks on it by the critical establishment, led by *New York Times* critic Bosley Crowther. Nevertheless, audiences flocked to it, copied its clothing styles, and made it one of the year's top grossers.

Vindicating the judgment of audiences over film critics is only one of the film's minor achievements. Its greatest success was in both introducing the ideas and techniques of the French "New Wave" into the Hollywood mainstream, and in firmly fixing the gaze of American filmmakers on the lives and styles of the alienated and discontented.

Written by two young *Esquire* writers, David Newman and Robert Benton, it was originally seen by them as a possible project for either François Truffaut or Jean-Luc Godard, a hope based on their appreciation of the French New Wave's understanding of the poetic and mythic nature of the American genre film. However, neither director was available, and the film was ultimately produced by Warren Beatty and directed by Arthur Penn.

Penn had also been influenced by the New Wave, so little was really lost by the change, and he was able to incorporate many of their techniques into the film. So along with free-intercutting of time and space, the use of slow and accelerated motion, he also used little vignettes ending in visual and verbal puns à la Truffaut and the alternating of comic and violent moments apropos of Godard. In fact, it was the irony and humor of *Bonnie and Clyde*—like the chase scene where careening and zigzagging cars comically pursue each other accompanied by a wildly twanging banjo sound track, or the gang's picnic with a middle-class couple, who though at first terrified, ultimately refuse to leave them—which helped prevent the film from turning into conventional social melodrama.

These techniques updated a story that was done before by Hollywood in Fritz Lang's *You Only Live Once* (1937) and Nicholas Ray's *They Live by Night* (1949). Yet this time-worn tale of two youthful outsiders who choose a life of crime held a powerful attraction for an audience who felt they were living cut off from the channels of power and incapable of bringing about social and political change.

This restless quality is caught right from the opening Depression-era scene in which the beautiful and bored Bonnie (Faye Dunaway) sees the limping, toothpick-chewing, handsome Clyde (Warren Beatty) attempting to steal her mother's car and, attracted by his bravado, she becomes involved in a life of crime. It takes them on a number of botched and bumbling robbery attempts, and after the addition of Clyde's crude, guffawing brother Buck (Gene Hackman), his bovine, pathetic wife Blanche (Estelle Parsons), and a nose-picking, hero-worshipping rustic driver named C. W. Moss (Michael Pollard), they go on a bank-robbing rampage that makes them celebrated and notorious figures.

Despite their violent and criminal acts, Penn never allows the audience's sympathy to leave Bonnie and Clyde. On the one hand, they are seen as outlaw-rebels (though never social victims) against an unjust social order represented here by the banks and police; on the other hand, they are innocent, awkward clowns, who in one robbery can't get the attention of their victims. Penn also attempts to reinforce our positive feelings for them through his use of shallow Freudianism. Clyde is sexually impotent, which supposedly provides the character with a measure of vulnerability, and gives his gun a crude, symbolic significance.

In depicting Bonnie and Clyde as ordinary folk, seeking to be immortalized, Penn sometimes catches the pathos underneath their posturing and bravado. For the sheepish, slow, inarticulate Clyde—match in mouth and permanent limp—and the slatternly, poetess manqué Bonnie—constantly looking at her image in a blurred mirror—are nothing more than a yokel sharecropper and a waitress who hunger for the American Dream of glamor and success. No matter how often Bonnie may dress in expensive clothes and obsess about her image and making the headlines, she still longs for her mother and settling down in a home. And though the scene where Bonnie returns to the family picnic is overly stylized and filled with soft-focused, sentimentalized, pastoral imagery (e.g., an almost too picturesquely weathered and stark-looking farm woman mother) it succeeds in evoking the rural and church-bound social world they both come from.

What is most striking in the film, however, is not their ordinariness or the social reality that helps shape them, but their mythic quality. It is a quality conveyed both by the glamor of stars like Beatty and Dunaway and by Penn's camera, which captures in long shot and close-up the outlaws' vitality, spontaneity, and style. Penn frames their actions with painterly, beautifully composed, melancholy images of sweeping wheat fields and prairies, and Walker Evans-like small towns. It is topped off by their slow-motion death, dressed in white (innocence?), twitching like rag dolls in a montage of violence. Their death is both mythic, the tragic death of a heroic duo, and concrete, for the bullets are real and leave them truly dead.

The myth of Bonnie and Clyde works for Penn in aesthetic terms—the beauty of alienation and outlawry—and captures something of how integral violence and the unfettered assertion of self and will were both to American mythology and the sixties. It is when Penn wants his outlaws to be seen as romantic rebels against an unjust social order—Clyde returning money he stole from a bank to a poor farmer or the gang being embraced as people's heroes at a migrant camp (straight out of *The Grapes of Wrath*) that the film becomes most simplistic and even dangerous. It is clear that Penn wants Bonnie and Clyde to stand as symbols for the rebellious and high-spirited youth of the 1960s while the banks, Deputy Sheriff Hammer and Pa Moss represent a callous, rigid, and hypocritical adult world. There are also suggestions, in the exaggerated, murderous use of police firepower (for example, a bloody shoot out where the police use an armored car), of the American military's penchant for overkill in Vietnam.

However, no matter that Clyde talks about protecting poor folk, their social consciousness is no more than a contrivance of Penn's. The only community Bonnie and Clyde are members of is the criminal one, and though the film might not have had any more pernicious influence than getting somebody to buy a snap-brim hat, it did give symbolic sanction to certain nihilistic values and strains permanent in both the counterculture and the New Left. The film fed the contempt many of the young had for the adult world and its work ethic. More significantly, by affirming crime as a viable means of social, political, and cultural protest, it fed the growing contempt that many of the young felt for more orthodox forms of political organization and action, and ominously romanticized sociopathic violence by confusing it with acts of social rebellion.[34]

These objections aside, *Bonnie and Clyde* was still the landmark film of the sixties. Along with revitalizing the formal dimensions of the Hollywood film, its focusing of attention on the young and the alienated gave some Hollywood luster to the 1960s revisionist impulse which saw American history and society from the bottom up. Once launched on this road the facile shibboleths about American society that had been Hollywood's stock in trade since World War II became harder and harder to sustain. And while much of this new perspective was transformed into films expressing a kind of bankable and facile pessimism accompanied by the same superstar actors as before, nevertheless, the films projected a vision of a fragmented America no longer as secure of itself and its values as had once been the case.

Nowhere is the crumbling of these values more clearly illustrated than in Mike Nichols's homage to the young, *The Graduate* (1967), a commercially and critically successful film whose most compelling moment is the post-nuptial abduction of the beautiful Elaine Robinson (Katherine Ross) by the romantically obsessed Benjamin Braddock (Dustin Hoffman in his first film). Not only did this scene break with a whole genre past that upheld the sanctities of the marriage vow above everything else, it was merely the shrewdest—it gave Hollywood a breakthrough into the eighteen- to twenty-five-year-old market—assault in a whole series of attacks on the values of the affluent, upper-middle-class American.

The embodiment of this challenge in *The Graduate* is somber, bright, and inexperienced Benjamin Braddock who returns to the emptiness and sterility of his parent's vulgar Southern California world of swimming pools and material comfort. Out of a sheer sense of ennui and alienation, Ben begins a sexually satisfying but emotionally starved and mechanical affair with the bored, cynical wife of his father's law partner, Mrs. Robinson (Anne Bancroft). It is the first stages of this affair that allow Hoffman to display his talent for giving richly textured performances. Before his transformation into a romantic hero, Hoffman's Braddock is filled with anxiety and self-doubt—speaking in half-finished phrases, wheezily expelling breath, and never quite sure of what his hands are doing—while fending off Mrs. Robinson's seductive wiles. The affair is simultaneously comic and pathetic and probably is the most poignant section of the film.

The deadness of his affair with Mrs. Robinson is contrasted with the spontaneity and openness he finds with her daughter Elaine. It is a relationship the predatory Mrs. Robinson violently objects to. And Nichols skillfully evokes empathy from the youth audience for both Elaine's freshness and vulnerability and Benjamin's truth-seeking and rejection of a plastic, unfeeling adult universe.

Combining the New Wave techniques of jump and flash cuts, extreme close-ups, and subjective view and telephoto lens shots (throughout, one senses Nichols's eclectic, stylistic borrowings from Antonioni, Fellini, and Godard) with the music of youth-culture heroes, Simon and Garfunkel, Nichols successfully creates a world of honest young people surrounded by stereotyped adults who are either predators or fools. The gilded surfaces of the adults predictably cover empty lives and dead marriages all echoing, in the words of Simon and Garfunkel, the "sounds of silence."

In such an emotional and moral void the mere act of honestly being in love is perceived as liberating and capable of shattering old taboos, even the supposed eternal links of "I do." Consequently, Mrs. Robinson's shriek at the runaway Elaine, that it's "too late," can be met with the reply, "not for me." This hardly guarantees a "they live happily ever after" fade out; and the film ends with the couple's blank and ambiguous stares as they leave the scene of the wedding in the back of a municipal bus.[35]

Regardless of this final seed of doubt about the future, The Graduate still remains a hymn to the young. Like Bonnie and Clyde it grants all energy, integrity, and life to the young. However, in contrast to the origins of Bonnie and Clyde's revolt, which was loosely tied to the poverty of the Depression, the reasons for Ben's alienation supposedly can be found in the sterility of upper-middle-class affluence. Taken together both films affirmed the discontent of the young. The Graduate underlined that dissatisfaction by locating it precisely at the moment when the American Dream seemed to have reached its peak of material fulfillment—creating a paradigm for the type of sixties film which attempted to subvert the values that had dominated American films since the 1940s. Not only were the language and sexual detail more frank in The Graduate, the insistence on a moral perspective which unambiguously repudiated social convention and mores was relatively new to Hollywood. With its oblique references to 1960s radicalism when its locale is shifted from Southern California to Berkeley (where a harried Benjamin follows Elaine) and a comic landlord who dislikes outside agitators makes a brief appearance, *The Graduate* hinted that there might be even more to Benjamin's anguish than alienation from the values of the upper-middle class and existential angst. However, *The Graduate* was based on a 1950s novel by Charles Webb and the film's few 1960s allusions did little to update the novel and illuminate the sources of student rebellion and alienation in the 1960s.

Still there was something about the intensity of *Bonnie and Clyde's* violence and the extremity of Benjamin's alienation which suggested that political events had some effect on the nature of the two films. The event which had the most profound effect on the politics of the young and American politics in general was the war in Vietnam. Aware of the divided nature of American public opinion about the war, producers hesitated to tackle the subject directly. However, for a right-wing super-star and patriot like John Wayne, a film about the Vietnam War, *The Green Berets* (1968), with himself as star, was a means of winning the hearts and minds of the American people.

Since the 1940s and films like *Wake Island* (1942), *They Were Expendable* (1945) and *Sands of Iwo Jima* (1949), John Wayne had become the symbol par excellence of the tough, efficient, patriotic, American fighting man. The Wayne image was indelibly imprinted on every American schoolboy's imagination and every raw recruit's dreams. Nor was there anything ironic or calculating in Wayne's own devotion to the image, as exemplified by his red-baiting leadership in the McCarthyite Motion Picture Alliance for the Preservation of American Ideals, and his support of bellicose right-wing politicians like Barry Goldwater and Ronald Reagan.

Choosing as the subject of his Vietnam film the elite, military unit, the Green Berets, Wayne was returning to the world of John Ford, his mentor. Ford's cavalry units, perched at the edge of the frontier, were bastions of communal honor, tradition, camaraderie and pride, fighting an often little-appreciated and less-understood battle for civilization and decency against the barbarians. Wayne's notion of the Green Berets was similar, he saw them as a fortress of muscular and professional anticommunist values whose most serious challenge came, ironically enough, not from the communists, but from a liberal, skeptical reporter, George Beckwith (David Jannsen). For Wayne, those soft liberals who undermined our patriotic will were far more dangerous than regiments of savage Vietcong. However, Beckwith's piddling doubts are suppressed as soon as he is exposed to the murderous brutality of a Vietcong raid on a desolate Vietnamese village.

If the first half of the film is mediocre John Ford—the Vietcong even scale with ladders the Green Berets' fort which is aptly named Dodge City—the film's second half is pure Richard Nixon. In this section Wayne uses all manner of advanced technologies and dirty tricks, including a Hollywood-style Mata Hari female decoy, and he kidnaps an enemy Vietcong general. The general's aristocratic and decadent values make even the revolutionary politics of the Vietcong suspect. Through all of this Wayne's hero (Colonel Mike Kirby) hovers about like a good paterfamilias, granting absolution to the liberal columnist for his political sins, providing fatherly comfort to a cute Vietnamese orphan who in Wayne's fadeout comment is "What this is all about."[36]

Although *The Green Berets* (1968) turned out to be financially profitable, rather than setting Americans' minds at ease about the righteousness of their cause, it produced new evidence of the national split on the war. Indicative of that polarization was some of the critical reaction to the film. In previous years a Wayne film rarely raised anything more that a critical ho-hum. However, *The Green Berets* provoked *New York Times* critic Renata Adler's withering comment that:

> *The Green Berets* is a film so unspeakable, so stupid, so rotten and false that it passes through being funny, through being camp, through everything and becomes an invitation to grieve not so much for our soldiers or Vietnam (the film could not be more false or do greater disservice to them) but for what has happened to the fantasy-making apparatus of this country.[37]

Adler's comment recognized that Hollywood's myth-making abilities had lost power and resonance, and consequently the old Hollywood formula could no longer capture and spur the nation's imagination to a greater commitment in the war. No longer could Wayne's war-loving, patriarchal figure, spouting the old patriotic and macho certainties and clichés about decent, freedom-loving Americans and brutal, totalitarian Vietcong, capture and dominate the moral center of the American imagination as it once had. Instead, Wayne's values existed in uneasy proximity to Hollywood's new revisionism featuring genre films that not only undermined Wayne's most cherished certitudes, but covertly and slyly evoked a Vietnam war which had horror rather than honor as its dominant motif.

One such film was Sam Peckinpah's (a descendant of pioneers) brilliantly cut and richly composed western *The Wild Bunch* (1969). Paradoxically *The Wild Bunch* drew much of its power from working against the Ford-Hawks tradition that had done so much for Wayne's reputation. For instance, *The Wild Bunch* took place when the frontier was closed physically, and the ethos of the Old West was disappearing fast in the wake of new technologies such as the motor car and machine gun. Also fading with it were the elite band of mythic professional good-bad Robin Hoods that often populated the moral landscapes of Hawks and Ford. In *The Wild Bunch* we have the interminable wranglings and whorings of Pike Bishop's (William Holden) gang of bank robbers and payroll snatchers, who are in turn pursued by a group of craven, rednecked, lumpen bounty hunters led by Pike's old confederate, the melancholy, trapped Deke Thornton (Robert Ryan). In addition, the traditional Hollywood western town, which often contained some people who could express communal pride, concern, and virtue, has been replaced by a passive, foolish citizenry, too cowed and confused to make even more than a token protest when the streets of their town erupt with bloody, chaotic violence. The only seemingly active members of the town are its children who mimic the shoot-out and are demonically amused by burning to death the scorpions and ants they have been playing with.

With society corrupt and rapacious and the mythic west gone, the film follows Bishop's bunch involvement in the Mexican Revolution (whose political issues Peckinpah cares nothing about) and in the process trying to establish some kind of rough set of principles. The one most valued is group loyalty, the kind embodied in Bishop's comment that "When you side with a man, you side with him all the way—otherwise you're an animal." Ultimately, this sense of loyalty grows among the outlaws and even includes the primal, savage Gorch Brothers (Ben Johnson and Warren Oates) and the Mexican bandit Angel (Jaime Sanchez). Almost as significant is the value placed on genuine authority in a world of corrupt betrayers where traditional institutional power is dominated by debauchees like the gross, murderous Mexican general Mapache (Emilio Fernandez) and the ruthless railroad executive Harrigan (Albert Dekker). Society's corruption makes it imperative, according to Pike's lieutenant Dutch (Ernest Borgnine), to heavily weigh the fact of not only giving your word (the old code), but also to considering "who you give it to."

However, whatever scrupulousness the outlaws exhibit toward their code is not matched by any restraint on Peckinpah's part in his depiction of violence in the film. For a supposed moralist, Peckinpah's use of graphic, elongated, and sensational violence throughout the film—a horse stomping on a woman and dragging a man along the ground and countless bodies falling in slow motion with blood gushing from them—raised again questions about the origins and effects of screen violence. The answer this time was not only the usual talk about the psychology of the director and Hollywood's tendency to indulge in and exploit blood and gore, but also a crediting of responsibility to the audience's increasing receptivity to violence, some of it caused by the nightly scenes of Vietnam bloodletting they saw on the television screen.

The climax of *The Wild Bunch*, with its stylized, orgiastic massacre, raised questions not only about the often incoherent blend of moralism and nihilism pervading Peckinpah's work, but also about the hopelessness reflected in many of the films of the late 1960s. Although *The Wild Bunch* ends on a supposedly revolutionary note with the last survivors both of the outlaws and of the bounty hunters, wise Old Sykes (Edmond O'Brien) and Deke Thornton, joining with the revolutionaries, the gesture seems a hollow afterthought following the more emotionally and aesthetically intense and compelling slaughter scenes. In fact, Peckinpah's deepest and most sentimental loyalties clearly have nothing to do with social commitment. It is men like Pike, seen in low-angle shots walking tall to a drum beat and resolving to die heroically, who elicit Peckinpah's deepest feeling. Pike and the men of the wild bunch may be brutal killers who belong to the past, but Peckinpah grants them a final, heroic eulogy (shades of Ford's *Fort Apache*, 1948) as he superimposes them over the film's last images, watching them, in their moment of transcendence, riding out of a Mexican village to the applause and serenades of its inhabitants.[38]

The Wild Bunch's mixture of intellectual incoherence and imaginative and powerful imagery was symptomatic (though in exaggerated form) of the problems that many of these late sixties films exhibited. The filmmakers revelled in the freedom they had to pursue previously forbidden subject matter and imagery but were often incapable of doing more than evoking a portrait of a world gone awry. They were clearly more at home with images and feelings of human corruption, alienation, confusion, and rebellion than with incisive and complex social and political critiques. And they were more attuned to feelings of anger and resentment toward established institutions and the desire for "freedom" from conventional mores than to any overviews of the social malaise and political and cultural movements of the sixties.

There were a number of films that touched on aspects of the counterculture. Films like Richard Lester's psychologically suggestive and self-consciously stylish *Petulia* (1968)—excessive flash cuts, a splintered narrative—were primarily interested in satirizing the callousness, crassness, and obliviousness of American society of the sixties. However, the film does provide brief glimpses of the counter-culture, but as a social alternative it holds out little hope. Lester depicts its adherents as being just as uncaring and mean-spirited as conventional middle class society. And Paul Mazursky's box office success, *Bob and Carol and Ted and Alice* (1969), gently satirizes the Southern California, upper-middle-class version of the counterculture. Mazursky's well-heeled professionals go to Esalen (for primal scream, twenty-four hour marathons and other pop therapies) smoke pot and struggle to achieve emotional and sexual liberation. The film has charm and wit and Mazursky conveys an insider's knowledge of his characters' foibles. It never, however, probes beyond the externals of their behavior, asking larger social questions about why they behave as they do—Mazursky playing it safe and muting his satiric jabs.

Arthur Penn's elegiac and loosely episodic *Alice's Restaurant* (1969) goes a bit further. Its prime purpose was to provide a critical but loving evocation of the counterculture. Using a ballad-like structure and centering the film around a solemn, honest, pure Arlo Guthrie (playing himself with consummate impassivity), the film touches on Arlo's relationship with the Old Left (via visits to his dying father, the legendary Woodie Guthrie); his conflicts with the establishment—college, police, army; and his involvement with the counterculture.

Arlo has long hair, plays a guitar, smokes dope, and takes refuge in a counterculture commune presided over by his more animated and complex surrogate parents, sensual earth-mother Alice (Pat Quinn) and her insecure, hostile, dreamer husband Ray Brock (played with manic intensity by James Broderick). Penn's sympathies are clearly with the counterculture as he wittily portrays Arlo's victories over the police (he beats a conviction for littering) and the draft. These scenes wryly and satirically (the film recreates the twenty-minute talking-blues hit "Alice's Restaurant Massacre") capture the estrangement between the generations in America. Nonetheless, though Penn likes the young's openness and spontaneity, he sees the counterculture having its own painful limitations. For though Arlo can serenely triumph over traditional institutions, another member of the commune dies of an overdose of heroin. And the image of the commune as a beatific refuge (they even reconsecrate an abandoned church) coexists with a profound sense of the whole venture's futility and failure. The film concludes with a despairing Ray desolately fantasizing about creating one more commune, and with Penn's camera tenderly panning around Alice, who stands vulnerable and alone with both the commune and her marriage heading for disaster.

Alice's Restaurant is filled with luminous, poetic, and painterly images and exhibits a real empathy for the counterculture. Penn can grace us with scenes that catch both the absurdity—the dim, cliched talk about getting one's head together—and the sense of human possibility and community of the counterculture. However, at times it seems that there are too many tones inhabiting the work—comic, pathetic, and ironic—ultimately dissipating some of the film's emotional and intellectual impact. *Alice's Restaurant* also never gets sufficiently close to the Brocks or especially to the other members of the commune—who are merely colorfully dressed, hippie extras—to get to the heart of the film's personal and communal breakdowns.[39]

If *Alice's Restaurant* is not a fully-realized and coherent portrait of the counterculture, a film like the left-leaning, strikingly cinematic *Medium Cool* (1969) tends to sacrifice its narrative and characters to the evocative documentary footage that its director had amassed. *Medium Cool's* hard-boiled, apolitical, hero is a TV cameraman, John (Robert Forster), who views contemporary events with professional detachment; he treats the nature and substance of the event as much less significant than the process of getting the story—until he discovers that the FBI is being allowed to use his footage to identify radicals. He suddenly realizes that the act of pointing a camera is itself a political gesture.

John's job as a TV cameraman allows *Medium Cool's* director Haskell Wexler to mix cinéma vérité—documentary and neo-documentary footage (a reconstruction of the assassination of Bobby Kennedy)—with a loose fictional narrative in order to create a telling portrait of sixties' social reality. And though there are scenes that go in for easy ironies (e.g., "Happy Days Are Here Again" can be heard on the sound track as protestors are beaten by Chicago police) and take facile potshots at targets like insensitive, white, middle-class liberals, the film is filled with incisive sequences depicting angry, knotted-up black militants subtly playing with white fears and guilt, Illinois National Guardsmen receiving riot training, and the chaos and repression of the Chicago 1968 Democratic Party Convention and police riot. However, the purely fictional scenes lack conviction, and are often left aimlessly suspended as the more powerful vérité scenes are inserted between them.

Even in the vérité scenes *Medium Cool* sometimes indulges in awkward Pirandello-like effects—the actors wandering past the Chicago police and protestors, and the audience viewing Wexler and his crew self-consciously shooting the final fatal accident scene and turning the lens toward the audience. That final scene, where John and a woman friend, Eileen (Verna Bloom), die in a car crash, ends the film on a dark note, which both conveys a sense of the fatality and destruction of the sixties,[40] and suggests that "we are implicated both as voyeuristic viewers and as potential victims of the camera's imaging of violence and death."[41]

Wexler is unambiguously on the side of the sixties protestors, but he knows full well that the exposure of repression on film, including his own, may merely titillate its audience. That "the whole world may be watching" on television the brutality of Mayor Daley's police, but their actions will probably arouse little concern in the audience. For a committed filmmaker like Wexler, the feeling that politically engaged films may ultimately make no more social difference than the most detached, commercial works was not a hopeful sign for the success of the sixties' movements.

Easy Rider (1969) which was the most culturally significant and commercially successful of cinematic attempts at capturing the rebellious and alternate lifestyles of the 1960s was no more sanguine about the future. Initially conceived of as a kind of American International Pictures' exploitation quickie about the hippie scene like the *Wild Angels* (1966) and *The Trip* (1967), it had to be finished with independent financing by its star Peter Fonda. Its subsequent box office success compared to its small initial investment made it a model for what became known as the New American Cinema. Their characteristic products were independently financed, low-budget films, made by non-studio-trained directors, who combined highly personal or politically radical stories that broke with conventional Hollywood narrative techniques while borrowing heavily from the respective styles of New Wave, cinéma vérité, and avant-garde films. Offshoots of this tendency were *Wild 90* (1968), Brian De Palma's *Greetings* (1968), *Hi Mom* (1970), *Putney Swope* (1969), *Coming Apart* (1969), *Ice* (1970), and other films of the late sixties and early seventies.

Crucial to *Easy Rider*'s enormous commercial success and cultural significance was its ability to capture on a visceral level certain prime themes and concepts of the counterculture and the sixties—mysticism, personal freedom, "the land," drugs, and communes. It begins as a reverse road film in which a pair of hippie motorcyclists—the cool, detached, oracular Wyatt (Peter Fonda) and the tense, angry, and comic Billy (Dennis Hopper)—sell a kilo of dope to a Los Angeles hippie capitalist and then head east to New Orleans for Mardi Gras in what ostensibly is a search for freedom. Along the way *Easy Rider* becomes a laid-back bildungsroman as the duo visit old-time ranchers and hippie communes, spend time in jail and in brothels, and take acid trips. The journey is enhanced by the film's exciting use of landscape, space, light, movement, and sound (especially the contemporary rock music of Jimi Hendrix, the Byrds, Steppenwolf, and others).

Unfortunately, the film is often painfully inarticulate, shallow, and pretentious when it forgoes its tracking camera and tries to turn its vision into words. Most of it takes the form of particularly banal and pretentious pronouncements by the hippie saint Wyatt who gives a benediction to a rural commune which has faced hard times—"they're gonna make it"—or pays pious reverence to the simple lifestyle of a toothless old rancher with a beaming Mexican wife who is "doing his own thing, in his own time."

However, in its depiction of Us against Them—the supposed free, long hairs versus the vicious, redneck straights, who universally treat Wyatt and Billy with murderous contempt—the film does strike a powerful social and emotional chord. In the process the film gave up its penchant for indulging in ersatz and sentimental beatitudes and connected itself to the disillusionment felt by many, especially the young, about sixties America. Its most poignant expression came in the comments of an articulate, witty, alcoholic lawyer, George Hanson (Jack Nicholson), who joins the two on their quest. After they are attacked by local goons Hanson points out that "this used to be a helluva country," but it seems to have lost its way. He adds that though the rednecks may ostensibly believe in the idea of freedom they are scared of free individuals.

Hanson's remarks set the tone of the second half of the film which is pervaded with as much of a sense of doom, failure, and despair as the opening half was a paean to the exhilaration of traveling on the open road. Wyatt's and Billy's own violent fate is prefigured in George's murder by a group of rednecks. And although they do make it to the Mardi Gras, and take an extravagantly filmed acid trip (fisheye lens, overexposed images, and overlapping dialogue) with some prostitutes in a cemetery, their pathetic destiny seems so sealed that we get hints of it in flash-forwards. It is a climax that not only acted as a judgment on their personal quest but seemed to extend to the American experience as a whole.

Such was the outrage of some critics at this judgment, that an elite, cultural custodian like Diana Trilling (who had not raised more than an eyebrow at films since her tenure as a reviewer for *The New Republic* in the forties and fifties) was moved to call the film "devious." She particularly questioned the appropriateness of Wyatt and Billy as symbols of our social and cultural condition and complained that "Wyatt and Billy lack the energy to create anything, comment on anything, feel anything, except the mute, often pot-induced pleasure of each other's company."[42]

However, though one may clearly quarrel with the presumptuousness of two dope-dealing drifters standing as symbols of freedom and making judgments on something as vast as the "American experience," there is little doubt that *Easy Rider* captured the sense of foreboding and doom that dominated many of the films of the sixties and heralded those of the seventies. In fact, the deaths of Wyatt and Billy seemed a reflection of what had been the fate of Martin Luther King, Malcolm X, and Robert Kennedy, and some felt could be the lot of anyone whose dissent and protest truly threatened the power structure of America.

Of course, Billy and Wyatt were far from being political rebels or critics, but in their dim, self-destructive way they were searching for some alternative vision to the dominant culture. *Easy Rider* is a tongue-tied film which succeeds in evoking the mood of a decade. In its mixture of intellectual simple-mindedness, striking imagery and editing, and conscious and unconscious intuition into the decade's confusion and alienation, it was one of the most representative of late 1960s films. In fact, Wyatt's despairing comment grants unintentional pop-cultural symmetry to a decade which began with the unequivocal optimism embodied in lyrics of songs like "Blowin' in the Wind" and ended with the pessimism of a line like "We blew it."

NOTES

1. William L. Langer, *Political and Social Upheaval, 1832–1852* (New York: Harper and Row, 1969).

2. Godfrey Hodgson, *America in Our Time: From World War II to Nixon, What Happened and Why* (New York: Vintage, 1978).

3. Ibid., pp. 491–99.

4. William L. O'Neill, *Coming Apart: An Informal History of America in the 1960s* (New York: Quadrangle, 1971), pp. 29–103.

5. Ibid.

6. Hodgson, *America in Our Time*, pp. 179–99.

7. Ibid.

8. Ibid.

9. Hodgson, *America in Our Time*, pp. 200–224.

10. Ibid.

11. Doris Kearns, *Lyndon B. Johnson and the American Dream* (New York: Signet, 1976), pp. 220–62.

12. Kearns, *Lyndon B. Johnson*, pp. 263–323.

13. Frances Fitzgerald, *Fire in the Lake* (New York: Vintage, 1973).

14. David Halberstam, *The Best and the Brightest* (New York: Fawcett, 1973).

15. Kirkpatrick Sale, *SDS* (New York: Vintage, 1974).

16. Morris Dickstein, *Gates of Eden: American Culture in the Sixties* (New York: Basic Books, 1977), pp. 51–88, 128–53.

17. Hodgson, *America in Our Time*, pp. 326–52.

18. O'Neill, *Coming Apart*, pp. 396–428.

19. Ibid.

20. James Monaco, *American Film Now: The People, the Power, the Money, the Movies* (New York: Oxford University Press, 1979), pp. 1–48.

21. Ibid.

22. Ibid.

23. Thomas Schatz, *The Genius of the System: Hollywood Filmmaking in the Studio Era* (New York: Pantheon, 1988), p. 489.

24. Pauline Kael, *Going Steady* (New York: Bantam, 1971), p. 115.

25. Gerald Pratley, *The Cinema of John Frankenheimer* (Cranbury, NJ: A. S. Barnes, 1969).

26. Susan Sontag, *Against Interpretation* (New York: Dell, 1969), p. 215.

27. Norman Kagan, *The War Film* (New York: Pyramid Publications, 1974), p. 142.

28. Norman Kagan, *The Cinema of Stanley Kubrick* (New York: Grove Press, 1975), pp. 111–44.

29. Pauline Kael, *Kiss, Kiss, Bang, Bang* (New York: Bantam, 1969), p. 79.

30. Albert Auster and Leonard Quart, *How the War Was Remembered: Hollywood and Vietnam* (New York: Praeger, 1988), p. 25.

31. Lewis Mumford, quoted in Kagan, *The Cinema of Stanley Kubrick* (New York: Grove Press, 1972), p. 132.

32. Donald Spoto, *Stanley Kramer: Filmmaker* (New York: G. P. Putnam's Sons, 1978), p. 2.

33. Norman Mailer, *Armies of the Night* (New York: Signet, 1968), p. 47.

34. Robin Wood, *Arthur Penn* (New York: Praeger, 1969), pp. 72–91.

35. Hollis Alpert and Andrew Sarris (eds.), *Film 68/69: An Anthology by the National Society of Film Critics* (New York: Simon and Schuster, 1969), pp. 235–41.

36. Alan G. Barbour, *John Wayne* (New York: Pyramid, 1974), pp. 121–22.

37. Renata Adler, *A Year in the Dark* (New York: Berkeley, 1969), pp. 199–200.

38. Joseph Morgenstern and Stefan Kanfer (eds.), *Film 69/70: An Anthology by the National Society of Film Critics* (New York: Simon and Schuster, 1970), pp. 148–56.

39. Wood, *Arthur Penn*, pp. 92–116.

40. Morgenstern and Kanfer, *Film 69/70*, pp. 165–72.

41. Robert Sklar, "When Looks Could Kill: American Cinema of the Sixties," *Cineaste*, xvi, 1–2 (1987–88), p. 51.

42. Diana Trilling, *We Must March, My Darlings* (New York: Harcourt Brace Jovanovich, 1977), pp. 175–86.

5

THE SEVENTIES

On March 18, 1969, newly elected President Richard Nixon ordered the secret bombing of neutral Cambodia. It was the first in a series of events whose consequences were to dominate American politics and society during the first half of the seventies. Given Nixon's past history—his hawkish foreign policy views and his gift for manipulating anticommunism to further his political career—there should have been little surprise that he ordered the bombing. But in 1968 Nixon had come to power primarily on the strength of the vague promise that he knew how to end the war in Vietnam, understanding that at this point in the Vietnam War neither Congress nor the public would approve its escalation.[1]

Despite his political promises, however, Nixon was clearly not ready to abruptly terminate American involvement. Nixon and his advisers had no use for the Johnson-Humphrey idea that the war was fought for democracy and "winning the hearts and minds" of the people, and displayed little interest in geopolitical rationales like the fear of toppling Southeast Asian dominoes. The Nixon-Kissinger justification for continuing U.S. involvement was summed up in the strategic concept of "credibility." They believed that the war was being fought to maintain America's reputation "as a guarantor"—to assure her allies, and more particularly her enemies, that the United States would be firm in confronting a crisis.[2]

Inextricably connected to the idea of "credibility" was the notion of "American will." The Nixon administration felt they had to assure the world that America would take the necessary painful steps, like the bombing of Cambodia, to back up words with action. After the American people finally became aware of the bombing the President affirmed the notion of credibility by stating, "it is not our power but our will and character that is being tested tonight."[3]

To the Nixon administration that will seemed badly shaken after years of interminable bloodshed, the investment of billions of dollars, and the often violent political debate and struggles of a profoundly divided nation. There were people in the administration that felt the national will had been permanently damaged not only by the war, but by social welfarism, government intervention in the economy, and the leadership of a decadent elite and establishment.

In order to renew America, Richard Nixon set about attacking the media, liberal-left intellectuals, and government bureaucrats—institutions which he viewed as bastions of an enemy establishment. It was a campaign motivated almost as much by Nixon's own sense of personal powerlessness and private grievance as by his ideological and political commitments. In the process of initiating this attack Nixon dismantled much of the "Great Society" legislation of the Johnson presidency, stacked the Supreme Court with supposed judicial conservatives (though Blackmun surprisingly turned out to be a liberal on a number of issues), and attempted the political mobilization of a segment of the American population he dubbed the "silent majority." They were supposedly ordinary Americans who adhered to traditional verities like patriotism and were antagonistic to the values of both the establishment and the war protesters.

Given that Nixon's policies were dependent on smears, innuendo, confrontation, and polarization, they succeeded only in fragmenting any semblance of an American will. They pitted race against race, old against young, class against class, and region against region, leaving division rather than unity in their wake. This further disruption of the American will did not contradict the goals of the Nixon administration, for what he and his associates were really interested in creating was not a harmonious and cohesive American society and spirit, but an administration which embodied and defined the national will. It was this confidence (megalomania?) that his administration really was an expression of the American will which provided Nixon with the rationale to indulge in whatever he felt politically necessary: to concentrate power in the White House; to use war methods against domestic enemies; and to use the power of the federal government to promote and maintain the image and reputation of the administration. In fact, for Nixon and his cohorts the image the administration projected was more significant than the substance, a notion which was far from new to American politics, but clearly gained much strength during the 1970s.[4]

In promoting their image the Nixon administration initiated a campaign of illegal activities. In 1971, after the release of the Pentagon Papers, the administration created a group of undercover operatives nicknamed "the plumbers." It was the covert activities of this group which led to the break-in at Democratic headquarters in June 1972 and the resulting Watergate scandal. The public revelation of the scandal and the administration's cover-up led to the resignation of Nixon—though even in his final days of power Nixon was unable to confront and admit his own responsibility in the whole affair. The forcing of Nixon and his hatchet man out of office (e.g., Vice President Agnew—for bribe-taking) undermined both the institution of the presidency and the whole American political ethos. The public began to distance itself from politics, expressing only cynicism about the rhetoric and programs that politicians proposed. By 1973 it was clear that the political passions and polarization of the sixties had died, replaced by a general sense of political alienation and apathy.[5]

Paralleling that shift in the public mood was the replacement of Nixon by his appointed Vice President Gerald Ford, the perfect figure to preside over a period of political stagnation. In 1976 Ford led a Bicentennial celebration of American independence. The frenetic activity and the overblown rhetoric were a self-conscious attempt by Americans to demonstrate their confidence in the country despite almost fifteen years of wars, recessions, riots, and the assassinations and resignations of its leaders. The most poignant expression of this need for self-congratulation occurred in New York City. In 1975, perhaps symbolic of American society and especially of its older urban areas, New York had been brought to the brink of bankruptcy by a combination of such factors as middle-class flight, rising crime, a reduced tax base, increased demands for public services from a growing poverty population, economic demands of municipal unions, and the callousness and rapacity of the city's major banks. Only a last-minute loan guarantee by the federal government staved off financial catastrophe.

However, despite, or more likely because of, these economic and social conditions, New York staged "Operation Sail," one of the most impressive of the Bicentennial ceremonies. During this celebration a fleet of white-sailed schooners and frigates from all over the world sailed up and down the Hudson River to the applause of immense crowds. Ne York's elaborate ceremony seemed to embody the nation's desire to affirm the power and resilience of the American will—no matter what the social realities were like.[6]

In fact, Jimmy Carter based his campaign for the Democratic presidential nomination in 1976 on just this national need to renew its belief in itself. Carter, a man of deep religious convictions (he was a "born again Christian"), was aware of the country's need for spiritual talk rather than political rhetoric and programs. In his standard speech he talked about a government as good as its people, implicitly affirming a belief that the American will and spirit were still strong and vital. He also shrewdly sensed that after Nixon, the "character issue" was a prime one for the American public, and he promised in Sunday School terms never to lie to the people.

In addition, Carter benefitted from other American social and political strains. A "New South" had emerged since the 1960s, for with de jure elimination of racial segregation, Carter no longer had to deal with the southern politician's albatross of the Civil War, Reconstruction, and Jim Crow. Secondly, Carter was not a national politician or party chieftain, he was an outsider (one term governor of Georgia) who could be projected as a fresh face untainted by Watergate. Finally, the all-pervasive power of the media had made it possible for a political figure to jump from obscurity to celebrity merely by making a number of successful television appearances.[7]

Carter's campaign avoided dealing with the issues or taking hard positions, and by invoking moral pieties and capitalizing on his outsider status he won a narrow victory over Ford in the 1976 election. However, though he was a skilled diagnostician of the public's yearnings, Carter's political talents did not seem to extend beyond the pursuit of power and the winning of elections. His first year in office was committed more to populist symbolism than to substance. Informal state dinners, telephone talks with ordinary citizens and spending the night at their homes, and wearing a cardigan sweater while announcing an energy plan which he conceived as the moral equivalent of war did not help him with Congress. Carter confronted an assertive Congress which after Vietnam and Watergate was profoundly wary of the executive branch. Furthermore, Carter carried over from his campaign a blurriness over issues and an inability to make hard decisions. He equivocated in the Bert Lance scandal, tarnishing his image for integrity, and seemed to lack control over his cabinet and his low-comic brother, Billy. More and more there existed a growing feeling that Jimmy Carter was too small a man to handle the presidency.[8]

In July 1979, after repeated attempts to untangle his administration, Carter tried to liberate himself from his ineffective and incompetent image by firing a number of cabinet members (Califano, Blumenthal, et al.) and making a speech updating his energy policy. It was more than just a speech about energy, it was in typical Carter style an expression of moral concern which attempted to rouse the American people from their malaise. It was a call to strengthen the American will by ridding it of its self-indulgence: "The erosion of our confidence in the future is threatening to destroy the social and political fabric of America ... we have learned that piling-up material goods cannot fill the emptiness of lives which have no confidence or purpose."[9]

Though this ministerial oratory was no substitute for a coherent energy policy, Carter's rhetoric did have cultural resonance and significance for the seventies. It paralleled the writing of culture critics such as Christopher Lasch and Tom Wolfe who had called the 1970s a narcissistic era, the "me decade." They conceived the age as a period when people went about polishing, cultivating, and doting upon themselves and their relationships without regard to politics, society, or posterity. The seventies had produced a culture built on a cult of personal relations which was often simply an expression and a result of a chaotic, destructive social order and devastated and empty private lives. This culture was characterized by a craving for intimacy without genuine human connection and sacrifice, material plenty without productivity, and success without real content or accomplishment. Hedonistic consumerism and the ethic of self-preservation—including an interest in the body ("working out," natural diets)—had become the order of the day.[10]

To some extent this collective narcissism was partially brought on by the failure and collapse of the New Left and counterculture in the early seventies. The "Movement" always differed from the Old Left by being concerned with problems of personal identity and authenticity. These problems, especially for those who were political or social activists, were rarely separated from their commitment to transforming American society. Of course, there were always activists who treated political action as merely a substitute for personal therapy. But by the seventies many of the survivors of the Movement had decided that one of the reasons for its failure (neglecting or dismissing historical and political explanations) was the nature of political commitment itself. What was now necessary to achieve some sense of peace and fulfillment was getting directly to the bottom of the self or losing oneself in various self-awareness movements (EST, Rolfing, and Arica), oriental gurus, and religious cults like the Moonies and Jim Jones' suicidal People's Temple and bioenergetics.[11]

The premise underlying this intense preoccupation with the self was the assumption that unlimited personal growth would coincide with unlimited material prosperity. The belief was based on the post–Second World War notion that continuous expansion was inherent in the very nature of the American economy, and though blatant racial and economic inequities existed in America in the years from 1945 through the early seventies, America had the resources to create an economy successful enough to satisfy the material needs and yearnings of the majority of the people. Within that expansionist framework, American capitalism could vitiate resentment by keeping unemployment low, increasing social services, and mediating between the interests of capital and labor.

However, in the mid-1970s a change in public consciousness occurred. For the first time in American history public opinion polls reported that the American people were no longer optimistic about the nation's future. The country was beset with an economic crisis, which in fact was an underlying cause of Carter's 1976 victory. But Carter was ultimately unable to turn the economy around. By the end of his term rising oil prices, a debt-laden balance of payments, and the lack of competitiveness of the motor and steel industries had again thrown the American economy into severe recession.

In the 1980 election Carter was soundly defeated and the ex-actor and California governor, Ronald Reagan, was elected by a landslide to the presidency. There were many reasons for the repudiation of Carter and the Democrats—a recoil from big government and liberalism (though Carter was no liberal), personal rage and resentment toward Carter's supposed weakness and incompetence, and most importantly the hope that Reagan would resurrect the American will from its malaise. The public craved a candidate untouched by a sense of complexity and ambiguity who could successfully package a simple belief in American might, power, and opportunity to right the ills of the nation. However, in 1980 the rebirth of the American will existed only in the realm of political rhetoric; the country was beset with perilous economic, social, and international difficulties which clearly would not be resolved by the intoning of patriotic and moralistic platitudes.[12]

During the seventies the film industry and its product reflected the confusion and malaise permeating the American will. At the beginning of the decade the industry was a chronic invalid, with studios losing a combined aggregate of $500 million between 1969 and 1972, only to renew itself financially during the second half of the decade with grosses of almost $3 billion. Early in the decade the old studios connected their fortunes to those of huge conglomerates like Kinney National Service. As a result, the men who produced the films had their eyes glued to the balance sheets rather than to the rushes. That meant fewer pictures, but those that were made had generous publicity budgets geared primarily to a youth audience between the ages of twelve and twenty-six.

Another element in this process was the changing relationship between the movie industry and TV. It began with a period of all-out-war in the fifties, moved to the casual embrace of the sixties, and by the seventies the film industry's relationship with television had become a passionate one; by pre-selling their films both to pay and commercial television, and cashing in on new video software (cassettes, discs, and so on), the possibility of Hollywood losing immense sums of money on films had become slight. No longer did a studio have to worry about possible bankruptcy if one heavily financed film failed.[13]

There was at least one beneficial result from the financial difficulties of the seventies. In groping around for any means to make a comeback, the studios began to take chances and reach out to relatively untried filmmakers such as Robert Altman, Martin Scorsese, Brian de Palma, Peter Bogdanovitch, Steven Spielberg, Michael Ritchie and Francis Ford Coppola.[14]

What distinguished these directors was their awareness of film history, technical competence (sometimes gained from working on small-budget quickies or being trained in university film schools), and self-conscious, personal visions. A number of these directors made films which were self-reflective in nature, and veered from the formal stateliness and order and even, at moments, the sense of verisimilitude of the classical narrative. For instance, Robert Altman directed films which were highly personal, idiosyncratic versions of popular genres (i.e., film noir) like The Long Goodbye (1973), engaged in social comment and satire in Nashville (1975), and made dreamlike, European-style, art films like Three Women (1977). Brian de Palma's varied output included the anarchic Hi Mom (1969) and the Hitchcockian Obsession (1976), and Francis Ford Coppola transformed the gangster film (Godfather I and II) into a tragic epic about the nature of Americanization.

In stark contrast to the old studio days when these directors and their cinematic styles and themes would have been subordinated to a whole battery of executive producers, they now retained a great deal more control over scripts and actors. They often even had the power of the final cut. The studios had become primarily financiers and distributors, treating film more as a business than an industry, and consequently taking more interest in profit margins than in the substance of their product.

The transformation of the studios and the success of this more personal form of filmmaking did not mean that Hollywood had opted for dispensing with the traditional genres. Genre films with their well-defined characters, actions, and iconography still resonated with American audiences. In the sixties a number of films (e.g., Easy Rider) both cut across and modified the traditional genres focusing on buddies (rather than Hollywood's usual solitary hero), the counterculture, and blacks. However, despite Easy Rider becoming a landmark for the directors of the seventies, these new genres did not sustain their audience appeal. A number of the seventies directors did make films which turned back to conventional genres like the gangster film and the thriller, but the effects of the counterculture and the New Left of the sixties and the sense of alienation and anomie were too great to make films which adhered to the structure and rules of classics like The Big Sleep (1946) and Little Caesar (1930). The genre conventions often existed now as a springboard for social commentary, psychological revelation, or parody and satire.[15]

The best example of this use of genre was the protean Francis Ford Coppola's The Godfather (1972) and The Godfather II (1974). In their emphasis on the murders, violence, and Machiavellian manipulations of criminals, these films indirectly reflected American involvement in Vietnam and the political crimes of Watergate. The films also echoed Balzac's famous comment that behind every great fortune there rested a crime. But beyond these images of American corruption, the two films used a driving narrative rhythm, a luxurious use of light and shadow, and voluptuous camera movements to evoke the destruction of the American Dream.

Coppola based the films on Mario Puzo's commercially successful pulp novel, and used it to invert the whole tradition of the gangster film. As Robert Warshow once wrote of the gangster film: "Since we do not see the rational and routine aspects of the gangster's behavior, the practice of brutality—unmixed criminality—becomes the totality of his career."[16] In *The Godfather* films Coppola begins with the very rituals and emotions that have been left out of the traditional gangster film—baptism and marriage, family solidarity and love—all of which serve as the foreground for the life of criminality, violence, and murder to which the characters remain committed.

The *Godfather I* centered on the idea of family and those rites of passage that celebrate and validate it. Dominating the film is gravelly voiced Don Vito Corleone (Marlon Brando), an almost mythological figure—a murderer who is totally at ease with his authority and power. He is a man whose prime goal is to keep his family from dancing to another's strings, and who is committed to maintaining their security, dignity, and independence. Don Vito is a powerful force who can absolve people of their guilt and protect them from hurt. He is a monster, but in Coppola's view an almost sacred one. In *The Godfather*, for every dark, shuttered room where business and murder are plotted, there are still scenes where children play, marriages are held and familial and communal warmth and light exist. The Don may live by violence, but Coppola allows him to die peacefully, playing with his grandson among the tomato plants in his garden.

Some of *The Godfather*'s audience appeal must have derived from the sense of order it evoked. During a time when many Americans felt the world had gone mad with assassinations, war, corrupt politics, and economic recession, there was a longing for a sane place where experience was relatively coherent and secure. In a nostalgic film like George Lucas' *American Graffiti* (1973) the time of innocence—of cruising and proms—is placed in the fifties, and in *The Godfather* that haven was the ethnic family. *The Godfather*, however, was a film drenched in blood and neither the depiction of strong family roots nor the Don's rough, natural sense of justice could quite cancel out the image of a family whose business and success were totally involved in intimidation, violence, and murder.[17]

In *Godfather II*, Coppola decided to pursue the underside of the American success ethic in much greater depth. Using Don Vito's son and heir, Michael (Al Pacino) as the central character, the film captures the transformation of the American Dream into a nightmare of alienation and dissolution. In *Godfather II* the old tribal Mafia of Don Vito's New York-based Genco Olive Oil Company—with its numbers, juke boxes, and prostitutes—has begun to transform itself into a Lake Tahoe-based, acculturated, depersonalized, multinational corporation. And with the abandonment of the old traditions, the quest for a veneer of corporate respectability and legitimacy has only tragic consequences.

Michael and "the family" have made it in America, and are powerful enough to command the support of a hypocritical and venal U.S. senator, and to gather with the heads of other ("legitimate?") multinational corporations to divide up the spoils in pre-Castro Havana. However, the family's mobility and new status has brought neither happiness nor repose, just pain and fragmentation. Michael is somber, remote and unfeeling; all his life energies are projected into the "business." His success results only in his sister Connie's (Talia Shire) hatred, betrayal by his ineffectual, envious brother, Fredo (John Cazale), and estrangement from his WASP wife Kay (Diane Keaton).

The decline of the family is filmed in dark, dimly-lit interiors and in sterile, luxurious rooms where people can often be seen only in silhouette. It is a joyless world, and by intercutting and counterpoi ting luminous flashback sequences of the life of the young Don Vito (Robert DeNiro), Coppola succeeds in vividly heightening the bleakness and desolation of Michael's universe. For though the immigrant world of Don Vito's Little Italy may be impoverished and murderous, it is enveloped in golden-toned colors and light and shot in soft focus, nostalgically evoking a world of warmth and community. Don Vito himself is depicted in a heroic mold, a venerated, urban Robin Hood—courtly, self-possessed, and courageous—a man who can help his fellow immigrants by frightening the rapacity out of exploitative landlords. Coppola does not hide the fact Don Vito is a criminal, but he is one whose profound familial feelings and natural grace make his criminality almost socially acceptable.

However, in the move from the world of tenements, pushcarts, and religious processions to the armed fortress in Lake Tahoe, the personal and the familial have been lost. The haven of the family and the ethnic community (however claustrophobic and prescriptive) cannot be sustained under the fragmenting pressures of the capitalist success ethic. Coppola depicts Michael as attempting to hold on to aspects of the code—he believes in machismo and the sacredness of the family—but they exist for him primarily as abstract and formal ideals, and he is never able to convey the love for his children that the young and old Don Vito basks in. In fact, it is Fredo who acts as surrogate father for Michael's unhappy, melancholy son, Anthony. By the end of the film the unforgiving Michael has murdered and lost almost everything he has cared for, and is seen in close-up sitting in tragic isolation, his face turned into a ghostly death mask.

The Godfather films did not pretend to provide a sophisticated Leftist critique of capitalism and its ethos. However, while operating within the genre conventions, they were able to convey some of the perniciousness of the American success ethic. The films projected an epic of dissolution conveying how Americanization and mobility turned the murderous passion and loyalty of the immigrant Mafia into an impersonal, rootless nightmare. Implicit in the films was the feeling that the nightmare extended far beyond the parochial confines of the Mafia into the center of American history and society itself.[18]

Another film that, in a similar fashion, was consciously influenced by the political and cultural ferment of the sixties was Robert Altman's Nashville (1975). The film was Altman's epic and ironic attempt at capturing both middle-American consciousness, and the perniciousness and life energy of America's popular culture that both helps shape and express it.

Indicative of the film's importance was that the *New York Times* assigned then associate editor Tom Wicker to write a think piece about it. In it he called *Nashville*, "a two and half hour cascade of minutely detailed vulgarity, greed, deceit, cruelty, barely contained hysteria and the frantic lack of root and grace into which American life has been driven by its own heedless vitality."[19] In *Nashville* Altman interweaves twenty-four characters who are both participants or who dream of entering the world of country and western music. Using an open-ended, improvisatory style that centers around the actors, *Nashville* is built on privileged, seemingly disconnected moments, filled with dazzling aural effects and visual images, and demanding close viewing from his audience (to pick up the elusive detail in frames packed with overlapping actions). Altman evokes a callous, grasping, violent world in which everyone either gropes for stardom or lives off the fantasies and myths popular culture creates. The country and western stars are manipulative, absurd, hysterical: in the main, empty, vain people obsessed by crowd applause and their own status, while their public's behavior ranges from breathless adulation and emulation to petulence and rage.

Among Altman's "Grand Hotel" of stars is the doyen of country western music, Haven Hamilton (Henry Gibson), a self-important, narcissistic, and petulent tyrant stuffed into a tailored, sequined cowboy suit with a slightly askew toupee. Hamilton is a tough, ambitious little rooster whose songs, "We Must Be Doing Something Right" and "For the Sake of The Children," embody the soporific and saccharine values of Nashville. The prime singing star, Barbara Jean (Ronee Blakley), a madonna dressed in white, is a child-like, fragile and neurasthenic figure. She is the film's symbol of how media success can help victimize and destroy a performer, exemplifying the agony that lies between an unstable private self and a star's public role. Altman's other characters run the range from a handsome, totally egoistical, stud rock singer who plays tapes of his songs while he sleeps, to a pathetic off-key singing waitress, a dim, bizarre-looking, promiscuous groupie, and a ridiculous and pretentious BBC journalist. They inhabit a world where relationships are subordinated to hustling for the main chance or to promiscuous scoring. It is a fragmented and alienated world where the characters, in the main, exist from moment to moment, and there is almost nobody in the film capable of listening to or caring about what another person is saying. Altman's cool sensibility succeeds in turning Nashville's country music world into a metaphor for American life; a chaotic din where everybody is struggling for or has their own gold record.

In *Nashville* everything is packaged, including politics. From the opening frame, when the sound track of the Replacement Party's presidential candidate, the pseudo-populist Hal Phillip Walker, patrols the predawn empty streets, to the final shot of his limousine leaving the climactic assassination scene, politics play a significant role in the film. It is a politics built on a canned voice and an invisible candidate (we never see Walker, just the detached, quietly contemptuous advance man, Triplette [Michael Murphy]). And the party, with its slogan "new roots for the nation" and platform calling for a new national anthem and the removal of lawyers from Congress, seeks national moral renewal by selling nostalgia and bumptious iconoclasm. The party is one more image without substance: boosters, and a sound truck hawking the vagaries of the platform in the same way as the record albums are hyped over the opening credits.

Altman has created, through dynamic and seamless cutting and unrelenting movement within his densely packed frames, a frenzied world. It is a landscape he simultaneously loves and despises. One thinks of Whitman's catalogues of America now gone amuck; sound tracks overlap as cars crash, planes roar, marching bands perform, and TV newsmen drone on. This grasping, frenetic universe has its apotheosis in the assassination of Barbara Jean at a benefit concert for the Replacement Party in Nashville's Parthenon. In this dazzling set piece of a finale, a seemingly innocuous boy with a guitar, acting out of some Oedipal rage or possibly out of the violence that permeates every pore of the society, shoots Barbara Jean. The act is an echo of the Oswalds, Sirhan Sirhans, and Arthur Bremers—the assassins and psychopaths that wander and menace the streets of contemporary America.

In the aftermath the crowd, stunned and milling about, begins to participate in the ironic and chillingly repeated lyric, "You may say I ain't free, but it don't worry me." What sounds at first like a stirring song of solidarity and the courage to go on is one more turn of the screw, accentuated by the fact that a black choir leads the singing. The camera pans to close-ups of people in the crowd giving voice to the words, and then zooms away to a long shot of the stupefied, acquiescent mass. The song is a hymn to apathy and accommodation, a metaphor for an America that unthinkingly accepts its bondage to the media's plasticity, artifice, and banality.

Altman is a director who is in love with the ambiguity and complex texture of his images, behavioral tics, and social surfaces. His work is built on observation rather than exposition, intuition rather than analysis, and on a vision of a society based on chance rather than on one whose values can be systematically traced to a set of causes. Consequently, Altman is not interested in exploring popular music's historical and cultural content or dissecting the power groups that help shape the music industry. But he understands just how bountiful and destructive American popular culture is, and how the world of appearances and hype often beguiles and rules Americans. When his suggestive metaphors and images come alive, as they do in Nashville, they conjure up a monstrous and irrational America which is vivid, resonant, and true.

Nashville's vision of the role of the media—especially in the political arena—has grown more apt and pointed with each passing decade, though there was no denying the power of the media to shape American public opinion during the late sixties and seventies. In fact, there were other films made during the decade like Michael Ritchie's *The Candidate* (1972) and Sidney Lumet's *Network* (1976) which criticized the power of the media.

The Candidate used a semi-documentary technique—natural sound, panning and tracking with a handheld camera, and a mixture of professional and non-professional actors—to richly evoke the mechanics of the political process and the power of the media to shape it. The film's protagonist is an idealistic, Kennedy-style, public service lawyer, Bill McKay (Robert Redford), who runs for the Senate in California against a glib, right-wing conservative. As the campaign evolves the frank-speaking, socially committed McKay acquiesces to being transformed into a handsome commodity who hedges on the issues and learns to speak in empty political slogans and vaporous rhetoric about "courage and compassion" so he can win the election.

The film does little with McKay's private self or marriage, but it has a political insider's knowledge of how to produce thirty-second spots, write position papers, win endorsements, and engage in campaign debates, rallies, and speeches. The television cameras are ubiquitous in the campaign, and the candidates must learn to gear their persona and positions to the camera eye and sound bite. *The Candidate* is satirical about the nature of a media-governed politics, but it's too shrewd and knowing to offer quick fix alternatives to a political process with a genius for co-optation.

Network—winner of four Oscars—is utterly different intellectually and stylistically than *The Candidate*. Written by Paddy Chayevsky, it is a dark, shrill, sometimes expressionist comedy filled with television lampoons, rousing monologues, collective primal screams, and savage portraits of freaked-out anchormen and TV revolutionaries. Shot mainly in close-up and medium shot, *Network's* images are totally subordinated to Chayevsky's speeches. In them he brings his wrath down on a corrupt and dehumanizing television world built on corporate jockeying and an obsession with Neilsen ratings. In Chayevsky's pessimistic vision the Left is totally absurd, "the people" mesmerized sheep, and there is only one weary, honest, news department head, Max Schumacher (William Holden as an Edward R. Murrow clone), to stand for what is honest and true.

Network is a moralistic, overstated film that strains for significance. But there are moments it draws blood—it is especially good on the media's capacity for turning everything into a marketable commodity, and conveying the feeling that the television image has become reality for many Americans. Though in its desire to be outrageous, the film ironically often seems to be doing what television does—merchandising iconoclasm.

The two films may have savaged the role of television, but it's clear that without TV the antiwar and women's movements in the seventies would have had a lesser impact. Television covered feminist sit-ins at leading women's magazines, mass marches, and demonstrations, and held debates on men and women's changing roles and identities. Of course, television also vulgarized and merchandized feminism in various sitcoms and commercials such as the one for Virginia Slims cigarettes.[20] And its underlying attitude toward women and feminism was at best ambivalent and at worst destructive, but it succeeded in forcing the movement into the consciousness of the American public.

Hollywood in turn had no journalistic function, so it had even more difficulty in dealing with women's issues; especially since they went far beyond equal rights and equal pay, and challenged sacred movie industry canons about the nature of sexuality and the family. For a time in the seventies Hollywood seemed to have banished most women from the screen and replaced them with buddy films such as *Little Fauss and Big Halsey* (1970), *Scarecrow* (1973), and *The Sting* (1973), works which concentrated on macho exploits and homoerotic bonds.

At the same time, however, Hollywood was being prodded to pay attention to changes in women's consciousness, both by the women's movement and by powerful and popular actresses like Barbara Streisand and Jane Fonda. In addition, the rise of an independent women's cinema which produced documentary films like *Joyce at 34* (1973), *Nana, Mom and Me* (1974) and *Union Maids* (1976) and features like Joan Micklin Silver's film about Jewish immigrants' adjustment to America, *Hester Street* (1975) and Claudia Weill's *Girlfriends* (1978)—dealt with women defining themselves through work and in other ways where their relation to men did not have primacy. These varied influences moved the mainstream film industry to make a stab at producing films where a women's exploration of identity was a central theme. One of the first of these, *Klute* (1971), was not only a box office success but an Academy Award-winner as well.[21]

Klute is John Klute (Donald Sutherland) a strong, silent, small-town policeman who comes to New York to pursue leads in the disappearance and possible murder of a close friend. The film is stylishly directed by Alan Pakula (*All the President's Men*, 1976), creating a paranoid, noirish New York of wiretaps, dark hallways, and lurking silhouetted figures. Pakula's compositions are nervous with his characters often placed on the extreme edge of the frame, and he often blacks out part of the screen to create feelings of isolation and tension. But the real focus of the film is not urban paranoia or the sadistic, murderous violence that lies behind respectable, corporate facades; it lies in the struggle for self-definition of a prime suspect in the case, a call girl, Bree Daniels (Jane Fonda).

Bree is a witty, seemingly confident, cynical, and self-destructive woman who wants to control her life, but can only maintain some equilibrium when she operates as a call girl. It is a life she knows is going nowhere. Nevertheless, as she tells her therapist, about her tricks: "I'm in control. When they come to me they're nervous, I'm not. I know what I'm doing. I know I'm good." In contrast to her power over the johns who share her bed, she has little control over the rest of her life. Although able to simulate sexual excitement and manipulate male fantasies as a call girl, she is merely an object or image, a commodity to be dismissed when she pursues her acting and modeling careers.

What little control Bree has in her life is increasingly threatened by her love for Klute, an emotion she tries to fend off by continually manipulating and hurting him. Some of the film's best moments take place during Bree's sessions with her therapist, where she describes how she tries to destroy her feelings for Klute for fear they will engulf her and she will lose whatever autonomy she has. It is one of the few times in the history of American film that a therapeutic session seems natural and irreducible to psychological clichés and magical resolution.

Unfortunately, Klute's character does not quite transcend Hollywood stereotypes. He is portrayed as a man whose self-sufficiency is merely a muted affirmation of traditional Hollywood rites of machismo, and whose passivity is a form of aggression. But the character of Bree gives the film a genuine sense of the problems of the seventies' "new woman." Breaking away from the old roles based on female dependency and commitment to domesticity and family means all sorts of new and anxiety-laden relationships and situations. At the end of the film Bree gives up her compulsive need to manipulate and control and leaves with Klute for his hometown. But she remains ambivalent about the relationship and informs her therapist in a voiceover: "I may be back in a couple of weeks."[22]

While Bree does not make the complete break with the traditional women's role in Hollywood—her possible happinesss is predicated on her having a man to emotionally support her—the film does provide some feeling of a woman's struggle for a new identity. In a faltering manner, the film industry made a number of other gestures toward confronting the social and psychological issues raised by the women's movement. Films such as Paul Mazursky's satiric sex comedy *Blume in Love* (1973) and Martin Scorsese's film about a working class widow who seeks to create a life of her own, *Alice Doesn't Live Here Anymore* (1974) reflected, in a compromised and commercialized fashion, the industry's struggle with constructing an image of the "new woman." There was also the lushly romantic—a great many soft focus close-ups and reaction shots—Streisand-Redford film *The Way We Were* (1973) about the doomed love affair of a passionate, Jewish Leftist with a cool, handsome, uncommitted WASP. Streisand's aggressive heroine is a committed activist who is willing to lose her love over a matter of moral principle, but the film subordinates its feminist and political strains to its romantic nostalgia.

Some of the women's films made during the second half of the decade tended to trivialize the problem by tying it to outworn genres like the "weepie" (*The Turning Point*, 1978) or a literate, female version of the buddy film (*Julia*, 1977). There were also films that dealt with supposedly liberated women, such as the comfortably feminist *An Unmarried Woman* (1978) and *Kramer vs. Kramer* (1979) which either provided talented, loving Prince Charmings to ease the pain of "liberation" or implicitly criticized the callousness of the newly emancipated women.

Kramer vs. Kramer was 1979's biggest commercial and critical hit, winning five Oscars (including ones for Best Film, Director, and Actor) and grossing over $60 million domestically. It was the kind of work that *Time* could tout as a minefield of contemporary social issues. And though it did indeed deal with the breakdown of traditional concepts of marriage and family and with the male assuming the maternal role, much of its massive success rested with its remaining human and cozy in the old Hollywood style. It is a film which keeps under control the despair and chaos inherent in the abandonment by the liberated wife-mother Joanna (Meryl Streep) of her husband Ted (Dustin Hoffman) and her son, emphasizing instead the growing warmth and love between father and son. It also comforts rather than disturbs the audience, assuring them that in a time of fragmentation where egoism had become a prime virtue, humane qualities such as loyalty, decency, and self-sacrifice still exist.

Despite these limitations, *Kramer vs. Kramer* is an intelligent and accessible work which succeeds in conveying fresh and unsentimental truths about parents and children; the relationship between father and son is evoked in all its anguish, pleasure and complication. The intensity of the father's love is most powerfully communicated in a scene where the boy receives a severe cut by falling off some playground monkey bars. The camera then focuses on Ted's despairing and guilt-ridden face as he races wildly with his son in his arms to the hospital. There are also perceptive scenes where Ted not only must try to be patient and compassionate with his son, but must feign affection and interest when he does not feel it or has his mind on other matters. And though Ted is clearly depicted as a caring, devoted father, he also can at times become prickly, tense, and easily irritated.

Nevertheless, *Kramer vs. Kramer* is a film which takes few formal or intellectual risks. Its emotions and images don't reverberate beyond what is presented within the frame. There is also a strain of antifeminism inherent in the film. It is Ted who garners the film's sympathy and applause by displaying the humanness and emotional strength (not without difficulty) that makes him capable of both pursuing a career and being a nurturing, committed parent. The wife's consciousness is never explored (except for the opening moments where in desperation and sorrow she prepares to tell her husband that she is leaving), and she is given relentlessly packaged feminist clichés (which in the context are unsympathetic): anguished-women-submerged-by-domesticity-career-ist-husband-in-search-of-self.[23]

Despite these limitations there were clear advances for women in the films of the 1970s. Women's issues were consciously foregrounded and built into the narrative of the films in ways the Joan Crawford and Bette Davis films about strong, well-defined women rarely did. For example, in *Norma Rae* (1979), a sentimental liberal film about a successful textile strike, the interest is more on the unformed heroine (Sally Field) realizing her potential than on labor issues. Spunky Norma Rae has spent much of her life being used and abused by men, but the strike grants her the opportunity to discover that she is a courageous, intelligent, and independent woman. Still it's a man, an articulate, aggressive, New York Jewish labor organizer, Reuben (played with broad, ethnic strokes by Ron Leibmen), who acts as her intellectual and political mentor and guide. Though Norma Rae does not end the film in a classic romantic clinch with Reuben—submerging her identity in his—the majority of the other seventies films still saw women usually back in place next to their man at the climax, despite the struggles for autonomy they engaged in through the body of the narrative.

In sharp contrast to the increasing number of films about women's quest for selfhood was the disappearance of the few serious films about black life (it was as if Hollywood decided to echo the Nixon-Moynihan notion of "benign ne-glect"). Black films had been commercially successful in the early seventies, with movies about heroic black studs and pimps like *Shaft* (1971) and *Superfly* (1972) ushering in a whole new genre called blaxploitation films (though they began to disappear by the mid-1970s).

There was also writer-director Melvin Van Peebles' more outrageous and controversial hit *Sweet Sweetback's Baadasssss Song* (1971) whose hero (played by Van Peebles) transforms himself from an apolitical black stud, who works in a whore house, into an indomitable avenging angel at war with and in flight from the police. The film is contemptuous of whites, who are seen as murder-ous brutes and buffoons, while it romanticizes the communal spirit of ghetto blacks. The anger and defiance at the heart of the film is more an expression of black rage toward whites than a coherent politics; the film is "dedicated to all those who have enough of the man." And among those who have had enough are a group of ghetto inhabitants—prostitutes, campy preachers, unwed moth-ers, and gamblers—whose lives Van Peebles does not prettify, but still affirms and even exalts.

Sweetback is an overheated, overdirected film—inundated with flash cuts, tilts, freeze frames, voiceovers, double exposures and the use of a split screen. However, it's a vivid and vital work, and though its politically counterproduc-tive to turn a sauntering pimp into a superhero and attempt to frighten and intimidate whites, the film's abrasiveness and rhetorical commitment to black power was successful in reaching a large black audience in 1971.

Films, in turn that involved much less action and dealt with less sensational aspects of black life, such as *Claudine* (1974), *Conrack* (1974), and *The Bingo Long Traveling All-Stars* (1976), did not do well at the box office. With rare exceptions, black films needed a star personality such as Diana Ross (*Lady Sings the Blues*, 1972) or Richard Pryor (*Greased Lightning*, 1977), to get the crossover audience—whites who would not normally go to see a film about blacks. And although these stars could generally sell a film, they tended to be well-crafted escapist works rather than films that dealt with the psychological and social reality of black life. Hollywood clearly sensed that in the seventies both white guilt about the social status and problems of blacks had begun to disappear, and black civil rights organizations had lost much of their political potency and power. As a result, beyond the few black stars who had crossover appeal, black actors mainly played minor character roles. Hollywood's decision to avoid dealing with the complexity of black life and lives was clearly in tune with the dictates of the market and the political and social climate of the 1970s.

Of course, early seventies' Hollywood films did not speak in one voice. Not all films engaging in a critique of American society and culture were made from the perspective of women or blacks or by people adhering to left-liberal politics or the counterculture. There were a great many people in the sixties and early seventies who were appalled by what they perceived as a period dominated by permissiveness and social breakdown. Their answer to the political protests and alternative life styles was a return to traditional values of home, family, and law and order. Part of this yearning was turned by Hollywood into a nostalgia for a lone man with a gun bringing law and order to an untamed frontier, only this time that frontier included the city as well. *Death Wish* (1974) and *Walking Tall* (1974) were two prime examples of this film genre, but the best and most archetypal one was Don Siegel's brilliantly edited *Dirty Harry* (1971), starring Clint Eastwood.

Dirty Harry was a film about an avenging knight, a San Francisco police inspector, Harry Callahan, whose major targets besides criminals were the liberals and politicians whose laws and sentiments helped create a permissive social climate. In the film Harry pursues a psychopathic, hippie killer who has tortured and killed a number of people, and culminated his series of atrocities by kidnapping a bus filled with children. Harry is a solitary, lean, indefatigable figure who will not be deterred by mere legalities, like civil liberties or police rules, until he has killed this personification of pure evil—there are no psychological or social explanations for the killer's behavior. Using heroic low-angle and full shots of the demigod Harry the film totally identifies with his perspective, making his superiors seem lame and weak, and Harry's skill at providing vigilante justice the only protection against a violent, demonic world. At the film's climax, in a scene reminiscent of *High Noon*, Harry throws his badge into the water where the killer's corpse is floating. Obviously, it is only a beau geste, for in sequels like *Magnum Force* (1973) and *The Enforcer* (1976), Harry continues to relentlessly wage all-out war against radicals, homosexuals, and other groups he perceives as flotsam of a permissive society.[24]

Many of the films of the early and mid-seventies nicely illustrated how long it took for major cultural changes and trends to register in Hollywood. Whether or not their points of view were inspired by the political right or the left, many of these films were a spill-over from the political conflicts and social tensions of the sixties. For example, Alan Pakula's *Parallax View* (1974) was a stunningly visual thriller (e.g., a wonderful use of wide screen space and unique settings) about a politically nebulous right wing conspiracy's assassination of a Kennedy-style politician, which a government commission (i.e., the Warren commission) whitewashes by attributing the murder to a lone psychopath. The conspiracy is all-encompassing, and the sullen, unflappable reporter, Joe Frady's (Warren Beatty) heroics are insufficient to defeat this omnipresent, evil power. Another skillful, paranoid thriller and commercial success was Sydney Pollack's *Three Days of the Condor* (1975) which evoked a desolate world of betrayers who work for the CIA. The film's last scene sees its isolated hero played by Robert Redford going off to take his story about this renegade organization that has gotten inside of the CIA, to the *New York Times*—a variation on Daniel Ellsberg and the Pentagon Papers. However, in this case, the film bleakly suggests that even the good, respectable *Times* could be part of the conspiracy, and may not publish the story.

One film which acknowledged some of the major political and social trends of the early seventies was Alan Pakula's big box office hit, *All the President's Men* (1976). The film was based on the Woodward-Bernstein book which painstakingly followed their investigation for the *Washington Post* of the Watergate burglary and all its more ominous political ramifications. Shot in the characteristic Pakula mode—shadowy night streets and apartment interiors, parts of the screen blackened out, the reporters seen isolated on the frame in extreme long shot or dwarfed by Washington's buildings—the film combines the style of the thriller and the television-style documentary drama which dramatizes actual events.

The two dogged, driven reporters—Woodward and Bernstein (Robert Redford and Dustin Hoffman)—are treated here as icons, using the freedom of the press to preserve our constitutional rights and democracy. Their private lives and individual personalities—except for sketching the surface of Bernstein's tense, aggressive, chain-smoking persona—are totally subsumed in the detailing of the investigation. The film tries and sometimes succeeds in adding drama to the endless car rides, phone calls, and meetings with the editors by creating an all-pervasive sense of danger. It sets a number of scenes in the murk of an underground garage—complete with threatening footsteps and screeching car tires—where Woodward meets his prime informant, Deep Throat (Hal Holbrook). In this Pakula film the conspiracy is, of course, defeated, and we are made to feel good about the press and the American system. Still, the film eschews a full exploration of the political motivation and institutional accommodation that was at the root of Watergate for the usual Hollywood emphasis on the courage of two individuals—Woodward and Bernstein.

Despite these conspiracy films, the industry sensed that the public sought some release from the years of Vietnam and Watergate. It turned, in the main, to mirroring political slogans like Ford's "time of healing" by relentlessly packaging escapist entertainment. Some of the films, such as the Bicentennial blockbuster, Rocky (1976), resurrected traditional American values like the Horatio Alger dream of "rags to riches." The fairy-tale dimensions of the film were projected both on and off the screen for it was written by an unemployed and practically destitute actor, Sylvester Stallone, who became an overnight sensation and superstar and won an Academy award.

Rocky was a film about a broken-down pug who also moonlights as an enforcer for a mob loan shark. However, in this fairy tale Rocky was depicted as combining the body of a circus strongman with the saintliness of St. Francis. He was kind to animals and small children, and gave a break even to those who were behind in their payments to the loan shark. Rocky's big moment comes when the black heavyweight champion grants him a shot at the title. The scenes of his training and his Dionysian struggle with the champion Apollo Creed turn into a crudely stirring evocation and endorsement of the importance of honesty, perseverance, and hard work.

Rocky not only revived the Alger myth, it made ethnic, working-class Americans the prime actors and agents of the dream. In Rocky the film had created a character who existed as some pre-psychoanalytic being, a man who could invoke nostalgia for a purer, simpler past. For the general film-going audience, working-class lives had, for the moment, become a preserve of spontaneity, warmth, and masculinity.

In fact, the success of Rocky made the white working class briefly fashionable in Hollywood again. The trend took off into solid, commercial hits like Saturday Night Fever (1978), and less successful films such as Paul Schrader's Blue Collar (1977), F.I.S.T. (1978) and Bloodbrothers (1978), all of which highlighted working-class characters and situations, though were more interested in exploiting genre conventions than in exploring class realities.[25]

In Saturday Night Fever the hero, Tony Manero (John Travolta), conveys on the surface much of the same mixture of macho charisma, gentleness, and vulnerability as Rocky. But instead of the heroics taking place in the ring, his arena is the dance floor, where he is the local king of the disco. His undulating energy and dynamism on the dance floor, however, aren't sufficient to grant him a way out of his neighborhood wasteland. Tony is bound to a world composed of a stereotypical Italian-American mother and unemployed construction worker father, both of whom spend much of their time either putting him down or shouting at each other; a pill-popping, gang-banging and fighting, oafish group of friends; and a job without a future as a clerk in a hardware store.

Saturday Night Fever is a more complex and suggestive film than *Rocky*. Though *Rocky* cannot escape touching on certain social realities such as decaying ethnic neighborhoods and racial conflict (Rocky as "the great white hope"), it still blurs, even obliterates, those tensions in a magical act of transcendence. However, *Saturday Night Fever* allowed much more of the anxieties of working-class life to intrude before submerging them in the romantic music of the Bee Gees and disco scenes shot through multicolored filters by a fluidly zooming and panning camera.

Tony, however, though more sensitive, decent, and perceptive than his friends, is not another saintly Rocky. His character is built on a blend of crude street humor, macho posturing, and self-absorption. He can use and dismiss friends (male and female) without much sensitivity to their feelings. The film also touches on working-class sexism, frustration, rage, and the sense of social inadequacy working-class people feel, when dealing with an upper-middle-class culture. *Saturday Night Fever* is still primarily a commercial, escapist work which does not delve too deeply into the full meaning of these problems and emotions. In fact, like *Rocky* (though in much more muted fashion), the film offers a second chance to Tony, a romance with an upwardly mobile secretary, Stephanie (Karen Lee Gorney), and the repudiation of his Brooklyn world for a supposedly more humane and exciting life in an upper-middle-class Manhattan.[26]

Along with *Rocky*'s affirmation of the American Dream came a revival of the traditional Hollywood theme of the uncommon common man. For example, in Steven Spielberg's *Jaws* (1976), the family man as hero is affirmed amidst blockbuster technical effects and a consummate building of tension and suspense. The most memorable elements in *Jaws* are the skillfully edited scenes of a killer shark's attack on a summer resort. However, though the ominous shark has a great deal of life, the film's central characters are thinly sketched. Among them is a middle-class, family man, police chief Martin Brody (Roy Scheider), who battles against the cover-ups of the town's corrupt mayor and ultimately kills the shark. He only does that after the upper-class technologisms of ichthyologist Matt Hooper (Richard Dreyfuss) and the working-class machismo of the Ahab-like sailor Quint (Robert Shaw) have failed. By turning Brody into the film's hero, *Jaws* implicitly celebrated the virtues of fidelity and family instead of glorifying the heroic loner.[27]

But even *Jaws* was touched with the anxieties of the real world. In George Lucas' *Star Wars* (1977), the ultimate in escapism was achieved by creating a magical world, somewhat similar to the American West, where heroic action could find its proper setting. The audience no longer had to be bothered by images of real streets, problems, and people; it could lose itself in outer space. In *Star Wars*, Lucas threw everything he knew into the picture—a catalogue of genre entertainments of the last thirty years—and capitalized on America's passion for technology. The film is populated with almost-human, cuddly robots, computers and alien beings (looking like an ape version of the *Wizard of Oz*'s Cowardly Lion), and scenes of glorified combat with rocket fighters right out of the Second World War films—all of it placed in a fantasy galaxy. Lucas' inventiveness is framed within a story of a "quest" for the "force" in a hierarchical world which does not only consist of robots, but contains knights, villains in black, princesses and priests, all of which were staples of adventure fiction, comic books, and fairy tales. Even if Americans were no longer willing to follow the lone cowboy as he eternally cleaned up the frontier, they flocked in record numbers to Luke Skywalker and his cohorts as they blasted through space and shot it out with Darth Vader.[28]

Shoring up this return to past values and genres were films evoking occult dread and divine power. Starting with *The Exorcist* (1973), a terrifying film directed by William Friedkin (*The French Connection*, 1971), these works began to denounce the sins of modernism and implied that only true faith could ensure peace and tranquility. *The Exorcist* was conceived by its scriptwriter, the Jesuit-trained, former USIA writer William Peter Blatty, as part of his "apostolic work."[29] The film describes how two gentle, heroic priests invoking Christ's name cured or exorcised (at the expense of their own lives) the young daughter of a free-thinking, divorced actress of demonic possession, after all else, including impotent doctors and psychiatrists had failed. Besides preaching the true faith *The Exorcist* and other similar works (for example, *The Omen* [1976], *Exorcist II* [1977]) also undermined the idea of individual or moral responsibility for one's behavior. *The Exorcist*, though primarily a work of well-crafted horror—using sound and elaborate makeup to evoke anxiety and fear in its audience—still projected in a cold and impersonal manner that the acts of human beings are determined by powerful demonic forces.

Though little intellectual credibility could be given to a belief in demonic forces, *The Exorcist* was symptomatic of a number of Hollywood films of the second half of the decade. In contrast to films of the first half of the decade, which either attacked American capitalism and culture for its corruption, murderousness, and creation of ersatz values, or saw criminality aided by liberalism overwhelming traditional institutions, many of the second-half films affirmed traditional American values such as a belief in mobility, family, technology, and religion.

That is not to say that there weren't a number of major films that didn't quite fit into either category. One of the best American directors of the 1970s and 1980s was Martin Scorsese whose work was built on emotional extremity, pulsating energy, and formal boldness. Two of his most original and imaginative works were critical successes and starred Robert De Niro. *Mean Streets* (1973) is an edgy, violent film which fuses realist and expressionist imagery to unsentimentally evoke the codes and rituals of "the boys" in New York's Little Italy.

Taxi Driver (1976) was a more murderous, alienated and hallucinatory film than *Mean Streets*. It centered on a paranoid, solipsistic, and strangely innocent New York City cab driver Travis Bickle (De Niro) who, isolated behind his glass partition, drives all night around nightmarishly beautiful Manhattan streets filled with junkies, pimps, and twelve-year-old hookers. Bickle is a man who carries "bad ideas in his head," and with an arsenal of weapons wants to clean the city—"an open sewer"—of its scum. *Taxi Driver* is not *Dirty Harry*—Scorsese is not advocating vigilante justice—neither is the film a social reformer's portrait of urban squalor and disintegration nor is it a critique of the condition of 1970s America.

Scorsese's obsessions are primarily psychological and aesthetic rather than social and political in nature. *Taxi Driver*, with its cinematic allusions, voice-over, restlessly moving camera, high overhead shots, semi-abstract sequences, extremely tight close-ups of Bickle's mad eyes, use of slow motion, and its sweltering, night city of shadows, neon lights, shimmering shapes, and manhole covers emitting steam, is not interested in providing a documentary or social realist view of the city. The emphasis here is on one alienated man's personal hell—most of the film shot from Bickle's point of view—which is shaped by the dark ambience of film noir and Scorsese's own personal demons and fantasies and fragmented view of the world. Scorsese has made a riveting, virtuosic work, where, breaking from classical Hollywood conventions, he creates no truly redeemable characters and concludes the film on an ambiguous, open-ended note.

Another major director of the seventies whose work could not easily be placed in either category was Woody Allen, America's prime comic auteur. By the late 1970s Allen's films were no longer nightclub-based, cartoon-style works filled with one-liners and pratfalls (e.g., *Bananas*, 1971), but comedies with serious moral intentions and characters capable of genuine suffering. The best of them was *Manhattan* (1979), a tragi-comedy with a coherent narrative and a distinctive visual style. The film opens with a glorious, loving montage of Manhattan icons and avenues—Lincoln Center, Park Avenue—the final image being a spectacular fireworks display over Central Park. Allen's New York is not Scorsese's; it's chic, comfortable, and romantic, and it sways to a Gershwin tune. His urban New Yorkers, however, may live in a city whose beauty can "knock you out," but they are neurotics—irresponsible and egoistic individuals—unable to sustain commitments to work or to other people.

Allen, of course, still remembers how to be funny. He wittily satirizes the cultural games New York intellectuals and demi-intellectuals engage in: Mary's (Diane Keaton) seamless flow of pretentious art crit jargon and talk of the wrong kind of orgasm at a MOMA fund raiser. But in Manhattan he never allows a sight gag or a one-liner to disrupt the film's moving, comic-pathetic portrait of intelligent people who are given over to self-deception and live unrealized lives.

Allen's film, like Scorsese's, could be read on one level as a critique of contemporary American urban life, but his perspective was neither shaped by nor derived from the movements of the sixties. As an antidote to contemporary moral decay, Allen constructs a personal pantheon which includes Willie Mays, Ingmar Bergman, Groucho Marx, and Louis Armstrong. His heroes aren't hip or politically radical; they have a sense of purpose, discipline, and genius—virtues that Allen clearly sees as having been lost by the often emotionally flabby and intellectually compromised characters that inhabit his cinematic universe.

Allen's and Scorsese's films were anomalies; Rocky came much closer to what the Hollywood mainstream was all about in the second half of the decade. The ultimate test of this renewed commitment to patriotism and the American Dream was to see how Hollywood would handle the Vietnam War. All through the war it had shied away from any films that dealt directly with the conflict. Despite some films (Bonnie and Clyde, The Wild Bunch) which could be seen as oblique metaphors for the war, there was doubt whether Hollywood would ever directly confront the issue. In an industry whose basic operating premise is that an appeal to the lowest common denominator is one of the keys to making a profit, dealing with a war that was so divisive and controversial was seen as a recipe for financial disaster.

However, as a number of successful novels and memoirs on the war came out, and people's passions about Vietnam cooled, films dealing with the war began to seem less risky. Moreover, books such as Tim O'Brien's National Book Award-winning novel, Going after Cacciato and Michael Herr's dazzling, feverish Dispatches, projected the feeling that only a film could convey the nightmarish and absurdist imagery of the war—making the ultimate statement about Vietnam and integrating it into the national consciousness. Consequently, after the release of a number of smaller films about Vietnam (Boys in Company C, 1978, Tracks, 1978 and Go Tell the Spartans, 1978), the war and its impact were treated in three big-budget films, Coming Home (1978), The Deer Hunter (1978) and Apocalypse Now (1979).

Coming Home directed by Hal Ashby was a film structured around a traditional love-triangle which mixed a touch of feminism and some painful Vietnam realities to give the film political and cultural significance. The prime focus is on a romantic affair between a Marine Corps Captain's wife and former cheerleader, Sally Hyde (Jane Fonda), and a parapalegic Vietnam veteran, Luke Martin (Jon Voight). Sally is transformed by her love for Luke from a repressed, conventional wife into a sexually liberated and somewhat independent woman, while Luke moves from an embittered, totally dependent cripple into an empathetic, politically and sexually active handicapped person. And the third person in the triangle, eager, ambitious Marine Captain Bob Hyde (Bruce Dern) goes off to Vietnam without any hesitation and returns submerged in suicidal despair, evoking the alienation and moral disintegration that often accompanied front-line service in Vietnam.

The romantic triangle and the radical transformations of character, in the main, seem simplistic and unconvincing. Sally's changes lack internality and are built on her achieving orgasm with Luke (aided by the Beatles' "Strawberry Fields" on the soundtrack) and are expressed primarily through stylistic changes in dress and hairdo. Luke's emergence as a caring, almost saintly figure is too sudden to be credible, and makes the film seem smug about America's capacity to turn the resentful vets into symbols of postwar hope.

Despite the facile Hollywood touches, there are moving moments where the film captures a great deal of the texture of the war's terrifying legacy. The scenes in the veterans' hospital of the crippled GI's oppressed by nightmares, talking unselfconsciously, and often with black humor, about the war and the pain they experience, seeing them being sponged, fed, and getting high, carries a great deal of emotional resonance and authenticity. The hospital's physical condition and medical care are no horror show, but the vets feel walled in—they see themselves as carrying too much of the war's reality for ordinary people to deal with except by treating them as objects of pity.[30]

Coming Home is a film openly critical of the war that never quite goes to the heart of the Vietnam experience. The nightmare of combat is left to our imagination and whatever can be gleaned from Bob Hyde's memories. More importantly, the film shies away from the war's political and historical context—emphasizing its link to American machismo—and tries to mute the specific terrors of the war by providing overly-neat moral and psychological transformations and an upbeat final image of Luke and Sally spending a joyous, sunny day on the beach.

The terror of Vietnam was clearly not purged from Michael Cimino's The Deer Hunter. Cimino's controversial epic was alternately condemned as being racist or a total distortion of the truth or praised for being cinematically brilliant and emotionally devastating by critics and Vietnam War correspondents. The film even brought on hostile demonstrations by antiwar activists when it won the Academy Award in 1978.

The three central figures in *The Deer Hunter* are three apolitical, young, Russian-American steelworkers—Michael the film's central figure (Robert DeNiro), Nicky (Christopher Walken), and Steven (John Savage)—from a milltown in western Pennsylvania who go off, without qualms, to fight in Vietnam. These are men who are linked to each other and their ethnic community not by words but by a number of visible and invisible strands of ritual and memory. Cimino is in love with their rituals and turns every experience (e.g., lip synching rock songs, drinking, and hunting) into an elaborate ceremony. And he is more concerned with constructing images of a warm, working-class community than with illuminating the social structure and culture of that world. The apotheosis of Cimino's homage to traditional working-class life is the ethnic wedding sequence. It is lovingly detailed with the camera dollying around the wedding participants, which include young children, stocky Slavic housewives, grizzled older workers, and all the film's major characters, evoking the joy, energy, cacophony, and brawling stupidity of the celebration.

Despite Cimino's use of long takes, natural sound, and non-professional actors to capture the formlessness of authentic experience, he gives a sentimental gloss to his working class milieu. It's a more intact and satisfied community than ever graced *Rocky*, *Saturday Night Fever* or factory towns in the late 1960s. *The Deer Hunter*'s steel mill is no "dark satanic mill" filled with alienated and resentful workers, but an elegant monolith where sooty, sweating workers labor with gusto and even pleasure amid intense noise and blast furnace flames. The three steelworkers are untouched by dreams of mobility and feel that all they have ever desired in life "is right here."

This almost Edenic image of the working class community serves to make what follows in the second half of the film in Vietnam even more horrific. The second half begins with the use of a handheld camera to make the audience viscerally feel the terror of Vietnam combat. There are no limits in this war—everyone, including civilians and soldiers, women and children, can be either shot or burned alive. However, Cimino's focus is not on combat, but on the emotional effects of the war on the three steelworkers, whose point of view the film embraces.

Vietnam's abattoir disrupts them all to different degrees, and their connection to each other and their community is almost totally torn apart. The only one of the trio who comes out of Vietnam able to function (though disoriented) is Michael, the deerhunter of the title. Cimino conceives Michael as a working-class superman in the romantic tradition of James Fenimore Cooper's *The Deerslayer*, a frontiersman who stood on the periphery of his society and struggled with nature to define his manhood. Michael, in turn, is still one of the boys who wrestles, jokes, guzzles beer, and has a deep link to his friends. But like Cooper's Bumppo he is silent, stoical, sexually chaste, and given to inarticulate poetic yearnings beyond the emotional understanding of his friends. He is also a man of almost superhuman will—an indomitable, fearless figure who is able to calmly confront and triumph over death. It is his will that saves the trio, by slaughtering their NLF captors, when they are tortured in an emotionally draining, politically manipulative, and stunningly edited Russian roulette session (purely a fictional conceit of Cimino's).

If the film lacks a conscious coherent political ideology, its total identification with Michael's rectitude and heroism has the politically invidious effect of inverting history, making the Americans innocent victims and the Vietnamese the aggressors in the war. In close-up the Vietnamese (including the South Vietnamese) are seen as "the other," demonic or decadent variations of "the yellow peril." The film suffers from a case of political and moral amnesia, forgetting that it was the Americans who were the aggressors and extended the basically civil and colonial conflict, who carpet-bombed and napalmed the Vietnamese and adulterated and destroyed the social fabric of South Vietnam. *The Deer Hunter* personalizes history, constructing a war where good Americans struggle to survive against bad Vietnamese, rather than one where political ideology, Cold War politics, and nationalism play a determining role.

The film's final scene provides a perfect illustration of Cimino's gift for moving us emotionally with action which is politically and intellectually callow. After Nick's funeral, Michael and his friends sit in numbed silence and suddenly begin to sing "God Bless America" in tremulous voices. Their singing uneasily affirms a tattered American will and community. One wants to believe that Cimino is providing, on one level, an ironic commentary on their continued patriotism, but there is no sign of it in the sequence. Given that *The Deer Hunter* gives no reason for Americans to be participants in the Vietnam charnal house it depicts, it is impossible to simply empathize with this ritual of reconciliation. Obviously, Cimino's strength is a gift for using mise-en-scène and editing to create striking images and arouse us emotionally. What he lacks is the kind of political intelligence that would allow for greater insight and coherence into the Vietnam experience.[31]

Despite its intellectual limitations and distortions, *The Deer Hunter* did convey a sense of the spiritual desolation and destruction that Vietnam caused for many Americans. However, the film not only raised a great deal of controversy, but was often taken by audiences as a homage to the American cause in Vietnam. As a result, it made the final release of Francis Ford Coppola's *Apocalypse Now* (1979) that much more eagerly awaited. There was a feeling that this film would provide for the public an emotional catharsis and be the final word about the war. Coppola reinforced these expectations when he equated the making of the film with the war itself. He said that he had made *Apocalypse Now* just the way America made war in Vietnam. That there were too many people, too much money spent and equipment used there, and little by little the cast and crew went insane.

Apocalypse Now was loosely based on Joseph Conrad's *Heart of Darkness*, particularly its evocation of the emotional and moral rot of imperialism. It opens with an image of apocalyptic flames superimposed over a sweating, drunken Willard—the novella's Marlow (Martin Sheen). Willard has the mad eyes and ravaged looks of a man who has lived and seen too much. In the film he is a burnt-out government hit man with six kills to his credit, whose mission is to terminate the life of Colonel Kurtz (played with little sign of real involvement by a bulging, mumbling Marlon Brando), a rogue Green Beret Colonel who had set himself up as a tribal god, engaging in a private war against the North Vietnamese and Vietcong in the Cambodian jungle.

Using Willard's pilgrimage as a framework, Coppola constructs a hallucinatory, surreal Vietnam—the war as absurdist epic. The film is filled with spectacular scenes touched with a sense of the absurd: an exhilarating *Gotterdammerung* helicopter attack led by Colonel Kilgore (Robert Duvall as an exaggerated version of General Patton) to whom napalm is the perfume of victory and the purpose of destroying a Vietcong village is to discover the perfect wave for surfing; the revolt of sex-starved soldiers as they rush the stage after being tantalized and provoked by a garish USO bump and grind show of undulating Playboy bunnies; and an officerless and forgotten platoon of anxious black GIs despairingly shooting into the darkness (accompanied by atonal music, disembodied voices on the soundtrack, and flares lighting up the sky) in the "asshole of the world"—the last American outpost on the border between Vietnam and Cambodia. These set pieces and a number of Coppola's other terrifyingly luminous images grant the film great visual power and a genuine feeling for the chaos and lunacy of the war. Still there is something excessive about much of it—not enough repose and moral balance to give some perspective on the almost unrelieved madness and abundance of special effects that fills the frames.

What hurts the film most is that the ultimate confrontation between Kurtz and an empty and exhausted Willard is anticlimactic. Willard is too saturated in death and a sense of nothingness to be morally transformed (as Marlow is in Conrad's version) by meeting Kurtz. In fact, there is little interaction between them, as an imprisoned Willard sits passively listening to Kurtz's gnomic and pretentious monologue which is permeated with literary allusions ranging from Eliot's *The Hollow Men* to *The Golden Bough*.

In Kurtz, Coppola has created a metaphysical abstraction—the superman incarnate—a man who speaks of himself as transcending conventional opinion and morality. He advocates, in almost Nietzschean terms, that judgment defeats us, and "we must make friends with moral terror." And Coppola's superman engages in the ultimate assertion of will: he wills his own and his followers' deaths.

Nevertheless, all Kurtz's philosophic musings and imperial posturing turn him into such a self-conscious symbol that the particular historical and social reality of the Vietnam War and America's role there is replaced by a vaporous notion of civilization's madness. The terror is universalized—it is seen as a part of the human condition, not as a product of concrete political forces. In constructing his version of Kurtz, Coppola strains for significance, trying to sum up the highly charged and sometimes overly-spectacular imagery of the film's first two-thirds with a symbol which has little emotional or political resonance.

In addition, Coppola demonstrates little critical distance from his conception of Kurtz. One senses that though Coppola may, on one hand, morally recoil from the war's murderousness and madness, on the other, he identifies, even embraces Kurtz's megalomania and extremity. So when Dennis Hopper's manic photojournalist speaks of Kurtz as a "great man," as an archetypal figure who has his own "dialectic logic," he is not parodied for his portentous babbling, but is seemingly expressing one strain in Coppola's vision. In *Apocalypse Now* that vision itself was often blurred, as Coppola sacrificed clarity for stylistic effects.

There is a German proverb that states that a war creates three armies: an army of cripples, an army of beggars, and an army of the unemployed. The Vietnam War had created a fourth army: one of filmmakers. But in the seventies these were directors who substituted a gift for inventive metaphors and symbols and startling images for an ability to penetrate the heart of darkness which was Vietnam.[32]

Of course, Hollywood has rarely tried to penetrate that heart—in either Vietnam or at home in New York or other American cities. It has usually used well-honed conventions and ceremonies to mute those profound anxieties and avoid looking too closely at what is. The Academy award ceremonies of 1978 was just the sort of occasion where Hollywood utilized its genius for shaping public rituals and neutralizing what was politically or emotionally threatening. John Wayne (in his last public appearance before his death) was called to present the Oscar for best film to Michael Cimino for *The Deer Hunter*. In the sixties and seventies Wayne had become synonymous with the traditional American verities and with virulent, jingoistic right-wing politics. Though *The Deer Hunter* was clearly no left-wing film, its alienated and maimed soldiers (though there was still a stoical, courageous hero) caught in a futile war were a far cry from the tough, confident, and uncomplicated fighting men portrayed by Wayne in *They Were Expendable* (1945) and *The Sands of Iwo Jima* (1946). The ceremony brought together the two Hollywoods: Wayne who had gone through the ranks from bit player to icon and Cimino, who without the long apprenticeship common to the old studio system (he had made only one previous film, *Thunderbolt and Lightfoot*, 1974) found himself with a multimillion-dollar picture in his hands. As it had done so often in the past, Hollywood had found the appropriate ceremony to absorb, exploit, or mute what could be seen in some ways as deviant and new.

Even without the death of John Wayne giving the decade a symbolic cap-stone, the seventies were an end to an era in American films. Gone forever were even the remnants of the old Hollywood production system, and in its place the studio had become a financial clearing house, dependent on inde-pendent producers rather than a rationalized assembly line. The old Holly-wood which could produce family pictures cheerily affirming individual mobility and success, family, and patriotism had almost disappeared. Its values were now open to question or even repudiation, and the films conveyed a greater sense of uncertainty about what was true and right than in the past. None of these changes, however, meant that much of the old Hollywood had not survived. It was still an industry where big-budget films were dominant, where stars called the shots as much or more than they ever did, and where television staples like situation comedies provided a large portion of the cre-ative models for filmmakers. And in a faltering and confused way, Hollywood still had the commercial magic and potency to create worlds which could si-multaneously hint at what American social reality was like and skillfully ob-scure it.

NOTES

1. Jonathan Schell, *The Time of Illusion* (New York: Alfred A. Knopf, 1976).

2. Godfrey Hodgson, *America in Our Time* (New York: Vintage Books, 1978), pp. 239–40.

3. Ibid., p. 398.

4. Schell, *The Time of Illusion*, pp. 77–134.

5. Theodore H. White, *Breach of Faith* (New York: Dell, 1975).

6. Gerald R. Ford, *A Time to Heal* (New York: Berkeley, 1980), pp. 378–80.

7. James Wooten, *Dasher* (New York: Signet, 1978).

8. Ibid., p. 298.

9. Ibid., p. 301.

10. Christopher Lasch, *The Culture of Narcissism* (New York: Warner Books, 1979).

11. Ibid.

12. Lou Cannon, *Ronald Reagan* (New York: G. P. Putnam's Sons, 1982).

13. James Monaco, *American Film Now* (New York: Oxford University Press, 1979).

14. Diane Jacobs, *Hollywood Renaissance: The New Generation of Filmmakers and Their Works* (New York: Delta, 1980).

15. Monaco, *American Film Now*, pp. 54–68.

16. Robert Warshow, *The Immediate Experience* (Garden City, NY: Anchor, 1964), pp. 38–39.

17. Jacobs, *Hollywood Renaissance*, pp. 115–18.

18. Leonard Quart and Al Auster, "The Godfather, Part II," *Cineaste*, VI, 4 (Winter 1976), pp. 38–39.

19. Tom Wicker, quoted in Judith M. Kass, *Robert Altman: American Innovator* (New York: Popular Library, 1978), p. 193.

20. Leonard Quart, "Altman's Films," *Marxist Perspectives*, I (Spring, 1978), pp. 21–33.

21. Molly Haskell, *From Reverence to Rape* (Baltimore, MD: Penguin Books, 1974), p. 366.

22. Ibid., p. 369.

23. Leonard Quart and Barbara Quart, "Kramer vs. Kramer," *Cineaste*, X, 2 (Spring 1980), pp. 37–39.

24. Stuart M. Kaminsky, *Don Siegel, Director* (New York: Curtis Books, 1974), pp. 268–83.

25. Leonard Quart and Albert Auster, "The Working Class Goes to Hollywood," in Philip Davies and Brian Neve (eds), *Cinema, Politics and Society in America* (Manchester: Manchester University Press, 1981), pp. 163–75.

26. Albert Auster and Leonard Quart, "Saturday Night Fever," *Cineaste*, VIII, 4 (Winter 1978), pp. 36–37.

27. Peter Biskind, "Jaws," *Jump Cut*, 15, pp. 3–4.

28. Dan Rubey, "Star Wars," *Jump Cut*, 18, pp. 9–14.

29. Josh Rofkin, "The Exorcist," *Screen Talk* (September 1975), p. 54.

30. Albert Auster and Leonard Quart, *How the War Was Remembered: Hollywood and Vietnam* (New York: Praeger, 1988), pp. 50–52.

31. Ibid., pp. 58–65.

32. Ibid., pp. 65–71.

6

THE EIGHTIES

The politics of the 1980s were dominated by Ronald Reagan's serene, amiable personal style and right wing politics. Reagan's political "philosophy" was built around aggressive anticommunism and an antagonism to big government and the welfare state. These commitments, ironically, made this enemy of state intervention into the best friend in government that the American military-corporate power structure ever had. The twenty-five percent tax cut enacted in his first year in office delighted business, as the almost ten percent increase over inflation in military spending pleased the Pentagon. And his cuts in domestic spending—health care, low-cost housing, and income maintenance programs—elated conservatives who saw them as the beginning of their long-hoped-for counteroffensive against five decades of the welfare state.

At first, however, Reagan's economic policy—critics named it "voodoo economics" as a contemptuous substitute for its original "supply side" title—resulted in the worst bout of unemployment (one factor in the creation of a subculture of homeless people who continue to wander and often sleep on the streets of American cities), bankruptcies, and corporate deficits since the Great Depression. Nevertheless, despite the growing income gap between the rich and poor and the failure of what were essentially his "trickle down" economic tenets, Reagan rigidly held onto his beliefs, shoring them up with anecdotes about welfare "cheats" and a philosophy of voluntarism that seemed to owe as much to Frank Capra (a Capra without a social conscience) as to Herbert Hoover.

Nor was this film-based political vision confined to economic affairs. In foreign policy, his "Darth Vader" speech, Reagan referred to the Soviet Union as an "evil empire," and extended the Star Wars metaphor even further by justifying his massive military build-up with allusions to as yet unbuilt space weapons that would presumably deter Soviet aggression. It seemed as if America had finally acquired a president who was deeply committed to all the crackbrained fantasies and mindless, empty rhetoric peddled by Hollywood ever since it became the center of America's popular culture.

Obviously, Reagan's saber rattling (which included the arming of a rebel force, the contras, against the leftist Sandinista regime in Nicaragua and the overthrow of an ultra-left revolutionary government on the island of Grenada in 1983) had a disquieting effect on America and its allies. If nothing else it helped relaunch antinuclear and disarmament campaigns that had lain dormant for a number of years. In small towns and large cities people all over the world began again to protest against the Strangelovian nuclear policies of the last forty-five years. In a similar fashion, by unleashing free-market forces, particularly on the air, land, and workplaces of America (dismantling the Environmental Protection Agency [EPA]) and placing people in charge who unblinkingly served the special interests, Reagan incurred the ire of the nation's environmentalists.

Nonetheless, despite these problems, mid-term election losses, and an unemployment rate of over ten percent, Reagan continued to gain the approval of the majority of Americans. Much of it had to do with his undoubted charm, his quickness with a quip, and his calming nice-guy demeanor, media assets which, when coupled with his actor's talent for assuming the presidential role and playing the "Great Communicator," led him to an easy election victory over a serious, uncharismatic Fritz Mondale in 1984. Reagan's triumph clearly demonstrated that the American public's obsession with imagery and personality went so deep that this politically unreflective and callow figure—this shallow man who seemed all persona—could do no wrong in their eyes.[1]

Of course, by 1984 the economy had revived, though there was an immense budget deficit, economic weak spots in the old industrial areas of the Northeast and Midwest, and blacks and the poor were clearly economically worse off. In fact, in the 1980s the living standard for the bottom fifth of the population dropped by eight percent while the top fifth's standard of living rose by about sixteen percent.[2] Wealth became increasingly more concentrated as a result of Republican policies. The public, however, cared little about the difficulties of the poor—the poor living at a great remove from most people's daily experience. They also felt that times were prosperous, and success was open in America to anybody who worked hard at achieving it. And even a precipitous decline of the price of farm commodities in 1985, and a trade shortfall of 170 billion in 1986—with protectionist Japan flooding America with better quality VCRs and autos (though it aroused the anger of unions and business groups)—did little to undermine the public's sanguine mood about the American economy. Of course, union opposition had little effect on Reagan's policies, as they had, in the main, allied themselves with the Mondale campaign and were in a weakened state, their membership declining by 1985 to nineteen percent of the work force. Reagan's base of support also included members of Protestant fundamentalist groups (e.g., the Moral Majority) whose prime political aims were not in the economic sphere, but in the active promotion of a social agenda including prayer in the schools, prohibition of abortion, traditional family values, and law and order. Reagan paid constant lip service to this constituency in innumerable presidential pronouncements, but did little concrete to put their program into effect beyond taking their interests into account in his Supreme Court nominations (e.g., Scalia and Bork).

The last years of his administration saw a scandal—"Irangate"—finally stick to Reagan (the "Teflon President") personally. This was a secret arms-for-hostages deal with Iran where profits from weapons sales were covertly shifted to the contras—a deal which broke the law and overrode the Constitution. Reagan attempted to deny his own reponsibility for the affair by claiming total ignorance of the activities of subordinates like Chief of the National Security Council, Vice-Admiral John Poindexter and superpatriot Colonel Oliver North. Of course, denying knowledge of the affair made Reagan look publicly like a bumbling, ineffectual figure incapable of controlling his underlings. Some of his diminished popularity was regained at the Gorbachev-Reagan summit conference in Iceland in 1986 when for the first time the superpowers agreed to eliminate a whole weapons system (all medium range missiles in Europe).

Nevertheless, by 1987 the Reagan administration seemed moribund: the president vague and detached; some former aides indicted for influence peddling; and the president and Congress at a stalemate over Star Wars, the budget, and other issues. But the Democrats were incapable of transforming the troubles of the Reagan administration into a victory in the presidential election of 1988. The Democrats, led by Michael Dukakis, an intelligent but inexpressive and rigid technocrat—who emphasized "competence" rather than social vision—ran an inept, defensive campaign which helped turn lightweight George Bush into a formidable candidate and Republican winner.

Bush was also aided in his victory by some skillful debate preparation and well-crafted, vicious, and racist negative campaign ads. In its first year the popularity of the Bush administration benefitted greatly from being in power as the Cold War wound down and revolutionary political changes in Eastern Europe, the Soviet Union, and Nicaragua took place (though the political and economic future of almost all these countries remains uncertain and even precarious). Bush demonstrated little talent or imagination for using the historical moment to project an inspiring vision of democracy, but his affable, cautious style also meant that he did not say or do anything that could undermine these momentous developments. On the domestic front, Bush's tepid, consensual, right-of-center politics muted much of the ideological abrasiveness of Reagan conservatism without breaking the faith on issues like abortion or tax policy. He also indulged in rhetorical gestures of concern for the poor and homeless and made a legislative commitment to educational and environmental reform—without any of it being sufficiently far-reaching to make even a dent in social problems (e.g., drugs, crime, housing, teenage pregnancy) that grew more profound and explosive with each passing year.

More significant than any specific Republican legislation during the eighties was Reagan's ushering in a culture of unbridled greed and materialism—where lining your own pocket was the primary goal. The public realm was devalued and treated negligently and contemptuously. There is, of course, the close to $2 trillion debt that the Federal Government built up over the last decade. More than that there is the corruption and influence peddling which permeated the Department of Housing and Urban Development, the money necessary to clean up waste from nuclear plants like Hanford in Washington, and the exorbitant cost (estimates run as high as $500 billion) to the public of the savings and loan spree that was supported by both the Reagan adminstration and Congress casting a blind eye to ongoing abuses. Conversely, the marketplace and the private realm and pleasure were deified. In a sense it was a second Gilded Age where conspicuous consumption was the norm—a great many stretch limousines and a great deal of nouvelle cuisine—an age whose commitment to profit, hedonism, and modern technology basically subverted its conservative political rhetoric. Its heroes—and Reagan's speeches promoting individual heroism—were vulgar, aggressive entrepreneurs like Donald Trump and sharp Wall Street pirates like Ivan Boesky whose operations skirted and went over the line into illegality. In fact, the people who did best financially during the decade were paper entrepreneurs (e.g., investment bankers) who made their money through deal making and asset rearranging—hostile takeovers, leveraged buyouts, junk bonds—rather than creating anything of value. The tone for the decade was set by Reagan's first inaugural which cost $8 million, opening with an $800,000 fireworks display at the Lincoln Memorial, followed by two nights of show business performances and topped off by nine inaugural balls serving 14,400 bottles of champagne. The inaugural exemplified both Reagan's aesthetic and his moral perspective, which was based on the notion that the "beautiful was the expensive, the good was the costly."[3]

This distorted moral vision gave sanction to an age of narcissism whose most representative figure was the yuppie. Yuppies may have been subjects of jokes and social satire, but in their emphasis on financial success, consumption, and self-development they embodied the period. The archetypal yuppie jogged, ate health food, was obsessed with brand names and what was fashionable, and was a workaholic. Work was a means to greater status and a more af-fluent life-style, and happiness only could be realized by relentlessly pursuing one's own needs. And little sense of larger social, moral, and communal con-cerns were allowed to intrude on this hunger for personal mobility. Of course, not every yuppie neatly fit this complacent archetype, or should I say stereo-type, but enough conformed to the type to help define the social character of the decade.

It was not clear, however, that his old industry, Hollywood, reaped any im-mediate benefits from the Reagan era. Not that times were bad—overall in-come and profits being up for most of the major studios. Yet, as always in an insecure industry, anxieties were heightened by Reagan's economic policies, especially since they swelled interest rates. Since the life blood of Hollywood is borrowed capital, the number of films produced each year suffered a severe cut-back. At the same time, Hollywood looked for economic shelters, usually in the arms of huge conglomerates that had enough internal excess capital to avoid high interest rates. So the conglomeratization of Hollywood that started in the sixties and seventies continued apace, with the gobbling up of previ-ously unattached studios like Columbia by Coca Cola in 1982 (the studio has just been bought by Akio Morita's Sony) and the mergers of old giants like MGM and United Artists. In the process tycoons like Kirk Kerkorian, Ted Turner, and Rupert Murdoch (he picked up Twentieth Century Fox in 1985) all got into the movie business.

The conglomerates positioned themselves to take control over some of the theatres they had lost long before—acquiring since 1985 more than 3,500 of the country's 22,000 screens.[4] They also took advantage of the explosion in new telecommunications technology—cable, cassettes, video discs—and their need for product by selling their old film libraries to them at a great profit. Despite the mergers, independent production companies (e.g., Island, Vestron) grew in the 1980s until the stock market crash of 1987.[5] But by 1988 many of these independent companies were on the verge of collapse unable to produce the box office hits that would keep them solvent. However, by the end of the decade Hollywood was under the tight domination of the entertainment combines, who in the main, eschewed innovative and risky filmmaking for conventional blockbusters with established stars—there were still independ-ent production and distribution companies like Miramax and New Line func-tioning and making films which were too idiosyncratic and personal for the mass market.

At the beginning of the decade, industry insecurity was heightened by the failure of Michael Cimino's intellectually vacuous and inchoate western epic, *Heaven's Gate* (1980), a total economic and critical disaster. Suddenly studios were calling into question the whole policy of allowing big-budget laissez faire to directors with only one or two hits to their credit. A search was initiated for highly marketable properties based on pre-sold reputations—sequels like *Superman II* and *Rocky III* (a film which exploits racial fears and stereotypes by creating a villain who is a brutal, black boxer with an intimidating, baleful look).[6]

It was perhaps this insecurity and the quest for bankable commodities that made it easier for Robert Redford to direct a film. Redford had been the producer of well-received and even financially successful films like *Downhill Racer* (1960), *The Candidate* (1972), and *All the President's Men* (1976), and this time around decided himself to direct a film based on Judith Guest's novel, *Ordinary People* (1980).

To some extent the material of *Ordinary People* was made to order for Redford with his Hollywood image of the WASP golden boy in films like *The Candidate* (1972) and *The Way We Were* (1973). The film evoked the dark side of an upper-middle-class, suburban WASP family—the Jarrets. The family's placid, comfortable life is disrupted by the accidental death of their eldest son, Buck, and the subsequent suicide attempt and hospitalization in a mental hospital of his guilt-ridden, bright, and sensitive younger brother, Conrad (Timothy Hutton).

The villain of the film is not the middle-class materialism or the conformist wasteland of the suburbs of a film like *The Graduate*, but WASP repression and control as epitomized by Conrad's handsome, compulsively neat mother, Beth (Mary Tyler Moore). She is conceived as a woman so obsessed with appearances and so fearful of allowing her emotions to get out of control that she deals with the family tragedy by remarking that: "We'd have been alright if there hadn't been any mess." The Jarret family "mess," and, in particular, the terror in self-lacerating Conrad's eyes, only begins to be worked out when Dr. Berger (Judd Hirsch), a warm, commonsensical, and iconoclastic Jewish psychiatrist, starts getting through to him. Berger not only helps Conrad, but as a bonus shakes his passive, somewhat unconscious, but loving father Calvin (Donald Sutherland) out of his bondage to his wife's rigidity.

Ordinary People is a small, intelligent film, which has an assured feel for the cocktail chatter and the green lawns and backyards of the insulated, all-white Lake Forest suburb where the film was made. However, the film is primarily a work of two shots and interiors, a domestic work much more interested in the tensions of family life than the world of the upper-middle-class (there is no evidence in the film that Calvin's values are much different from Beth's). Despite subtle touches such as Dr. Berger's office becoming darker as Conrad gains more insight into his problems, the film is marred by Redford's habit of sometimes reducing the complexities of familial conflict to pat formulas.

From Conrad getting just the right, jargon-free psychiatrist, to his meeting up with the most understanding and loveliest of high-school co-ed girlfriends (Elizabeth McGovern), the film has a tendency to be too pat. What helps *Ordi-*

nary People transcend some of its clichés and melodramatic contrivances (the boating accident itself) is Redford's gift for having his actors use their faces and body movements to convey a wide range of emotions. In an especially inspired bit of casting, Redford garnered Mary Tyler Moore (America's sitcom sweetheart) to play against type, giving a performance which avoids turning her frigid, golf-playing, napkin-folding mother into a mere stereotype. She is able to successfully communicate the profound desperation and insecurity that lies underneath her need to cleave to the surfaces of life and to coerce the people around her to do the same.[7]

However, though her ability to project feelings of anxiety adds nuance and dimension to the role, the mother is still the film's villain, bearing primary responsibility for Conrad's problems. It is Beth who is unwilling to contemplate changing and going to therapy, and incapable of giving any love to Conrad. And it is the mother's cold-bloodedness and egoism that links the implicit point of view of *Ordinary People* with sophisticated, often unconscious feminist backlash strains inherent in films like *Kramer vs. Kramer* and even *Tootsie* (1982). Like the wife in *Kramer*, Beth flees home and familial responsibility and leaves her husband to assume the nurturing, maternal role—the family becoming a male preserve. In both films the central female characters are portrayed as being either irresponsible or uncaring, with Beth carrying the added burden of being insidious as well.

Tootsie, of course, is a very different sort of work from the other films we have linked it with. It was one of the big box office hits of 1982, a genuinely clever and funny film with beautifully timed gags, witty one-liners, and a virtuoso performance by Dustin Hoffman. It is built around the classic comic gambit of the man who dresses up as a woman, and then cannot have his identity revealed (for example, *Some Like it Hot*, 1959). However, Hoffman and the film's director, Sydney Pollock, were not satisfied with merely making a film which left audiences howling, and they began to make serious claims for the film as an exploration of gender and sexual roles.

Tootsie is the sort of film that baldly states that each of us carries both maleness and femaleness, and that a man can acquire greater sensitivity and humanness by getting in touch with his femaleness. It also touches on other feminist issues and insights by dramatizing the insults and patronizing behavior constantly bestowed upon women at work by their bosses and, of course, asserts that women must stand up for their dignity. However, despite the film's self-conscious feminism the reality of *Tootsie* is much more conventional than its ambitions. As Dorothy Michaels, soap opera star, Hoffman continuously affirms his maleness beneath the female impersonation; there is little sense of Hoffman having truly experienced his female side. And Dorothy Michaels' feminism is troubling since it ends up that the strongest and, in fact, the only feminist in the film is a man, the other female characters being either neurotically insecure or vulnerable and dependent on a man to provide direction. *Tootsie* is a skillful, entertaining film which breaks little new ground, for it ultimately demonstrates how a man can become a feminist and leave the traditional sexual patterns in place. Just as in *Kramer vs. Kramer* and *Ordinary People*, the new hero-heroine of *Tootsie's* brand of feminism turns out to be a man.[8]

Though small personal works like *Ordinary People* and a farce with pretensions to social significance like *Tootsie* were popular in the early eighties, probably more symptomatic of the period were the works of Steven Spielberg. In the seventies Spielberg directed blockbuster hits like *Jaws* and *Close Encounters of the Third Kind* (1977) and almost singlehandedly resurrected the fortunes of Columbia Pictures. But after the failure of his comedy *1941* (1980), his career seemed on the wane until, aided by his friend and USC schoolmate, George Lucas (the film's Executive Producer), he directed *Raiders of the Lost Ark* (1981).

As in his previous films—the hunt for the malevolent shark in *Jaws*, the extraterrestrials in *Close Encounters*, and the Japanese submarine in *1941*, *Raiders* is essentially a story about a quest. The search focuses on the competition between an intrepid and invulnerable American archaeologist, Indiana Jones (Harrison Ford), and the Nazis to find the lost ark of the covenant, which will give its possessor unlimited power.

Although the film does go in for an awesome, though nonsensical, religious display at its finale, and there is talk of the gleaming gold ark having infinite power, the film's appeal and even its subtext aren't built around religious belief. *Raiders* is a reflection of the old Hollywood and its skilled manipulation of an audience's need to feel anxiety, lose itself in harmless fantasy, and become nostalgic.

In fact, from the film's opening credit, where the Paramount fades into a snow-covered Andean peak, to a fadeout, where it recreates the final scene in *Citizen Kane*, we are treated to a whole host of images and themes borrowed from old Hollywood—particularly the cliffhanging serials of the thirties. Following the genre conventions, the whip-snapping, unreflective Indiana and his hard-drinking, tough but dependent girlfriend, Marion (Karen Allen), face down poison darts, snakes, rotting corpses, assorted gun-toting villains, and finally out-smart and out-fight the inhuman Nazi hordes. The upshot of it all is not so much to reassure us about good triumphing over evil—Indiana's only real commitment is to adventure and acquiring the ark (even Marion is an afterthought)—but to enclose us in a claustrophobic world of action for its own sake. The result is that *Raiders* comes as close as a film can to being a children's comic book.[9]

It is that very same child that exists in all of us that Spielberg appealed to so imaginatively and skillfully in *E.T.* (1982). Written by Melissa Mathison, who wrote the scenario for the lyrical children's film *Black Stallion*, *E.T.* managed to hit on a mine of primal fantasy. It is basically the story of a benign extraterres-trial (who looks very much like one of the aliens in *Close Encounters*) who is left behind when his spaceship takes off without him, and a young boy, Elliot (Henry Thomas), who befriends, protects, and helps him return to his home. The story is as simple and familiar as any about a boy and his pet dog. However, there is more to the film than a bare sketch of the plot would suggest. *E.T.* con-tains numerous references and images invoking children's films (i.e., *Bambi*, 1943; *Peter Pan*, 1953; and *Mary Poppins*, 1964). The film also carries a feeling of religiosity that alternately transforms the cute, doll-like extraterrestrial into a loving father substitute and, possibly pushing its significance a bit too far, a Christ figure (E.T. dies and is resurrected in the midst of a family where the mother's name happens to be Mary).

Of course the qualities that made *E.T.* a great commercial success—within less than a year of its release it was assured of becoming one of the top grossing films of all time—went far beyond its *Bambi*-like forest imagery or its possible religious resonances. Among the most significant of these was the emphasis it gave to the need that all of us have for unwavering affection, which is con-veyed in the spiritual union between E.T. and Elliot. Pervading the whole film was Spielberg's commitment to child-like innocence, reinforced by his ability to visualize the world the way a child does.

As a result of the film's emphasis on a child's perspective, adults and adult authority are either treated warily or distrusted altogether. Even Keys (Peter Coyote), the benevolent and sympathetic head of the government scientists sent out to find E.T., wants to subject him to scientific scrutiny, and that alone places him in the adult realm. None of the adult males in the film, including Keys, are ever shown beyond their midriffs, they are a faceless, ominous, almost malevolent group—the real aliens. Elliot's mother is portrayed as ineffec-tual—she has difficulty coping with being a single parent. And his father as ir-responsible—he causes Elliot distress by running off to Mexico with another woman. In *E.T.* the children ultimately triumph over the adults, helping E.T. to elude their grasp and reach his home—the victory of feeling over rational and scientific thought.

E.T. was essentially a fairy tale, sometimes a bit too cute and sentimental for its own good—a film whose meaning is much less significant than the feelings it elicits. Still its general mood paralleled a number of cultural tendencies in early eighties America. In its affirmation of innocence, its simple optimism, and its distrust of authority, particularly the state, it unconsciously mirrored some of the certainties and pieties offered to the American public by Ronald Reagan. Indeed both E.T. and Ronald Reagan were eminently lovable, and just as Spielberg's Elliot found solace from his problems in a fantastic creature Rea-gan mouthed platitudes about traditional values, and fled the complexities in-herent in bringing about social change or reshaping the economy.[10]

The fact that the audience also shared this nostalgia for old verities need not rest solely on the election returns, but can be confirmed from the grosses and awards to a film like *On Golden Pond* (1981). In fact, if nothing else, *On Golden Pond*, with its saccharine shots of rippling water and loon-filled lakes, evoked the sterile aura of a Norman Rockwell illustration. Despite the banal imagery, the film did have an important theme and moments of truth about a rite of passage—aging and the confrontation with the imminence of death. Nevertheless, by casting Henry Fonda and Katherine Hepburn in the leading roles as the eighty-year-old, ailing Norman Thayer and his radiant, vital wife Ethel, the film paid less attention to gerontology than to Hollywood iconography.

It is not that Fonda's portrayal of the dying Norman was not a fitting culmination to a brilliant career. In fact his characterization of the surly curmudgeon with a soft streak, who delivers lines like, "I think I'll read a new book—see if I can finish it before I'm finished. Maybe a novelette," is letter perfect. Likewise is his confusion and anxiety when a well-known path suddenly becomes unknown to him, due to his failing memory.

It was not the characters or the neatly turned, sentimental narrative that drew audiences. What did was the teaming of Fonda and Hepburn, and the cinematic memories it evoked of her co-starring roles with icons like Grant, Tracy, and Wayne and their combined five decades of starring roles from Mary, Queen of Scots to Tom Joad and Mr. Roberts. In addition, in casting herself as his estranged daughter Chelsea, Jane Fonda stirred resonances of her real-life, often embattled relationship with her father. Finally, it also gave Hollywood the chance to make amends to an actor who had given so much to the industry and audience over the years by granting him an Academy Award for best actor.

The long overdue award to Fonda (Hepburn also won for best actress) was yet another symptom of Hollywood doting on its past. The problem was that this tendency was more than mere nostalgia, for it indicated not just a sentimental longing for the past, but an active use of its ideas and images in lieu of any new subjects, themes, or forms. Hollywood's yearning after its past almost seemed symptomatic of a more general longing for an America of a vigorous work ethic and powerful, growing industries, whose policy of speaking softly and carrying a big stick was enough to keep any foreign government, at least the Latin American ones, in line. It was a simpler, more buoyant and heroic past which stood in sharp contrast to a contemporary America where smokestack industries decayed and closed leaving its workforce standing on unemployment lines, and a seemingly growing number of Central American Fidelistas thumbing their noses at American power.[11]

To some extent it was this yearning after a heroic past that contributed to a decidedly peripheral, but still a minor, trend in the early eighties—the impulse to make epic films dealing with grand themes. It was a thread that ran through *Heaven's Gate* (1980), a muddled, inarticulate attempt to deal with class warfare in the American West, and Milos Forman's respectful, intelligent but stolid effort in *Ragtime* (1981), based on E. L. Doctorow's jaunty, ironic, cinematic novel of the same name, to deal with the American success myth and American racism—a trend that finally regained some critical if not economic respectability with Warren Beatty's *Reds* (1981).

In many ways *Reds* was as much a personal film for Warren Beatty as *Ordinary People* was for Robert Redford. Like Redford, Beatty's previous successes as the producer-star of *Bonnie and Clyde* (1967), *Shampoo* (1975), and *Heaven Can Wait* (1978) insured him the industry clout necessary to make a film about, of all things, an American radical and communist. Also in line with Redford's work, Beatty's film was inspired by personal experience. In the late sixties Beatty had taken a trip to Russia where, whenever he met older communists, they told him how much he physically resembled John Reed. When he returned home, Beatty delved into doing research about Reed, which set off an almost two-decades-long campaign to do the film about him.[12]

Ultimately, it was a combination of this personal obsession coupled with his awareness of what made for success and failure in the film business that deeply influenced *Reds*. First of all, Beatty (who won an Oscar for direction) decided to limit the focus of the film to the last four years of Reed's life; concentrating on his love affair and marriage to Louise Bryant (Diane Keaton); their experience and reporting of the Russian Revolution; and Reed's subsequent commitment to building an American Communist Party. Of course this left out important aspects of Reed's life: his equally intense involvement with wealthy Mabel Dodge Luhan, who ran a literary salon in the Village, and his participation in the Mexican Revolution and the First World War, struggles of which we get only brief glimpses. Also Beatty's decision to portray Louise as a poor little woman who clings to her man, offended many feminists who saw her as much more forceful, defined, and talented than the Keaton role conveyed.

Significant as these omissions were, even more glaring was how basically safe the film truly was—especially on a formal level. Of course Beatty faced an insurmountable problem in making a commercially viable film with a $35 million budget which at the same time treated two American communists sympathetically. In making *Reds*, except for his inspired use of the "witnesses," Beatty never strayed beyond the conventional romantic epic. In fact, despite its links to Stieglitz photos and Eisenstein's *Ten Days That Shook the World*, it owed its greatest debt to David Lean. In one episode Beatty had Louise, in her attempt to unite with an imprisoned Reed, doing a pointless reprise of Dr. Zhivago's trek across the frozen tundra to Lara. The film also had a tendency to transform the chaos of the Revolution and the squalor and poverty of war communism into Hollywood operatics and glamor. In *Reds* historical credibility is sacrificed so that the Revolution can become a carefully choreographed magical tableau.[13]

Unfortunately, in this quest for commercially viable elements Beatty often skirted perilously close to romantic comedy, complete with cute puppy dogs, and running gags like Reed bumping into a chandelier. The most problematic element, however, was the film's depiction of two main characters and their relationship. Keaton is able to bring some complexity into the role of Bryant when she communicates both her insecurity and her resentment at being treated as a mere adjunct to Reed during their early Village days—especially when Emma Goldman curtly dismisses her as she painfully struggles to find the right words. Still there is nothing in her performance of the passion and sensuality of the woman whose touch, according to Eugene O'Neill, could set you afire. Indeed the only time she conveys a bit of that intensity is in her scenes with O'Neill, played with great brio and force by Jack Nicholson. In addition, the scene where Bryant begins to offer trenchant political criticism of the relationship between the American Communist Party and the working class feels utterly incongruous, as if a ventriloquist's dummy is doing the talking.[14]

Beatty in turn struggles to capture a life of the scale that Reed lived—his romantic individualism, his contentiousness, and the passion and intensity of his political commitment. Though he makes him an attractive figure, nowhere does one get the sense of a man whom Walter Lipmann described as "Many men at once . . . there is no line between the play of his fancy and the responsibility to fact: he is for the time the person he imagines himself to be."[15] Beatty with his boyish charm, winsome smiles and sheepish looks is not so much protean as eager to please. And the complicated, painful, and contradictory relationship between Reed and Bryant, which is made the focus of much of the film, is superficial and seen primarily from the outside, through meetings, partings, and passionate reconciliations, rather than through illuminating its intricate internal life and motivation.

Despite these limitations *Reds* remains both stirring and provocative. It was one of the rare times a Hollywood film had both at its center an appealing hero who was fully committed to left politics, and made the history of the American left accessible and engaging. And though the film may concentrate too much on the Bryant-Reed relationship, *Reds* successfully captures the feeling of two people living on the rim of a new world which will usher in a cultural and sexual revolution as well as a political one. Of course, it may be absurd to hear *The Internationale* played with such exaltation while Reed and Bryant make love and at the same time the Bolsheviks take over the government. But it is also striking to see an image of politics, more American sixties than Communist Party, which merges the personal and the political—as much a revolt against bourgeois culture as against capitalism itself.

Coinciding with this image of a utopian—thoroughly romantic, impulsive, and exhilarating—political commitment is the most incisive and lucid political dialogue to appear in an American film. Undoubtedly the contribution of

Beatty's screenwriting collaborator, British leftist playwright Trevor Griffiths (*Comedians*), there are moments, particularly in the film's second half, chronicling Reed's political battles within the American left and with the Comintern, that carry a dialectical electricity. For instance, in one especially insightful moment a weary and disillusioned Emma Goldman (Maureen Stapleton) and Reed debate the effects of the Russian Revolution. Goldman attacks the decline of the revolution into tyranny, stating that "The dream we had is dying, Jack. The centralized state has all the power. They're putting anarchists like me in jail, exterminating all dissenters. I want no part of it." To which, justifying himself, Reed replies, "What did you think anyway? It was all going to work right away? It's war, Emma. And we have to fight it with discipline, terror, firing squads—or give up." Then pausing, and expressing his own internal conflicts and misgivings, Reed ruefully says something with as much relevance to himself as to her, "Otherwise what has your life meant?"[16]

Unfortunately, when this sort of exchange is fused with brief portraits of Reed's political struggles with Comintern ideologues and political Czars Zinoviev (played by chic, Polish-born novelist Jerzy Kosinski) and Radek, there was not so much the image of a man analyzing and brooding over the nature of the revolutionary process, or of a man conflicted between the bohemian writer and the disciplined revolutionary in himself, but the simpler, less introspective question of whether or not Reed was ultimately disenchanted with the revolution. It was not that Beatty did not bravely begin to pose the other questions, but the film never truly pursues them. Of course, even the question of Reed's disenchantment is never really answered, and is made to seem less significant by the only genuine unconventional formal technique in the film (a chorus and self-reflexive device)—the use of real "witnesses" who were contemporaries of Reed and Bryant.

Like "petals on a wet black bough,"[17] as one critic, quoting Ezra Pound, referred to them, the poignant, intelligent, aged faces and voices of Adela Rogers St. John, Rebecca West, Dora Russell, Henry Miller, and other famous and once-famous figures comment on Reed and Bryant ("I'd forgotten all about them. Were they Socialists?") and their times ("There was as much fucking then as there is today."). And the one inescapable conclusion drawn from these meandering and fragmented comments is the elusiveness and selectivity of human memory. Whether Reed would have turned against the revolution (as many of his friends like Max Eastmen did) is probably less important than the larger truth that a person's historical place and role is difficult to discover and define. If nothing else *Reds* at least rescued the figures of Reed and Bryant from historical obscurity and assured them a place in popular mythology.

There were other films during the Reaganite 1980s that dealt with the nature of the American left. Writer-director John Sayles made his first feature film *The Return of the Secaucus Seven* (1980)—a low budget ($40,000), independent work about a group of sixties activists who get together for a reunion in the late seventies. The group were never hard line, movement ideologues, nor had they been hippies. In Sayles' words, "they were the people who went to the marches, not those who planned them"[18]—strongly committed, issue oriented activists who liked to smoke dope. By the time of the reunion most of them are no longer activists—they are teachers, doctors, folk singers, speechwriters for liberal politicians. But the political values and culture of the sixties still have a powerful effect on their lives, without their ever losing a sense of perspective and some ironic feelings about the period.

Sayles's film had little camera movement, contained a number of scenes that needed editing, and was generally very raw and awkward on a technical level. However, it was a fresh, authentic, and open-ended work, made by a man who understood the sixties from the inside—capturing its consciousness, language, and humor—and who did not dismiss or parody the significance of the experience. Sayles's wondrously attuned ear and eye for the way different people speak and behave was extended also to a "straight" liberal visitor and two working class townies. Almost all his characters carried the kind of behavioral nuance that defied stereotyping.

It was, however, Lawrence Kasden's popular hit *The Big Chill* (1983) rather than *The Return of the Secaucus Seven* that conjured up memories of the sixties for the general public. Using a somewhat similar plot device to *Secaucus*, Kasden structures the film around the reunion of a group of sixties friends for the funeral of their friend and guru, Alex—the only one who kept the 1960s faith—who has committed suicide.

Starring rising Hollywood stars like William Hurt, Kevin Kline, Glenn Close, Tom Berenger, and Jeff Goldblum, Kasden's film is slicker, better acted, and more dynamic—a great deal of neat and rhythmic crosscutting between characters, witty one-liners, and a rousing 1960s soundtrack (e.g., "I Heard it Through the Grapevine" and "You Can't Always Get What You Want")—than Sayles's work. Almost all the characters have achieved some semblance of upper middle class success—pop journalist, shoestore chain owner, real estate lawyer, and television actor. None of them works in social activist professions, and though they express some feeling about betraying their past ideals and a few pangs of conscience about their mainstream careers, there is little sign that these characters ever had any real politics to betray, except smoking dope, wearing long hair, and attending the odd antiwar rally. In fact, the malaise most of them feel has more to do with their own psychic make up than with conflicting values and ideals

In fact, the film basically affirms yuppie values and rejects holding on to the ideals of the past. It's their generous weekend host, Harold (Kevin Kline), the owner of a chain of shoestores, who is the most sympathetic and dominant character. Harold is lean, athletic, a loving father, and the only one of the group who is happily married. He is at home in the eighties—an investor and money maker, an integral part of his small town, and utterly realistic about what it takes to survive in the present. His antithesis is Nick (William Hurt), a bitter insomniac, a graduate school dropout and, for good measure, a Vietnam vet who was wounded and, as a result, became impotent during the war. Nick sells drugs out of his run-down sports car, feels totally adrift, and hates his life. He inherits Alex's cabin and girl, but clearly there is nothing in his fragmented life which offers an alternative vision to Harold's complacent sense of well-being.

The Big Chill is an intellectually thin, well-crafted film which gives little sense of what the sixties were all about. The politics and culture of the period are reduced to fashionable tag lines, and the only sixties' legacy they have kept seems to be a capacity for greater emotional and sexual spontaneity and ease. That easy, bantering style separates them from the stiff, dull, workaholic ad man who is unhappily married to one of the group. It provides them with a feeling of superiority based on their hipness, but these feelings are based more on matters of personal style and sensibility than on some ultimate difference of values.

The Reaganite eighties were really the wrong historic moment for Hollywood to revive the politics of the sixties. But The Big Chill's embrace of yuppie realism had strong links with aspects of the 1960s counterculture which emphasized "doing your own thing" and giving all one's energies to developing the self, with little consciousness that a society needed some idea of social interdependence to be at all cohesive and whole. In fact, The Big Chill was a perfect expression of the "temporary truce between bourgeois and bohemian individualism as they joined together in a celebration of private life"[19] during the 1980s.

If it was difficult to make films which projected the political critique and culture of the 1960s in the period, still films critical of American politics were produced. Missing (1982), a box office hit, was the first American film made by French director Costa-Gavras (e.g.,The Confession [1970], State of Siege [1972]). The political thriller plot centers around the disappearance of a young American writer Charlie Horman (John Shea), and the arrival of his naive, apolitical, conservative businessman father, Ed (Jack Lemmon). The purpose of the narrative is to indict the United States for the CIA's collusion in the right wing military coup of 1973 which overthrew the elected Marxist government of Salvador Allende in Chile. And that end is achieved here by personalizing the experience for an American audience by having them identify with the pain of an American Everyman, Ed Horman. He undergoes a political transformation, and becomes enraged with American policies after discovering that the government was involved in his son's execution.

The film's power does not lie in its political critique, which neither illuminates what the Allende regime stood for or what the particular political dynamics of the coup were. Or is Costa-Gavras particularly gifted at creating complex characters—the reasons for innocent Charles Horman and his wife Beth's presence in Chile (though Sissy Spacek gives an extremely natural performance) are never made clear. What is most striking is Costa-Gavras's gift for creating the terrifying atmosphere of a night city under martial law. It's a city where the sound of sirens and volleys of gunfire pierce the eerie silence, where pedestrians beg strangers for sanctuary, and a stadium's bleachers are filled with people rounded up because of suspected leftist connections.

Costa-Gavras embeds his unambiguous political critique within the conventions of the thriller, but a film like Mike Nichols' *Silkwood* (1983), eschews melodrama for a muted, ambiguous account of the dangers of nuclear power. Based on a true story about a woman who had become a political heroine, Karen Silkwood, the film uses very different aesthetic strategies from both *Missing* and the earlier nail-biting, Oscar-winning entertainment about a demonic nuclear power industry, *The China Syndrome* (1979).

Silkwood avoids turning the problem of nuclear power into a schematic conflict between people of good will and a profit-hungry industry. Its heroine, Karen Silkwood (Meryl Streep in a natural, unselfconscious performance), is a tranquilizer-swallowing, chain smoking, sexually promiscuous blue collar worker, whose three children are being raised by her husband. This tense, crass, unsophisticated protagonist can alternately be both abrasive and deeply feeling. And the film spends more time, using long takes and medium two-shots, to capture atmospheric detail—the clutter of her collapsing house—and realistically limn her difficult relationships (there are tedious moments as well as evocative ones) with her lover Drew (Kurt Russell) and her lesbian roommate, Dolly (Cher), than in conveying the machinations of the nuclear power industry.

Silkwood's focus is on the feelings of ordinary people rather than on issues, and most of the workers are either too unaware or too frightened about the possible loss of their well-paying jobs to speak out about the plant's disregard for their safety. The workers are no heroic mass out of Eisenstein, the local union is ineffective, and the workers don't suddenly turn into angry, articulate critics of nuclear power. It's Karen who courageously and heedlessly takes the main role in agitating against the company and trying to bring to *The New York Times* evidence of falsified safety records—activity which is not simply aimed at changing company policy, but also motivated by an unstated desire to realize a greater sense of self. The corporation itself isn't conceived as a group of avaricious, stock villains, but as an impersonal, opaque and ultimately more insidious organization. *Silkwood* is a restrained work, which leaves the cause of Karen's death in an auto wreck an open-ended question—it's either an accident or a cold-blooded murder by the company. And the fact that the company is ultimately shut down is only seen in a postscript without any inflated theatrics about the triumph of individual courage and virtue over the evil corporation.

Besides nuclear power other 1980s political and economic problems were touched on by Hollywood. During the early 1980s there was a run of farm bankruptcies, resulting in some suicides and even in the murder of a few mortgage-holding bankers by angry, frustrated farmers. A cycle of films like Robert Benton's *Places in the Heart*, Mark Rydell's *The River*, and Richard Pearce's *Country* (all in 1984) reacted to these events by focusing on small farmers—all of them strong women—struggling against the elements and the banks.

Places in the Heart was the most popular of the three films and won Academy Awards for its star Sally Field and scriptwriter Robert Benton. Set in rural Texas during the depression—the world of Benton's youth—the film has a wonderful feel for the Texas landscape, climate, and the church services and dances which are at the heart of small town life. The film's narrative, however, is a thoroughly soft and sentimental fable, Sally Field playing a gutsy widow with two children who must make a profit on her cotton crop to save her farm. She is magically aided by two outsiders—a bitter, blind veteran, Will (John Malkovich), and a kind, black drifter, Mose (Danny Glover). It's soft-spoken, heroic Mose whose knowledge of the land helps save the farm, though the local KKK drives him off the land right before the film's conclusion. Benton's childhood memories are essentially sweet ones, and though racism pervades town life, and the local banker is unctuous and manipulative—the communal ethic remains strong, and even a defensive Will becomes less bristly and more emotionally open. The film concludes on a moving, phantasmagoric grace note with a church service where all the film's characters—living and dead, black and white—gather to affirm Christian and communal love.

Places in the Heart was basically an affirmation of the human spirit's capacity to triumph over adversity, but the other two farm films did make a stab at a political statement. The more interesting of the two was *Country*—a muted, unsentimental film about a farm family whose husband (Sam Shepard) collapses when their government loan is called in. The determined wife (Jessica Lange) maintains the family and organizes a group of small farmers to resist the government, resulting in her winning a temporary stay of foreclosure. The film's strength is its fidelity to the reality of farm life, and it uses few close-ups or dramatic scenes to distort the daily texture of that experience. However, though it attacked Reagan farm policy, the film blurred the nature of the political enemy by portraying it nebulously as "monolithic bureaucracy" and apathetic government.[20]

Besides making films like *Silkwood* and *Country*, whose liberal values were at odds with Reagan policies, Hollywood also began to make films which projected right wing political views. It was a trend which only gained momentum after Reagan's landslide victory over Mondale in 1984. The first of these films was John Milius' *Red Dawn* (1984), a paranoid action movie about the invasion of the United States by a combined Russo-Cuban force, and the defense of the country left in the hands of a group of young patriots. It revived the spectre

of the Soviet threat, and demonstrated that anticommunism fused with exciting, reconstructed tank battles could sell.

Following *Red Dawn*'s lead, Hollywood indulged in some Vietnam War revisionism with a series of films that exploited the remaining cause celebre, the
2,500 purported MIAs left behind in Vietnam. In the process Hollywood did
nothing less than rewrite history and gave America a second opportunity to
win the war, at least on the screen.

Of the reported 2,500 MIAs many were presumed dead, but others were
considered to be alive and held captive by the North Vietnamese. Anguished
relatives and supporters initiated a campaign to obtain their release. And one
former Green Beret colonel, James B. Gritz, was not satisfied with lobbying
and led an abortive raid into Laos whose most notable accomplishment was
that Hollywood could turn it into a film, *Uncommon Valor* (1983).

In its us-against-them portrait of a powerfully linked group of Vietnam vets
against a craven government, *Uncommon Valor* reflected a pessimistic right
wing populism sharply critical of an uncaring society and government. In addition, the film provided a retrospective affirmation of Vietnam as a noble cause,
whose only seeming limitation was that we didn't win the war. The narrative
structure of *Uncommon Valor* also provided a model for other revisionist Vietnam works.

Uncommon Valor leaned heavily on one of America's most-enduring archetypical forms, the captivity myth, which originally evolved from the Puritan
fear that the American wilderness would corrupt them spiritually. The myth
was built around a tale of pure white men and women taken prisoner by barbaric Indians who tempted them into sins of the flesh and spirit. The Indians
don't succeed in subverting their piety, and, in fact, the prisoners rediscover
God's will.

As these tales were modified in the nineteenth century, there emerged a
fearless, stoic hunter-hero—Davy Crockett, Hawkeye—whose intimacy with
Indian and wilderness lore gave him the skill to wrest the land away from the
Indians, and projected into the future the vision of a white man's agrarian Ar-
cadia as the nation's destiny. That destiny helped justify our expropriation of
the wilderness through methods that historian Richard Slotkin called a "re-
generation through violence."

In films like *Uncommon Valor* the Indians became the Vietnamese and the
MIAs the prisoners of the captivity myth, but the central figure in the film,
Marine Colonel Jason Rhodes (Gene Hackman), was too much the dignified,
stoic professional soldier to become a hunter-hero. Hollywood, however, had
other aspirants for the role, the first being half-Indian, karate champ Chuck
Norris, who had already established a screen persona of a mild-mannered, taci-
turn loner who puts to rout hosts of sleazy villains (e.g., *Force of One* [1978]).

In films, constructed in the captivity narrative tradition like *Missing in Action* (1984) and *Missing in Action 2: The Beginning* (1985), Norris (Colonel Braddock) plays an inexpressive, solitary hunter-hero who liberates MIAs at the expense of literally hundreds of Vietnamese soldiers. This hunter-hero is indomitable in the superman mode of a Michael Vronsky, and is able to use the enemy's own guerrilla combat tactics like wearing a camouflage suit to triumph over them. And the films were extremely successful with the public, because they guaranteed a great deal of bloody action, little extraneous dialogue, and, for the politically unconscious, even the illusion of final victory in Vietnam.

The *Missing in Action* films served as a warm-up for the apotheosis of this developing cycle, *Rambo: First Blood Part II* (1985)—a sequel to *First Blood* (1982), an extremely popular film about the bloody visit of John Rambo, (Sylvester Stallone) an alienated Vietnam vet and Congressional Medal of Honor recipient—to a small town in the Pacific Northwest. *Rambo II* was not only a box office success—$57 million in the first two weeks—but became a political byword after President Reagan referred to it in a number of his speeches. For Reagan, Rambo was a symbol of American machismo and patriotism, and the film's crude Russophobia and narcissistic camera worship of its star Sylvester Stallone's glistening, Nautilus-crafted body provided perfect fodder for Reagan's Hollywood brand of populism.

The film opens with Rambo being freed from a prison stockade, where he was incarcerated after his *First Blood* rampage, so he can be sent on a secret mission into Vietnam to prove the existence of MIAs by photographing them. From that moment on, the film becomes a rant against the U.S. government, embodied by an opportunistic bureaucrat, Murdock (Charles Napier), who both inspires the MIA mission and wants it to fail so he can bury the embarrassing political issue for good. Murdock is seen by the film as Rambo's prime enemy and a cartoon symbol of a soulless and impotent American government that ostensibly betrayed its own troops because it lacked the will to win. And Rambo's uncontrolled Luddite-style outburst at the film's conclusion—using a machine gun to destroy Murdock's computers—supposedly spoke for all the ordinary GIs that suffered the callous manipulations and rationalizations of these government experts in Vietnam.

Coupled with this populist, superpatriotic backlash was a revival of the Soviet menace. The real enemy in the film are the Russians, not the North Vietnamese—the Soviets acting like an update of the Nazi SS, even to the point of being racists who view the Vietnamese as "yellow scum." And Rambo here is both a working-class echo of Colonel Kurtz, mumbling such aphorisms like, "to survive a war you must become a war," and a hunter-hero, who moves through the jungle, stripped to the waist, looking like an Indian brave or a scowling noble savage.

There is an undercurrent in the film suggesting that the Rambos of the world will never receive justice from the American government, and that the only possible alternative is destructive rage. The film's dominant strain, however, is one of an America truly regenerated through violence—a resurrected nation bursting with pride, power, and unabashed aggression that can humble any enemy.

Nevertheless, by providing a touch of primitivism to the archetypes of the superman and hunter-hero, Stallone linked the character so close to his inarticulate persona that there was little possibility left for other films to work out new variations on the character. As a result, though Stallone succeeded in adding another mythic hero, along with Rocky, to his personal pantheon of America Redux, he helped bring the MIA cycle to a standstill. Of course, desiring better economic and diplomatic relations, the North Vietnamese themselves began to permit U.S. inspection teams to search for the remains of the missing—the kind of pragmatic behavior which made it difficult even for Hollywood to go on constructing aggressively patriotic fantasies.[21]

Still there were other films which fueled America's military build-up and Reagan's patriotic rhetoric. In 1986 Tony Scott's revved-up *Top Gun*—a film exulting in the military and in macho heroics—became one of the top box office hits. Its arrogant, adolescent hero, Maverick (a grinning Tom Cruise), is obsessed with becoming "top gun," the best of the best pilots, at the U.S. Navy Fighters Weapons School. The film's strength is its virtuosic and lengthy flying scenes and simulated dog fights shot from a variety of camera angles, but the rest is laughable dialogue, a contrived plot, and an unbelievable passionate romance between the narcissistic Maverick and his aeronautics instructor (Kelly McGillis). Still the film would only be as disturbing as a glossy and banal navy recruiting ad, if, at the film's climax, Maverick did not become a hero by engaging an unnamed enemy in a real war situation over the Indian Ocean. That narrative twist turns *Top Gun* into a film which is dangerously unable to distinguish war games from real war—reducing life and death situations into a plaything for male egos.

Films like *Top Gun* and Clint Eastwood's *Heartbreak Ridge* (1986), where a career gunnery sergeant (played by Eastwood) follows the tradition of old World War II movies turning raw rookies into men—readying them for a triumphant invasion of Grenada—may still have been produced in 1986. But that year also would see the first Hollywood film to really confront the concrete realities of the Vietnam war, Oliver Stone's Oscar winning *Platoon*. Stone was a Vietnam War veteran, whose film of remembrance and mourning had a cathartic effect for many Vietnam vets and nonvets alike. *Platoon* is most powerful and successful when it uses minimal dialogue and telling close-ups and medium shots to convey with great immediacy the war's everydayness: the stifling discomfort of the ants, heat, and mud of jungle and brush; the fatigue of patrols; the murderous cacaphony and chaos of night firefights; and the boredom and sense of release of base camp. Stone also understood just how fear, fatigue and rage could undermine some GIs' sense of moral restraint and balance, and turn them into savages who massacre civilians and torch villages.

Stone's Vietnam is a bleak, horrific world where the GIs face an almost-invisible, ubiquitous enemy. It's all seen through the eyes and voiceover narration (a number of self-consciously literary letters back home) of Chris Taylor (Charlie Sheen) an upper-middle class, Yale dropout and patriot, who like Steven Crane's hero in *The Red Badge of Courage* is initiated into manhood and transformed by the war. Taylor discovers not only Vietnam's terrors, but a gallery of working class and underclass GIs that are given a bit more nuance than the norm for Hollywood war films. There is baby-faced, beer-can-crunching Bunny (Kevin Dillon) who loves war and killing; gum-chewing Sergeant O' Neill (John MacGinley) whose obsequious attempts to find safety only lead him to greater danger; and a group of blacks of whom the earthy, wise King (Keith David) is balanced by the the perpetually whining and malingering Junior (Reggie Johnson). The blacks are never turned into an anonymous mass, though the film's prime focus, as in most Vietnam films, is on the experience of white soldiers.

If the strength of *Platoon* is its ability to portray Vietnam as a world free of self-sacrificial heroics, where mainly angry, disengaged and divided GIs try to survive the madness in one piece and just get on the plane back home—its main weakness is its penchant for overblown literary conceits. For besides his ordinary GIs inhabiting a realist film, Stone created two mythic lifers, the headband-wearing doper saint Sergeant Elias (Willem Dafoe) and the war-loving, demonic Sergeant Barnes (Tom Berenger), whose Manichean, melodramatic struggle tends to subvert the film's verisimilitude.

Both of them are constructed in larger-than-life terms: Elias is depicted as a gentle, Christ figure, critical of the war he has become weary of, and given far too many self-consciously significant close-ups by Stone; while Barnes, his face crisscrossed with scars, is portrayed as a closet superman who asserts "I am reality" and is shot too often from a low angle to underline his forbidding character. These two portentous figures, on one level, serve as symbolic fathers warring for the soul of Taylor (a somewhat bland character who doesn't have too vivid a soul) and on another, supposedly reflect the political divisions within American society.

Platoon, however, lacked a genuine political perspective. It was neither a film that dealt with the mixture of nationalism and Marxist-Leninism that underlay the North Vietnamese military effort nor did it explore the political culture and specific policies involved in American intervention. When Stone ventures to make a political point, as he does in the film's final moments, it's as vaporous as the physical world he conjures up is grittily alive. He has Taylor indulge in a sermonizing voiceover, which projects the facile, ethnocentric notion that the "enemy was in us" (as if America had fought the war to purge its own destructive impulses) and adds the harmless, banal sentiment that we must try "to find a goodness and meaning to this life."

Although *Platoon* was clearly not the final word on the war, it was an antidote to mindless political cartoons like *Rambo* and metaphysically confused works like *Apocalypse Now*. If Stone had little gift for capturing the political and social meanings of the war, he had at least echoed the dominant public feeling about Vietnam, that it was a self-destructive march into some kind of purgatory. Stone's authentic depiction of the mad and murderous world of combat was also so powerful an achievement that one could say that he had taken the first real cinematic step in Hollywood's coming to terms with Vietnam.

Platoon marked, after years of avoidance, wavering and regression, Hollywood's total acceptance of Vietnam as a serious subject for film. In 1987 three films dealing with different aspects of the war were produced—*Hanoi Hilton*, Coppola's *Gardens of Stone*, and the only one worthy of a critical stir, Stanley Kubrick's *Full Metal Jacket*. Kubrick's work had grander aspirations than *Platoon*, dealing less with the concrete reality of Vietnam than with the military as an institution that breeds killers, and projecting a vision of an innately brutal and corrupt human condition.

That vision of all human beings as potential destroyers and lovers of death coupled with an Olympian, detached style pervades almost all of Kubrick's work, notably *Clockwork Orange* (1968), where a futuristic, delinquent gang engages in orgies of destruction. In *Full Metal Jacket* Kubrick brilliantly uses his unique style—overbearing close-ups, drained colors, harsh white and cold blue lighting, minimal dialogue, and an unnaturally severe barracks set—to choreograph the transformation of unformed recruits into trained Marine killers.

Directing this dehumanization process is an obscenity-spouting, bullying drill instructor, Sergeant Hartman (Lee Ermey), whose relentless, sardonic barrage is so oppressively effective that it strips the men of their past identities and provides them all with new ones, naming one of them Private Joker (Matthew Modine) and still another Cowboy. Hartman's harrangues often attain the imagistic richness of a poet of the profane, and they are permeated with a sense of menace. Kubrick has never been clearer about the links between sex, aggression, and death—in this case, cocks and rifles.

Unfortunately the compressed power of the forty-five-minute prologue makes the film's second half—the Vietnam section—pale in comparison. Kubrick still dreams up inspired visual images and aural effects—a desolate, lunar landscaped Hue constructed out of an abandoned gasworks outside of London, and after killing a female sniper, the chilling image of the Marines marching into a blazing sunset singing "The Mickey Mouse Club Song"—sardonically fusing the carnage of war with the synthetic innocence of the popular culture that shaped the young Marines. However, much of *Full Metal Jacket*'s second half is either conventional—a sniper sequence where one Marine after another dies in blood-cascading slow motion is merely a more idiosyncratic variation on World War II films battle action—or given over to heavy-handed ironies. The central, chorus-like figure Private Joker is a wry, ironic, less defined character than Sergeant Hartman. Joker's detachment is a projection of Kubrick's, but his exercise of irony feels too often like an overly literal cataloguing of the war's absurdities—the army newpaper "Stars and Stripes" attempt to provide happy news by calling search and destroy missions "sweep and clear" expeditions—than the kind of Brechtian mordancy that could get to the heart of the war's madness.

The ultimate and most striking irony implicit in Kubrick's version of Vietnam is that the film's most vital figures are its most lethal and brutal. Though Kubrick may not endorse the world of a Sergeant Hartman, he clearly has sympathy for characters who are at home in a nihilistic world. For Kubrick it's the misanthropic who dominate and often triumph amidst the war's barbarism.

The most problematic element in *Full Metal Jacket* is Kubrick's Hobbesian view of human nature. Blaming it all on the savage nature of human beings may aptly describe some of the behavior on all sides in the war, but it is an evasion of its historical context. There was all too much anguish present in the Vietnam abattoir to totally conceive it in terms of pitiless irony and black humor. It was a war whose intense torment demanded more than Kubrick's cool genius.[22]

At the end of the decade Oliver Stone returned to the subject of Vietnam, and made a film which centered more on the cultural roots of the war effort than on the horrors of battle combat. *Born on the Fourth of July* (1989) was based on the autobiography of Ron Kovic, a paraplegic veteran who the war transformed from a macho, working-class patriot into an articulate antiwar activist.

The film's opening scenes sketch in bold, underlined strokes how Kovic's (Tom Cruise) values were formed in the Long Island suburbs by a mixture of repressive Catholicism, John Wayne films, patriotic parades, and the American obsession with competition and victory. In depicting Kovic's coming of age, Stone eschews subtlety for both images which are almost operatic, even vulgar, in their intensity and a swelling musical score to accompany them. Nevertheless, despite its sledgehammer style, the film captures with great poignance and power Kovic's horrific experiences in a slum of a Bronx Veterans Hospital, his uneasy, angry return to his forbidding mother-dominated, conservative, pro-war home, and his descent into alcoholism and self-degradation which reaches its apotheosis in a wild fight with another vet Charlie (Willem Dafoe), while sitting in their wheelchairs in the middle of the Mexican desert. Stone is also much more adept at orchestrating emotional fireworks than in delineating the psychic and intellectual changes that Kovic goes through before he appears as a full-blown radical spokesman at the 1976 Democratic convention. The transformation is too abrupt, but *Born on the Fourth of July* marks the public's acceptance of the fact that it was more than just a mindless, suicidal war. That, at least in Vietnam, America's intervention was a consequence of our need to assert our national will, and demonstrate to the world our imperial power.[23]

Vietnam was clearly not the prime subject of 1980s film. Hollywood also spawned a flood of teen comedies like Amy Heckerling's successful and sometimes funny and fresh *Fast Times at Ridgemont High* (1982) about a group of high school students who spend their time surfing, hanging around the local mall, and obsessing about sex, which is never treated as a real problem. Another was Paul Brickman's *Risky Business* (1983) starring Tom Cruise (Joel Goodson) as a straight, careful suburban high school senior who lives in a comfortable, white Chicago suburb with the usual foolish and unseeing parents who populate teen films. Most of his time seems spent indulging in elaborate masturbatory fantasies and worrying about what college he'll attend. Joel's parents leave on vacation, and he decides to take a risk for the first time in his life—to say, "what the fuck." He gets involved with a pretty, shrewd hooker who provides sex and solace, and then to make money hosts a party which provides hookers for all his friends and even for a Princeton recruiter who is there to interview him. Insecure, guilt-ridden Joel has overnight become a daredevil-driving, smooth-talking middle-class pimp with shades, and the film cynically affirms this sleazy persona and his new-found talent for making the quick buck.

Risky Business is a perfect film for budding Reaganites. There is no danger here of Joel's risk-taking to lead him to question or break from his upper-middle-class world; it actually helps him get into Princeton—where he'll major in business—and gives him a good start at learning what it takes to become a "future enterpriser." The hooker-girlfriend is a sharp, tough businesswoman who will clearly be of help to Joel in acquiring a Porsche of his own, and, after graduation, organizing hostile take-overs on Wall Street. *Risky Business* evokes a morally bankrupt world,[24] where any action is justified if it will help you get ahead. It romanticizes both prostitution and cynical opportunism and endorses the success ethos—without a hint of irony.

The master of the teen picture, John Hughes, produced and directed a whole slew of films during the eighties (e.g., *Sixteen Candles* [1984], *The Breakfast Club* [1985], *Weird Science* [1985] and *Ferris Bueller's Day Off* [1986]), which conveyed some feeling for the social tensions and frustrations created by high school clique and life style divisions—nerds, jocks, preppies, druggies, valley girls. Sometimes even class barriers are alluded to—someone coming from "the wrong side of the tracks"—but in 1980s America, despite the contin-

uing reality of class, that idea had little emotional or social resonance for adolescent moviegoers.

Hughes' films were cute, decent, and relatively innocent—none of them as
hedonistic or cynical as *Risky Business*. The only culture that exists in his films
is a white, suburban adolescent one—the films treat with contempt an absurd
adult and parental world—and Hughes seems to be able to enter totally and
unselfconsciously into a world of teenage mating rites, dress codes, and argot
(e.g., "asswipe," "geek"). Rebellion in a Hughes film is rarely anything more
than a brash and spoiled kid hero like Ferris Bueller (Matthew Broderick) ingeniously and successfully flaunting school and other institutional rules, but
without ever deviating from a world that keeps him living a comfortable, pos-
session-filled existence. All Hughes' films end neatly and happily, and in
Elaine Rapping's words Hughes' "kids are sui generis members of a self-suffi-
cient, mysterious universe which operates not by the laws of capital but by
magic, good Magic."[25]

One of the most popular teen films of the mid-eighties was Robert
Zemeckis's *Back to the Future* (1985) (there have been two sequels so far),
which combined teen comedy with science fiction. Starring television sitcom
star Michael J. Fox (Marty McFly), the film combines time travel, a wild-eyed
scientist (Christopher Lloyd) and his Rube Goldberg inventions, and nostalgia for the relatively innocent small town of the fifties. Diminutive and clever
Marty travels back thirty years to the time when his parents met in high school,
and inadvertently alters his own and his parents' future. The film is inventive
and has some charm—playing with the emotional-Oedipal problems involved
in time travel—Marty's mother is at first attracted to him rather than to his
spastic, timid father. But Marty succeeds in averting the danger of this incestu-
ous connection, and pairs them off. In doing so he leaves a legacy for the future
which transforms his seedy home and comic-pathetic 1980s parents—an over-
weight mother who is puritanical and drinks, a father with a lunatic laugh, who
allows himself to be mercilessly bullied—into a smooth, tennis-playing pair.
The parents are now confident and successful and have moved up a couple of
steps in class—the appropriate social background for a conventional teenage
hero like clean-cut Marty. And though the film clearly endorses this Reaganite
success story—Marty's time-travelling intervention aside—his father's ability
to painfully assert his own will is the main reason he is able to create a new persona for himself; the parents are much more interesting as ineffectual, sham-
bling failures than as stereotypical success stories.

During the Reagan years many black economic and social gains of the 1960s
and 1970s, ranging from the rate of college attendance to the proportion of
two-parent families to relative income levels, began to decline while poverty
and crime rates escalated. Hollywood, of course, was not interested in depicting these harsh, ominous realities, but in finding black performers—who assert

their black identity—like Richard Pryor (*Stir Crazy* [1980]) and Eddie Murphy, who still would have crossover appeal.

In the 1980s it was Murphy who was the big box office draw in films like Martin Brest's *Beverly Hills Cop* (1984). The film actually opens with a graphic montage of Detroit which evokes a predominantly black ghetto world of windowless bars, abandoned buidings, polluting smoke stacks, and empty lots. The film, however, is not about the social reality of Detroit, but about a rule-breaking, undercover cop, Axel Foley (Murphy), who sets out from its impoverished, violent urbanscape to find the murderers of a boyhood friend amidst the glitter and wealth of Beverly Hills.

The nonsensical plot, filled with soporific car crashes and shoot-outs, is merely a vehicle to provide the fast-talking, profane, homophobic Murphy a chance to do a number of routines and try out a number of voices. In his sweat shirt and sneakers he plays the irrepressible bad boy who tweaks authority and convention, but is, at the same time, utterly apolitical and safe. Murphy's Foley may coolly manipulate and dominate his fellow white cops, but the edge of his behavior is muted by the film projecting a vision of interracial camaraderie and ease between them. And when it comes to white women, Foley is utterly chaste. Murphy is an aggressive, hip and funny comic, and *Beverly Hills Cop* is the perfect medium for him to reach a white audience—making them feel good so that they can both root for a quick-witted black at the expense of dim whites (it also helps him hold a black audience) while preserving the racial status quo.

One of the rare films made during the early 1980s dealing with race was Norman Jewison's adaptation of Charles Fuller's prize-winning play *A Soldier's Story* (1984). The film stars a predominantly black cast, and perceptively explores the question of racial identity—what it means to be a black in a world dominated by whites—but it is set back in time in the deep South of 1944. Another, more popular and commercial work, directed again by a white, was Steven Spielberg's adaptation of Alice Walker's Pulitzer Prize-winning novel, *The Color Purple* (1985)—a film about growing up a female victim in the Deep South.

Like the novel, the film is more about the oppression of black women by black men than about white racism. Celie (Whoopie Goldberg) is passive, subservient, and not very pretty. She is sexually and emotionally abused by almost all the men in her life—brutal, callous males who express their own rage against being demeaned by viciously scapegoating women. But Celie ultimately gains self-respect, becomes independent, and achieves happiness by forming a communal house dominated by women. And the women are the powerful, luminous figures here—loving, supportive, nurturing and indomitable—while almost all the men are depicted as cruelly unseeing and uncaring.

The repressive, degrading nature of Southern white racism is evoked, but the whites are peripheral to this feminist fable of female triumph. Spielberg's style tends to prettify, turning rural black poverty into a picturesque landscape filled with purple flowers, clear blue skies, green fields, and buzzing insects. There is also too much flashy editing, too many dramatic close-ups, and a couple of inflated musical sequences that look like they come from the MGM vault. Spielberg also played it safe politically, merely skimming over Celie's passionate lesbian love for a sensual, free-living, blues singer Shug (Margaret Avery). *The Color Purple* may be a sentimental, overdirected film, but the portrayal of Celie's assertion of self and liberation from male domination leaves one emotionally stirred.

A more typical Hollywood treatment of racial issues was Alan Parker's *Mississippi Burning* (1988), dealing with the 1964 disappearance of three civil rights activists during Mississippi's "Freedom Summer." Parker, a sincere, socially conscious director, decided that the only way he could make a viable commercial film about the black civil rights struggle was to invert reality and feature whites and the FBI as heroes (the FBI's role in the South was essentially antagonistic to the movement, often spying on rather than protecting activists) and turn blacks into mute victims—obliterating the basic fact that the movement was built on black collective action and courage.

Parker's film was "simply the latest in a long line of historical films which subordinate complex political and social processes to individual heroics and spectacular set pieces."[26] In this case, the civil rights movement is denuded of all political and social nuance, and replaced by excitingly edited action sequences and close-up confrontations between good FBI men—Anderson (Gene Hackman), a tough, local boy who is willing to bend the rules and Ward (Willem DaFoe), a by-the-book Yankee—and the ignorant rednecks who are Klan members and unadulterated scum. That makes for a film which is strong on small town atmosphere and the recycling of buddy film conventions, and devoid of any feeling for historical fact or reality.

It was only in the last half of the decade that the films of a group of young black directors—Robert Townsend, Keenan Ivory Wayans, the Hudlin brothers, and the most original, Spike Lee, began to appear. Their works were rooted in black concerns and language, and possibly signaled "the emergence of a new esthetic sensibility within Black America."[27] And despite the fact that they were centered in the specificity of black reality, they were able to appeal to white, mainstream audiences.

Spike Lee's films, the low budget *She's Gotta Have It* (1986), *School Daze* (1988) and *Do the Right Thing* (1989), were personal works about complex aspects of black life that the larger public almost never saw before on the screen. The most politically controversial and formally imaginative of his films up to now is *Do the Right Thing*, which received both a great deal of critical praise and was virulently attacked by some black and white critics. There were white critics who saw the film as stirring up race riots and as a black racist work, while a number of black critics saw it as being insufficiently militant or given to stereotyping black life. Lee's film elicited the kind of charged, extremely varied responses that clearly went beyond its mise-en-scène and touched a raw nerve in black-white relations.

Do the Right Thing was flawed: a bit too many film school tics (e.g., gratuitous oblique angles and tight close-ups); a tendency to sanitize some of the more destructive aspects of black inner city life by eliminating both drugs and crime from the street; and a sexist depiction of its central female character, Tina (Rosie Perez)—Mookie's (Spike Lee as an underachieving, intelligent, pizza deliveryman) undulating, nagging, foul-mouthed wife. Flaws aside, the more one views the film, the more its political complexity becomes apparent. One sees that Lee's film projects a genuine sense of political ambiguity, avoiding being either politically facile or polemical; he is a director genuinely groping for social answers—looking at Malcolm X and Martin Luther King as offering two alternative political visions and strategies. And the choice made by Lee's conflicted protagonist, Mookie, to hurl a garbage can through Sal's Pizzeria's window is not seen as a heroic act, but one that leaves him perplexed and saddened. The film's conclusion carries no answer to what it means to "do the right thing"—just more questions.

Do the Right Thing ultimately was a rarity among American films; it was a serious, dynamic work about something substantial—successfully fusing realism and stylization to evoke a kaleidoscope of black community life and problems on one Brooklyn street during a summer heat wave. And Lee truly loves and knows how to grant cinematic life to the physical texture and language of the street. Using an episodic narrative and a great deal of rapid cutting, point-of-view shots, talking heads, characters who skirt the edge of being cartoons and other distancing devices like the disc jockey Love Daddy who provides commentary and narration during the film, Lee touches on a number of prime social issues that face the black community. They range from police brutality and white racism to gentrification, black hostility toward white and Asian storeowners, and the way black pride should be manifested. Lee's Brooklyn street, enveloped in artificial light, has clearly been sweetened and romanticized, but he doesn't totally avert the camera eye from some of the painful realities of black inner-city life. For example, Mookie continually evades his responsibility as a father, and many of the black characters lack a work ethic, spending a great deal of time merely jiving, hanging around, and indulging in the kind of race rhetoric and idle fantasy which become substitutes for any sort of coherent, decisive action—be it political or personal.

Given Lee's profound identification with the black community and culture, it was a sign of his skill that the character granted the most dimension in *Do the*

Right Thing is Sal (Danny Aiello), the Italo-American owner of the neighborhood pizzeria. Sal is depicted as an earthy, decent man whose life is his store. He has an amicable relationship with his black customers, who he treats, despite an undercurrent of paternalism, as individuals. But Sal is also a product of a sub-culture where the use of racist epithets like "nigger" are not unusual. Enraged, Sal spews out racist invective, but Lee never dismisses or calcifies him as just a bigot. He treats him sympathetically (even a bit sentimentally)—an honest, feeling man in a frightening situation, whose dimensions he doesn't quite fully understand, responding the only way he knows how.

Lee's film may have heralded a breakthrough for black directors into the mainstream, but 1989 also saw a racially sensitive film like *Glory* evolve from more traditional and white Hollywood sources. Directed by Ed Zwick (creator of television's *thirtysomething*), the film dealt with the Civil War's 54th Massachusetts Infantry, an Afro-American volunteer unit led by a white abolitionist Robert Gould Shaw (Matthew Broderick) who shed their lives in the cause of freedom. *Glory* would have likely been more profitable, if it had centered the action on the idealistic white officer. This time around, however, Hollywood gave more than equal time to the courageous members of the black regiment (e.g., Rawlins [Morgan Freeman], Trip [Denzel Washington]), who, if not richly nuanced characters, are never reduced to stereotypes—racial or military genre film ones.

There was one other extremely popular mainstream 1989 film to touch on racial issues. Bruce Beresford's luminously acted, Oscar-winning *Driving Miss Daisy* (Jessica Tandy won an Oscar for best actress) deals with the warm relationship of a crotchety, elderly Jewish lady and her gracious, wise, black chauffeur Hoke (Morgan Freeman again) who serves her. Set in the South of a couple of decades back, the film is a too neatly calibrated work which intelligently choreographs the nuances of their relationship without disturbing an audience either politically or psychologically. The relationship is an inequitable, mistress-servant one, but Daisy's power is muted by age and her dependency on Hoke. The friendship permits a white audience to feel emotionally and socially at ease because Hoke is a courtly and restrained man that they like, and who almost never directly challenges the social status quo. The audience's sympathetic identification with this nostalgic, safe relationship makes them feel virtuous and liberal, without their ever having to confront the pain and tortuous complexity of present-day black-white relations.

Though the late 1980s saw the production of relatively sophisticated films about black life and black-white relationships, this heightened cinematic consciousness did not find a parallel in the society-at-large. General Colin Powell may have become the first black to head the Joint Chiefs of Staff under President Bush, Bill Cosby's sitcom one of the top rated television shows of the period, and Spike Lee a popular director and pitchman for athletic shoes, but, in the main, white acceptance extended to talented, elite blacks, not to the vast majority of the black population. In fact, during the 1980s the Reagan presidency signaled, by word and deed, that racism was acceptable; "decent," upper-class George Bush used coded racist appeals as part of his presidential campaign; there was a marked increase in general racial tension, and even a proliferation of racial incidents on college campuses. What films like *Glory* possibly signified for a white audience was an affirmation of those democratic ideals which represented their best selves on questions of race. It was much less painful for the public to connect with this moral vision on film than to try to actualize these ideals by wrestling with all the complex social variables surrounding everyday racial issues.

The 1980s not only saw several black directors finally get the chance to make films, but there was a minor renaissance of women directors as well. From its inception, male-owned and -controlled Hollywood had closed off the opportunity for women to play a significant role behind the camera. There were only a handful that were allowed to direct films—Alice Guy-Blache, Dorothy Arzner, Ida Lupino, and Elaine May—none of their work explicitly feminist. The feminist movement, however, changed the situation for younger women directors, and in the mid- and late 1970s overtly feminist films like Joan Micklin Silver's *Hester Street* (1975) and Claudia Weill's *Girlfriends* (1978) were made.[28]

After these films appeared, women directors could move away from expressly feminist content while rooting their work in the assumption that female characters no longer perceive themselves solely in terms of their relationships with men; and as a corollary that they would live more independent lives based on their own individual choices. Some of the most interesting 1980s films made by women directors were commercial, mainstream works like Barbra Streisand's *Yentl* (1983) and Susan Seidelman's offbeat second feature, *Desperately Seeking Susan* (1985), about two very different women switching identities (Madonna and Rosanna Arquette), while others were low budget films like Joyce Chopra's *Smooth Talk* (1986), an adaptation of Joyce Carol Oates' story about an adolescent girl's frightening sexual initiation and Donna Deitch's film about a passionate lesbian love affair set in the middle America of 1959 Reno, Nevada, *Desert Hearts* (1986).

Yentl, the most mainstream, was the result of Streisand's fifteen-year dream to adapt an I. B. Singer story for the screen. Streisand, in the megalomaniacal mode of an Orson Welles, produced, directed, starred (she sings every song), and even co-wrote this big-budget, overly orchestrated and sometimes bathetic work about a rebellious, intellectually avid, Jewish shtetl girl, Yentl, who dresses up as a boy in order to study the Talmud. (Women were excluded from the world of learning in the orthodox Jewish religious tradition of the shtetl.) Streisand loves to underline, using split mirrors to connote Yentl's split self and a bird as a symbol of her flight, panning to a chicken as a metaphor for gossipping women, and bathing every sacred object (e.g., a talis) in a golden light.

Nevertheless, despite its heavy-handed and bloated images, Yentl is an ambitious, sometimes suggestive work which raises questions about the role of women, and about female bonding. Yentl, in her male disguise, establishes a link with a beautiful, deferential, traditional woman Hadass (Amy Irving), which is more intimate and tender than any male-female relationship in the film. The relationship is open to a variety of interpretations: as a homoerotic passion; as a non-sexual affirmation of female bonding; as an appreciation of the role domestic, supportive women play which would appeal to Streisand's more conventional fans; and the underside of her appreciation of Hadass—an independent woman's revulsion with Hadass's passivity and capacity for shape-changing.[29] The film also concludes on a feminist note, Yentl sacrifices the man she loves—the kindly, manly, Talmudist Avigdor (Mandy Patinkin), who wants her to stay at home and be a traditional wife, maintaining that a wise woman knows everything without opening a book, and heads for America to try out her wings and find room to grow.

Besides Streisand there were other women who had an impact on Hollywood as producers. Jane Fonda formed a production company and made China Syndrome and Nine to Five (1981), Jessica Lange produced Country, Sally Field, Places in the Heart, and Goldie Hawn together with Anthea Sylbert produced shallow, pop feminist films like Private Benjamin (1980) and Protocol (1984). Though there is no guarantee that the fact of some women achieving power in Hollywood meant that a more profound feminist perspective would inform its product, the bottom line is still profit, and risk-taking is usually left to filmmakers outside the system.

Not only did the 1980s see a minor breakthrough for women directors and producers and for films projecting a feminist perspective, but also for films dealing with gay and lesbian sexuality as well. Until the 1960s most Hollywood films submerged, displaced, or hid any mention of homosexuality. Then, with the relaxation of the Production Code, films like The Boys in the Band (1970) and The Killing of Sister George (1968) were made which dealt with openly gay and lesbian characters, but tended to perpetuate the most blatant, negative stereotypes—hysterically effeminate men and muscular and sadistic male hustlers, and angry butch or sleek predatory lesbians. In these films gay or lesbian characters were also rarely given the chance to have a happy, full life. However, in 1980s films like Bill Sherwoood's Parting Glances (1985) and the aforementioned Desert Hearts, a gay and lesbian cinema that defined itself in its own terms and voice made its appearance (e.g., best exemplified by the openly lesbian Cay's [Patricia Charbonneau] remark in Desert Hearts, "I don't act that way to change the world, I act that way so that the world doesn't change me.")

The films were a hopeful augur of future works which would authentically portray gay and lesbian life and consciousness, and neither romanticize nor denigrate it.[30]

Despite the clear shift in Hollywood's attitude toward women, and greater openness to unstereotyped images of gay life, the last years of the decade saw films which evoked strains of an anti-feminist backlash. In very different ways films like *Baby Boom* (1987), *Fatal Attraction* (1987), *Broadcast News* (1987), and *Working Girl* (1988) affirmed marriage and often projected negative images of independent career women. *Baby Boom* reverses the pattern of feminist films, centering on an ad executive, played by Diane Keaton, who leaves her high-powered job in Manhattan for a fulfilling life as mother and apron-clad housewife in small town Vermont. Adriane Lyne's slick, overheated, manipulative *Fatal Attraction* skillfully creates frissons of suspense and fear, while constructing an implicitly regressive, anti-feminist vision. In *Fatal Attraction*, Dan (Michael Douglas), a New York attorney with a loving home and happy marriage to a beautiful, thoroughly domestic wife, has an intensely sexual, weekend affair with a seductive, single, book editor, Alex (Glenn Close). Afterward he tries to brush her off, but the career woman, who lives in an inferno-like apartment, becomes vindictive and turns out to be a wild, murderous figure. Though basically a well-made, predictable thriller, the image it conveys of the unmarried, professional woman as pathetic and mad, reaffirms the value of marriage and home as havens of warmth and stablity, and acts as a warning to women of the unnaturalness of living independent, solitary lives.

The backlash elements in writer-director James L. Brooks' (creator of the Mary Tyler Moore Show) *Broadcast News* are more subtle. This briskly paced film is filled with witty one-liners, and has an insider's knowledge of how television deals with the news and newscasters. However, *Broadcast News* is much less a critique of the content, role, and value of television news than an updated portrait of a love triangle, whose emotional life is no deeper than the wisecracks and the well-honed set pieces that permeate the film. The romance is salvaged a bit by extremely strong performances by the film's leads: Albert Brooks as Aaron—a knowlegeable, committed reporter, who was born with Woody Allen's whine, insecurity, and self-deflective humor; William Hurt as Tom—a handsome, decent, intellectually limited anchorman whose pleasing and natural television persona make him the darling of the media executives; and Holly Hunter as Jane (an Oscar-winning performance)—an extremely effective, bright, bossy news producer, who has an unhappy private life. Implicit in the film is the notion that any woman like Jane who is a driven, successful, morally serious professional, would, by necessity, live a tearful and solitary existence; that for a professional woman to have a happy personal life she would have to submerge some part of herself into a conventional female persona.

Even Mike Nichols's glossy, populist fable, *Working Girl*, projected an anti-feminist strain. Nichols's slight fairy tale about a sweet, working class, Staten Island secretary, Tess (Melanie Griffith) whose financial wizardry both wins the heart of a Wall Street broker and turns her into an executive with a secretary and office of her own, is, on one level, a scenario for Reaganism—creating a world where overnight success and the big money (especially of the Wall Street variety) are available for anyone who has confidence, drive, and can appropriate the style and accent of the upper-middle-class. On another level, the film is a put down of the type of cold, manipulative superwoman—Tess's boss Katherine (Sigourney Weaver), whose lack of softness and femininity help lead to her fall.[31] *Working Girl* is not interested in engaging in a serious critique of the corporate world or of feminist claims, but in Tess it found a heroine who combines ambition, shrewdness, and female vulnerability—a perfect alternative to all those hard, threatening women whose supposed female virtues and characteristics disappeared with success in the public world.

Films containing strains of anti-feminism were just one of a number of cinematic currents during the last years of the decade. A popular, Capraesque fable like *Field of Dreams* (1989) sees the film's hero, Ray Kinsella (Kevin Costner)—a sixties activist turned Iowa corn farmer—resurrect what the film sees as the purity of the past by following the instructions of a heavenly voice and transforming a cornfield into a baseball diamond filled with old ballplayers like Shoeless Joe Jackson. Kinsella does this not only to recover an idyllic America, but to ease the pain of a disenchanted writer so he can rediscover his muse, and to bring about his own reconciliation with the father he once rejected—baseball becoming both a social and psychological panacea.

Field of Dreams provides a great many simplistic soliloquies about both the need to dream and to recreate the innocence of childhood—a mixture of 1960s counterculture spirituality combined with the myth of the American rural past. It also attacks the utilitarian money culture and smalltown censorship (an easy target), but its alternative vision is apolitical and nebulous, consisting of little more than a set of greeting card platitudes.

The soft-minded, nostalgic *Field of Dreams* was just one of the popular successes of 1989 which included a disparate group of films. Among them were the previously discussed, *Do the Right Thing*, *Driving Miss Daisy* and *Born on the Fourth of July*, a relentlessly middlebrow and pop homage to poetry and freedom like the *Dead Poets Society*, and big budget, summer films like the imaginatively designed (influenced by Fritz Lang's expressionist *Metropolis* and Reginald Marsh's painting) and totally impersonal, comic book epic *Batman*, and Spielberg's *Indiana Jones and the Last Crusade*—the third and most human (which is not saying much) of the playful boy's adventure trilogy. Clearly no single political and social trend could be gleaned from such radically different works, but the variety itself was a sign that Hollywood had become a touch less dependent on a teenage and action-oriented audience, and could make a few films that would appeal to literate adults, albeit that most of these films took few formal or intellectual risks.

NOTES

1. Lou Cannon, *Ronald Reagan* (New York: G. P. Putnam's Sons, 1982), pp. 329–413.

2. Nicolaus Mills, "Culture in an Age of Money," *Dissent* (Winter 1990), pp. 11–17.

3. Ibid., p. 13.

4. Gregg Kilday, "The Eighties," *Film Comment* (November-December 1989), p. 65.

5. Ibid., p. 66.

6. Budd Schulberg, "What Makes Hollywood Run Now?" *New York Times Magazine* (April 27, 1980), pp. 52–88. See also Leslie Wayne, "Hollywood Sequels Are Just the Ticket," *New York Times* (July 18, 1982), pp. 1–17.

7. Veronica Geng, "Pearls Before Swine: Review of Ordinary People," *Soho Weekly News* (September 17, 1980), pp. 58–59.

8. Barbara Quart, "Tootsie," *Cineaste* XII, 4 (Summer 1983), pp. 40–42.

9. Richard Schickel, "Slam! Bang! A Movie Movie," *Time* (June 15, 1981), pp. 74–76.

10. Michiko Kakutani, "The Two Faces of Spielberg—Horrors vs. Hope," *New York Times* (May 30, 1982), pp. 1, 30. See also Pauline Kael, "The Pure and the Impure," *The New Yorker* (June 14, 1982), pp. 119–22.

11. Richard Schickel, "At Last, Kate and Hank!" *Time* (November 18, 1981), pp. 112–13.

12. Aaron Latham, "Warren Beatty, Seriously," *Rolling Stone* (April 1, 1982), p. 19.

13. Belle Gale Chevigny, Kate Ellis, Ann Kaplan, and Leonard Quart, "Talking 'Reds,'" *Socialist Review* 12, 2 (March-April 1982), pp. 109–24.

14. Ibid.

15. Robert A. Rosenstone, *Romantic Revolutionary: A Biography of John Reed* (New York: Alfred A. Knopf, 1975), p. 4.

16. Richard Grenier, "Bolshevism for the 80's," *Commentary* (March 1982), pp. 56–63.

17. Joy Gould Boyum, "'Reds': Love and Revolution," *Wall Street Journal* (December 4, 1981), p. 35.

18. Al Auster and Leonard Quart, "Counterculture Revisited: An Interview with John Sayles," *Cineaste* XI, 1 (Winter 1980–81), pp. 16–19.

19. Fred Siegel, "Blissed Out and Loving It," *Commonweal* (February 9, 1990), p. 76.

20. Terry Christensen, *Reel Politics: American Movies from Birth of a Nation to Platoon* (New York: Basil Blackwell, 1987), pp. 165–66.

21. Albert Auster and Leonard Quart, *How the War Was Remembered: Hollywood and Vietnam* (New York: Praeger, 1988), pp. 99–112.

22. Ibid., pp. 131–45.

23. Christopher Sharrett, "Born on the Fourth of July," *Cineaste* XVII, 4 (Spring 1990), pp. 48–50.

24. Elayne Rapping, "Hollywood's Youth Cult Films," *Cineaste* XVI, 1–2 (Winter, 1987–88), pp. 14–19.

25. Ibid., p. 18.

26. Editorial, *Cineaste* XVII, 2 (Fall, 1989), p. 2.

27. Eric Perkins, "Renewing the African-American Cinema: The Films of Spike Lee," *Cineaste* XVII, 4 (Spring 1990), p. 8.

28. Barbara Koenig Quart, *Woman Directors: The Emergence of a New Cinema* (New York: Praeger, 1988), pp. 37–38.

29. Ibid., pp. 83–85.

30. Andrea Weiss, "From the Margins: New Image of Gays in the Cinema," *Cineaste* XV, 1 (Fall 1986), pp. 4–8.

31. Caryn James, "Are Feminist Heroines an Endangered Species?" *New York Times: Sunday Arts and Leisure* (July 16, 1989), p. 15.

7

THE NINETIES

In his magisterial historical study of the twentieth century, *The Age of Extremes*, the British historian E. J. Hobsbawm refers to the period between 1914 and 1991 as the short twentieth century—the decades from the beginning of World War I to the fall of the Soviet Union. From this chronology one can assume that Hobsbawm considered two key landmarks of that period the rise of communism in Russia, and its ultimate disintegration.[1] Consequently, our chronology of the nineties in American film begins on November 9, 1989, the day the Berlin Wall fell. On that date irrevocable changes occurred for Americans and for people throughout the world, and the old Cold War certainties passed into history and a new post–Cold War era began.

Hardly anyone could foresee the end of communism in Russia and in Eastern Europe. Throughout the whole Cold War era there had been rumblings of discontent in Eastern Europe from the Berlin Riots of 1954, to the Hungarian uprising in 1956, to the Prague Spring and its suppression in 1968, and the rise of Solidarity in Poland in the eighties. Nonetheless, Soviet tanks had little trouble in repressing these acts of rebellion.

With hindsight, there was even evidence of increasing discontent in the Soviet Union. Nikita Khrushchev's 1954 denunciation of Stalin's crimes may be said to have been the first step in what would ultimately lead to the demise of communism. But along the way there had been an increasing vociferous if not very powerful band of Jewish refuseniks and dissidents, led until his death by the physicist Andrei Sakharov. There was also a small but very brave underground movement of literary, political and philosophical samzidat, which if they hadn't shaken Soviet power, at least gave evidence a real opposition existed.

However, when the Soviet Union collapsed there were those who quickly took credit for its demise. In America one theory held that it was President Ronald Reagan's defense strategy, which practically tripled defense spending and encouraged surrogate wars against the Soviets in places like Afghanistan, that forced the Soviet Union into economic and then political bankruptcy. While this hypothesis could serve as a potent campaign slogan, it was far from the truth.[2]

A far more important reason for the break-up of the Soviet Union was the unwillingness of the moribund Communist Party to carry out economic and political reform. Reform was necessitated by decreasing economic productivity during the so-called years of stagnation under Leonid Brezhnev's gerontocracy, and the need to combat the overweening power and privilege of a corrupt bureaucracy—the "nomenklatura."

Reform was initiated under the leadership of Mikhail Gorbachev. After he came to power in 1985, Gorbachev began a campaign of glasnost and perestroika. The former was an opening to the intellectual and cultural expression that had been suppressed throughout the entire history of the Soviet Union, and the latter was an attempt to restructure both the economy and the political culture.

Unfortunately for Gorbachev, his reforms opened a Pandora's box of previously repressed demands among the East European countries and Soviet Union nationalities. This resulted in pressure from nationalities like the Latvians and Georgians for independence, and East European satellites demanding freedom from Soviet domination. The response by communist hard-liners to these demands and to Gorbachev's policies was the ineffectual 1991 coup attempt, easily resisted by liberals led by Russian President Boris Yeltsin and ultimately resulting in the end of Soviet power.[3]

The demise of the Soviet Union left the United States the sole remaining superpower, a position that carried its own risks and problems. Nationalism, which had ironically been so long repressed in Eastern Europe by communism, reared its tribal and savage head. In the nineties, the United States watched, at times impotently, as the former Yugoslavia descended into a series of chaotic and bloody wars of secession in Croatia, Bosnia, and Kosovo. The latter forcing the United States and its NATO allies into a seventy-eight-day air war to coerce the increasingly genocidal Serbs to retreat back to their homeland.

Europe wasn't the sole venue for the rising tide of nationalism. In the Middle East, Iraq, under the ruthless, quixotic, and cunning leadership of President Saddam Hussein, invaded the oil-rich kingdom of Kuwait, only to be turned back by a forty-two day air and ground campaign led by an outraged United States and a large contingent of its European and Middle Eastern allies.

Far more threatening in the Middle East than the increasingly isolated Saddam Hussein was the dramatic rise of Islamic fundamentalism and its weapon of choice, terrorism. The United States had already been badly hurt by that weapon in 1983 when 241 U.S. Marines were killed when Islamic terrorists drove their explosive laden truck into the Marines' billet in Lebanon. But at home Americans had the illusion they were immune to attacks. That is, until the February 1993 bombing of New York City's World Trade Center, in which six people were killed as a result of bombs set by a group of Islamic terrorists from a number of Arab countries. By the end of the decade Americans trembled far more at the name of Osama bin Laden, an Islamic fundamentalist terrorist, whose fanatic followers had bombed two American embassies in Africa in 1998, than they ever had at the military power of Saddam Hussein.

Although Saddam Hussein and Osama bin Laden might give Americans nightmares of bomb plots and poison gas attacks, a far more potent threat to American stability came from the quickening pace of financial and business globalization. With companies like McDonalds and Nike represented all over the world and foreign companies buying American ones (DaimlerChrysler), as well as American companies merging with and taking over foreign ones (Merrill-Lynch), business was becoming far more international than it had ever been. So much so that a dip on the Hong Kong stock market or the Japanese Nikkei securities index was almost certain to cause trouble the next day on the American financial markets. In fact, in 1998, America's almost-decade-long prosperity was placed in serious jeopardy by the domino fall of Thailand's currency, followed in swift succession by the collapse of the Indonesian and South Korean economies and a deep Japanese recession. Were it not for the efforts of the American Federal Reserve quickly lowering interest rates in the United States and the International Monetary Fund pumping funds into these bankrupt economies, there might have been a worldwide financial collapse rivaling that of 1929.[4]

Prosperity and an almost decade's long soaring of the stock market (the Dow Jones stood at 3500 in 1993 and was at 11,000 by the year 2000) was one of the hallmarks of the eight years of Bill Clinton's presidency. Clinton, then the virtually unknown governor of Arkansas, seemed to come out of nowhere in 1992 to challenge a popular incumbent president. He skillfully used the slogan, "It's the economy, stupid," with its explicit message that the economy is in decline as a brickbat to defeat President George Bush in the 1992 election.[5]

More important, Clinton staked a claim as a New Democrat, moving away from the politically and economically untenable New Deal consensus that emphasized expanding the welfare state and increasing social spending, and recasting the Party's appeal after years of Republican dominance. He embraced free markets and the balanced budget and committed himself to the shrinking of government programs. He also took away all sorts of wedge issues from the Republicans, like crime and welfare, by providing Democratic alternatives that spoke of greater individual responsibility for one's life without obliterating the notion that government had some obligation to create a more equitable and just society. Clinton's creed could be best summed up in this statement when he began his campaign for the presidency in 1992, "Government's responsibilty is to create more opportunity. The people's responsibility is to make the most of it."[6]

Consequently, Clinton committed himself to a limited social contract that offered social reforms like national service, school construction, the assault weapons ban, a higher minimum wage, earned income tax credits for the working poor, and welfare reform, whose meanest provisions Clinton has tried to modify. (On the whole, welfare reform was a necessary though flawed move away from traditional liberalism that has so far worked somewhat better than expected.) He also carried out his campaign promise to choose "an administration that looks like America," with the appointment of unprecedented numbers of minorities to major administrative positions, including the first black Commerce Secretary—the consummate political insider Ron Brown—the first female Attorney General and Secretary of State, and a second woman to the Supreme Court.[7]

Of course, there were failures like the FBI siege of the Branch Davidian compound in Waco, and the defeat of the highly touted but unwieldy attempt at healthcare reform presided over by first lady, Hillary Clinton. And the 1994 election saw the Democrats lose control of both houses of Congress, and the president seemingly being pushed into irrelevancy. Clinton, however, was blessed with enemies like Congressman Newt Gingrich, who became Speaker of the House in 1994. Gingrich, a plump, silver-haired, demi-intellectual conservative devised a strategy ("Contract with America") where business groups would work closely with social conservatives like the Christian Coalition to build a common agenda of deregulation, privatization, tax cuts, school prayer, and opposition to abortion and gun control. Gingrich and his band of House conservatives (many of them from the South), overreached themselves, and soon the strategy began to break down. Voters may have felt a distrust for government, but they didn't want to turn the clock back to the 1950s and they didn't share Gingrich's antipathy towards Medicare, the EPA, and the Department of Education. In addition, when the Republicans tried to pass a budget bill over presidential vetoes, and allowed the government to shut down, they went too far and gave Clinton a weapon to beat them with in the 1996 election. The ultra-conservative wing of the Republicans did not disappear, but the Party in the 1996 election, by choosing a traditional Republican—Bob Dole—to run against Clinton, opted for a less ideological form of conservatism.[8]

Though Clinton may be remembered primarily for his domestic achievements, he also helped broker and stage the signing of an interim Middle East settlement (including the handshake between PLO Chairman Arafat and Israeli Prime Minister Rabin), played a role in settling the conflict between the eternally warring parties in Northern Ireland, the negotiation of the Dayton accords which ended the Bosnian war, and the successful conclusion of the Kosovo air attacks. Though none of these conflicts can be said to have been fully resolved and can blow up again, still the United States successfully exerted its power in all these conflagrations.

Domestic and foreign policy achievements aside, it was Clinton, the complex personality, who dominated the politics of the nineties. Clinton was a charismatic man of preternatural political gifts, impressive intellect, and policy expertise, with a talent for public empathy possessed by few other American politicians. Talents that were marred by a flawed character that seemed to lack a genuine emotional or moral center. One often felt when listening to him that feelings and political arguments and positions, even if he believed in them, came too easily, and that more reflection, introspection, and social commitment were in order. Also, Clinton's inability to tell the truth went beyond the professional politician's normal prevarications, and he had a sexual appetite that led him into politically irresponsible and self-destructive actions.

Perhaps nothing illuminates his personality than these two statements made by Clinton, one during his first presidential campaign and the other during his presidency. The first was a memorable moment in Dover, New Hampshire in February of 1992 just before election day of the New Hampshire primary. It was a period when Clinton's candidacy seemed about to unravel as a result of the Gennifer Flowers sex scandal and the controversy over his Vietnam era draft status. Talking to the audience about their problems and not mentioning his own, Clinton said in closing, "I'. be with you till the last dog dies."9 It's the kind of comment that was emblematic of Clinton's empathetic form of populism.

The second was the humiliating moment almost six years later in January of 1998, when a red-faced Clinton told a press conference, "I did not have sex with that woman—Miss Lewinsky." He was forced to retract that comment seven months later when he acknowledged that he did have the infamously "inappropriate relationship" with her. The confession revealed Clinton at his worst—hiding his adulterous conduct behind euphemisms like "inappropriate relationship" just as he had tried to cloak his extra-marital affairs with nebulous remarks like "problems in our marriage" in his appearance with his wife Hillary on 60 Minutes in 1992 at the time of the Gennifer Flowers scandal.10

For a president whose fondest desire was to leave a brilliant and noble legacy, it is especially galling that perhaps the one thing that the Clinton presidency would be remembered for most was that he was the third president in American history ever to be impeached. Again Clinton was saved by the booming economy, a shift in the public's attitudes toward sexual transgressions, and the nature of his enemies. The economy's unprecedented success caused many Americans, who might otherwise have disapproved of his moral conduct, to nevertheless give him high marks for his presidential leadership and refuse to support his removal from office. In addition, the nineties public consumed vast quantities of celebrity gossip, confessional entertainment, and self-help advice which blurred the distinction between fame and notoriety, and also made them more forgiving of misbehavior. The other element was the grim self-righteousness and clear political motivation and ineptitude of his gang of impeachment stalkers led by the implacable special prosecutor Kenneth Starr.

Clinton's struggle against impeachment was also helped by the tin-eared House Managers of impeachment. These die-hard conservatives led by avuncular Henry Hyde, chairman of the House Judiciary committee, refused to listen to the American people who had indicated repeatedly by public opinion polls and in the 1998 elections (where the Republicans lost seats in the House and Senate) that they did not want Clinton impeached. The committee Republicans were obsessed with ousting a Clinton who they abhorred as a baby boomer representative of the 1960s draft-dodging, pot-smoking culture of permissiveness, and more important, as the man who helped prevent the triumph of conservatism.[11]

Impeachment aside any final evaluation of the Clinton years was sure to note that its most significant political characteristic was a skillful shunning of radical change and bold solutions. Clinton's Third Way political perspective became a model for European social democrats like Tony Blair and Gerhart Schroeder in their ascent to power. Nonetheless, there was one area where radical change had occurred and this was just as likely to have been spurred by the Clinton administration as it was to have occurred despite it. Never before had the United States had as long a period of economic expansion as under Clinton. What's more, that expansion included low unemployment (the lowest in thirty years) with virtually no inflation, and increasing productivity. In addition, an economy was taking shape that was more and more reliant upon the computer and cyberspace related e-commerce. No further evidence of this is needed than the fact that when Clinton took office in 1993 there were fifty web sites on the internet and by the year 2000 there were fifty million. Economists and entrepeneurs more and more referred to this economic state of affairs as the "New Economy."[12]

The Clinton administration had helped this New Economy come into being because of its economic plan to reduce the deficit and by spurring free trade with agreements such as NAFTA. But it had also helped it by removing the last vestiges of government regulation in many sectors of the economy. Among these were the Telecommunications Act of 1996, which leveled the economic playing field for television, cable, and telephone companies, and in the waning days of the century the repeal of the Glass-Steagal Act, a piece of depression era legislation which had erected an impenetrable firewall between the financial activities of banks, stock market companies, and insurance businesses.

The film industry was enormously affected by some of these economic changes. One little noticed change was the expiration of the FCC's Financial Interest and Syndication rule in 1995. This rule had prevented networks from having any financial stake in programs produced in prime time. With the fin/syn rule gone, the old studios that had made television production a mainstay of their profits suddenly felt these profits threatened. Similarly, the Telecommunications Act of 1996 removed the prohibition against owning in excess of twelve TV stations.

As a result a series of mega-mergers began to convulse Hollywood. The first of these in 1995 was the Disney studio's merger with Capitol Cities/ABC, which owned the ABC-TV network. The following year Time Warner, which owned a Warner's movie studio, saw its holdings greatly expanded by the addition of Turner Broadcast Networks, which owned cable TV and sports franchises and the Castle Rock movie production company. In 1999 Viacom, which owned Paramount studios along with the Blockbuster Video store chain, MTV, Nickleodeon cable networks, and the publisher Simon and Schuster, merged with CBS. These mergers created synergistic companies which could conceivably buy books from their publishing arms, produce movies from the scripts, advertise them over their networks, and then turn the more successful ones into miniseries or sitcoms.

While the influence of these mergers was undoubtedly profound on an economic level, on an artistic one, Hollywood was dramatically transformed by the growing significance of the independent cinema movement. Though always a factor in American film as a training ground for new talent or as a medium for directorial experimentation and political and social criticism by idiosyncratic and original artists like John Cassavetes and John Sayles, the independent movement had never been able to gain the attention of large audiences.[13]

However, after Robert Redford's founding of the Sundance Film Festival in 1984—a festival devoted almost exclusively to independent documentary and fiction films—the movement blossomed. The independent American cinema's breakthrough moment, however, didn't come until 1989 when Steven Soderbergh's independent film, Sex, Lies and Videotape, signed up with an aggressive distribution company—Miramax—won a best film prize at the Cannes Film Festival, and then went on to rack up large box office grosses in America. Suddenly, studio executives who had long ignored the independent cinema descended on the Sundance Film Festival with open checkbooks and long term development deals for recent graduates of film schools or precocious filmmakers who had maxxed out their credit cards in trying to make their dream film. When they got there they found that a number of small companies like Miramax, New Line, and October had already monopolized the situation by creating relationships that assured them the pick of the independents. The response of the studios was to buy these companies and let them function in a boutique arrangement within the larger studios (e.g., Disney/Miramax, Warners/New Line), an arrangement that was sometimes referred to as "Indiewood."

Nonetheless, these smaller companies did have a bracing effect on Hollywood. They funded movies that dealt with issues (lesbianism, AIDs, suburban life, racial and ethnic minorities, etc.) that Hollywood had long since ignored in favor of romantic comedies, high concept works about ghosts and children inhabiting adult's bodies, and action films with lots of car chases, explosions, and special effects. The defining moment for independent cinema came at the Academy Awards ceremony of 1996 when four of the five nominees for best picture were produced by independents (e.g., *The English Patient*, *Shine*, *Secrets and Lies*, and *Fargo*). However, perhaps the most striking achievement of the independents came in 1998 when Miramax studio's stylishly light period piece, *Shakespeare in Love*, beat out the highly acclaimed favorite, Steven Spielberg's patriotic epic *Saving Private Ryan*, receiving the Academy Award for best picture.[14]

It was a victory that undoubtedly owed as much to the marketing genius and chutzpah of Miramax's reigning mini-mogul Harvey Weinstein as to the movie's quality, demonstrating how much the independents had come to resemble the studios. The independent success story was achieved as much by deal-making, media manipulation, and by playing hardball, as by talent. Many of the directors had less interest in creating original works—expressing something they can't say within the system—than in using their films as a path to fame and the big dollars of the Hollywood mainstream. Still, with the advent of digital video—a format that will permit anybody with $50,000 to make high production value films—there will be no diminution of fledgling directors making independent films. The quality of them, not their quantity, is the question.

The Hollywood mainstream, however, still had to churn out film in accord with its traditional, audience-pleasing formulae. Like everyone else, Hollywood was ill-prepared for the end of the Cold War and the post–Cold War era. Even a year after the fall of the Berlin Wall, the film industry was still producing films that reeked of the Cold War, albeit with faint hints of the coming collapse of communism. The most popular of these was action-film director John McTiernan's (e.g., *Die Hard*, 1988) *The Hunt for Red October* (1990). The film is based on a Tom Clancy techno-thriller that remained on best-seller lists for over two years and sold as many as five million copies. *The Hunt for Red October*'s narrative revolves around the Soviet Union's highest ranking submarine commander, a gruff, authoritarian Marko Alexandrovich Ramius (Sean Connery) and his officers who plot to defect. Their plan is to take with them the most sophisticated hi-tech Soviet submarine ever built—one with such speed and undetectability that it could hover near the coast of the United States without ever being discovered.

When a patrolling United States sub discovers the Red October, the reflexive response of American leaders is that this is the beginning of a Soviet first strike. This notion is successfully challenged by a bright CIA analyst, Jack Ryan (Alec Baldwin), who believes the commander wants to defect. Predictably he joins Ramius and a U.S. sub commander and helps thwart the best efforts of the Soviet sub fleet to destroy the Red October. The film is all cross-cutting between sub interiors, close-ups of advanced technical equipment, intercuts of the immense Jaws-looking Red October, and reaction shots of anxious Soviet and American naval personnel. The film's emphasis on submarine technology dwarfs its utterly flat characters and perfunctory, banal dialogue.

What is most interesting about a mechanical film like The Hunt for Red October, especially in light of the Cold War's end, are its political assumptions, not its aesthetics. The most striking was that Soviet naval officers, certainly among the most privileged group in their society, had become so disillusioned with their country and its ideology (the sub's political officer, who mouths the Party's line is killed by Ramius) that they felt compelled to defect. (Ramius' background as a Lithuanian provides added resonance with its reference to the disgruntled Baltic nations, and their desire for independence from Russian domination.)

Of course these assumptions are Clancy's responsibility, since he always took a tough line on the Cold War. They point to the widely held belief, even before the fall of the Berlin Wall (the book appeared before the collapse), that faith in the Soviet system had almost disappeared. They also implicitly acknowledge the fact that despite this the Cold War left such a dangerous residue of mistrust that one mistake might still lead to catastrophe. And that there was a need for reasonable men like Jack Ryan and Marko Ramius to overcome the last vestiges of Cold War paranoia.

The intensity with which American cinema still pursued Cold War narratives and scenarios is in sharp contrast with the lack of interest in constructing stories that dealt with post–Cold War events such as the Gulf War. Since the war in 1991, only two studio-produced-films specifically dealt with it, Courage Under Fire (1996) and Three Kings (1999). This is especially odd in view of the tremendous hoopla that greeted the victorious end of the war, especially the declarations that the so-called "Vietnam syndrome" was finally dead and buried. Perhaps the reason was that Americans took little pride in defeating a country with the gross national product of Kentucky, and that the victory remained tarnished by the fact that after all the smart bombs and stupid politicians, Saddam Hussein still remained in power in Baghdad, outmaneuvering all the international weapons inspectors sent to Iraq to try to enforce UN sanctions.

Courage Under Fire, though an earnest attempt at dealing with the Gulf War, was hardly the kind of film to strike many imitative sparks. Directed by Edward Zwick (*Glory*, 1989) and starring Denzel Washington and Meg Ryan, it depicts Lieutenant Colonel Nathaniel Serling's (Washington) search for the truth about Captain Karen Walden's (Ryan) possible Medal of Honor Award-winning heroism during the war. Beside the introduction of certain contemporary politically correct tropes—like a black officer investigating the battlefield field actions of a white woman officer—the film used an old fashioned *Rashamon*-like structure as the basis of the narrative. (Some of Captain Walden's troops claiming she was a coward, others affirming her courage.) *Courage Under Fire*, however, offered very little insight into the nature of the war itself except for Serling's own guilt and remorse over a "friendly fire" accident where he killed American soldiers during it (the majority of U.S. casualties in the war having been killed by friendly fire). Ultimately, *Courage Under Fire* doesn't go much further than the liberal problem film of the forties—personalizing the social problem and settling for an angry sexist villain, and leaving out any sense that the military as an institution may have its own difficulties in dealing with women officers.

Three Kings, directed by an independent film director David Russell (e.g., *Flirting with Disaster*, 1996), is a hybrid work—on the one hand an imaginative absurdist take on the war, on the other, a conventional action film. Three reservists, solid, straight family man Sergeant Troy Barlow (Mark Wahlberg), glowering, Jesus-loving Chief Eldin (Ice Cube), and a sweet comic redneck Conrad Vig (Spike Jonze), find the map to Saddam's hidden stash of stolen Kuwaiti gold bullion. Led by Special Forces Major Archie Gates (George Clooney), they go on a postwar expedition to steal it for themselves, and on the way become involved in their own mini-war against the Iraqi army units. Russell shoots the war with a hand-held camera, and it chaotically explodes on the screen with scenes popping out of other scenes, and with stark close-ups of what bullets can do to a soldier's guts. It's a media war the film keeps reminding us, where the army totally collaborates with the media, and ubiquitous television reporters build their careers by frantically, racing around competing for stories. It's a war where most of the American soldiers never see combat, and learn most of what they know about the war from CNN.

The film's political perspective is conveyed by the heroic Clooney character, playing a variation on his macho, anti-authoritarian, unbelievably adept television doctor. He lectures his American cohorts on how the war was for nothing, since the United States encouraged the uprising against Saddam but then refused to support it when we defeated Iraq. It's a war that American troops engaged in, presumably to help a nation, Kuwait, preserve its independence, but also to protect America's oil sources. Russell depicts it also as a war whose legacy is not freedom, but a country of mines and car hulks littering the desert, innocent Iraqi children killed in bombing attacks, Shiite rebels being shot, and cranes black with oil from the burning wells. The film is most incisive when it satirizes the power of globalization exemplified by an Iraqi army torturer, trained by the U.S. military, having a discussion with the imprisoned Troy on the pros and cons of Michael Jackson's cosmetic surgery. In fact, everybody in the film—Americans, rebels, Iraqi army—is obsessed with brand names, opening businesses, and American mass culture. In one scene when the Americans descend upon an Iraqi bunker they discover rooms filled with goods stolen from Kuwait including everything from jeans to Cuisinarts to cell phones and TV sets playing the Rodney King video.

Three Kings alternates between scenes of derring-do—the Americans blowing up Iraqi helicopters and storming bunkers—and sometimes trenchant black comedy about a senseless war. It ends like any conventional action film with the likable Americans eschewing their avarice for discovering a conscience. They jettison their load of booty to help the Shiite rebels get safely across the border to Iran. The final message of the film, despite all the absurdities and contradictions of the war (the final one being that Iran, for at least a decade America's greatest antagonist in the Middle East, serves as safe haven for the refugees), is that the Americans are the good guys.

With the collapse of the Soviet Union, and the ambiguous victory in the Gulf War offering very little comfort, Hollywood faced a dearth of credible foreign adversaries who could be utilized to build conflict and fear into its films. One option that existed was a holdover from fifties cinema which was to look to the skies and other planets for fictional enemies from space as possible antagonists. *Independence Day* (1996) provided just such an enemy. The space invaders depicted in Independence Day aren't the messianic Giacometti-like aliens depicted in films such as *Close Encounters of the Third Kind* (1977) or the cuddly little *E.T.* (1982). They are repellent-looking space meanies who are reminiscent of the Mars invaders in *War of the Worlds* (1953).

Independence Day is a combination of fifties alien invasion film and seventies disaster film—much of the film a pastiche of other works (e.g., *Star Wars*, 1977, and *The Towering Inferno*, 1974). The aim of these fiends from outer space is to destroy civilization. So they quickly lay waste to most of New York (including the Statue of Liberty and the Empire State Building), Washington, and Los Angeles. And if anyone still doubted their malevolence they also obliterate a bunch of Los Angeles New Agers who foolishly welcome them as saviors.

Everything looks bleak, until the President Thomas J. Whitmore (Bill Pullman), a former Gulf War veteran pilot, who until then has been perceived as a Clintonian waffler joins forces with brash, quick-witted, top gun fighter pilot Captain Steve Hiller (Will Smith), and evironmentalist, computer genius David Levinson (Jeff Goldblum) to deal these alien invaders their comeuppence.

Thrown in for comic relief is Judd Hirsch as David's unshaven, sneaker-wearing Yiddish-accented father, and a wild-haired, mad scientist played by *Star Trek: The Next Generation*'s Brent Spiner.

It hardly matters that all this is utterly derivative. What is significant is that in this cheery cartoon of a film, the brotherhood of man, symbolized by the world forces, combine to oppose the aliens. And a quartet that contains a white Protestant president, a former black rapper, an intellectual Jew, and an alcoholic ex-pilot Russell Casse (Randy Quaid) right out of *Dr. Strangelove* defeat the forces of intergalactic evil accompanied by a final montage of people all over the world rejoicing.

It was this sort of patriotic rainbow coalition—unifying the world under American command—that prompted Senator Bob Dole (no movie critic or fan), the 1996 Republican candidate for president, to laud it by saying, "Bring your family. You'll be proud of it. Diversity. America. Leadership."[15] This extravaganza of special effects soon became one of the highest grossing films of all time, proving that for Hollywood affirming American patriotism by saving the human race from alien extermination would prove an apt substitute for fighting Reds.

If intergalactic fiends weren't sufficient, there was always the patriotic trump card of World War II. Interestingly enough, it was in the Soviet Union that World War II had first become known as "The Great Patriotic War." In the United States it was not only the war that everyone could agree was the last "Good War" (given the ambiguities and dark side of the Korean War, Vietnam War, and Gulf War), it was also fast becoming the American equivalent of the "Great Patriotic War." It was seen as a war fought against powerful, purely evil enemies that threatened our very existence as a nation, required a total national commitment, and ended in unambiguous victory. So on the roster of Hollywood's international evildoers (now that the Red Menace was out of the way) the Nazis and the Japanese could still be relied upon to invoke a frisson of fear and a patriotic surge of pride from the American public.

There was no one better to arouse these feelings of fear and pride than Hollywood's most successful director, Steven Spielberg. With the completion of *Saving Private Ryan*, Spielberg had already directed six of the top twenty box office grossing films of all time. Furthermore, ever since 1993 and his Academy Award-winning *Schindler's List* (to be discussed later in the chapter) he had aspired to make films with moral and social content that, at the same time, would appeal to wide audiences. Spielberg was a master of film technique and Hollywood genre conventions, who often brought great stylistic inventiveness to his films—leaving audiences with a sense of visceral excitement, as well as nostalgia for older forms of cinematic storytelling.

Spielberg's *Saving Private Ryan* strikes a patriotic note right from the start, with a giant American flag rippling in the breeze accompanied by John Williams's mournful score in the background. The camera then slowly tracks after an aged veteran and his family on his return to the battlefields and cemeteries of Normandy, and then in flashback dissolve from the veteran at a gravesite to a squad of wet, vomiting, and frightened soldiers landing at Dog sector of Omaha Beach on June 6, 1944. What follows is what one military historian, John Keegan (*The Face of Battle*), has called, "the most terrifying, realistic thing ever done in the cinema."[16]

The first twenty-five minutes of the film are probably the most brilliant evocation of war's horrors ever filmed. Shooting with his camera low to the ground like a combat photographer, so that blood and water frequently splatter the lens, and seen from the points of view of a German machine gunner and from the soldiers themselves, and using diffused light and unsaturated colors, Spielberg presents a staggering portrait of the randomness and chaos of D-day's violence. He fills the screen with terrifying moments such as a wounded soldier searching for his arm, another whose face is blown apart, a GI screaming for his mother as his intestines spill out onto the beach, others engulfed in flames, and the blood of the wounded and dying turning the ocean red. Spielberg shoots much of the horror in close-up and jagged tracking shots, and concludes the sequence with a long overhead shot of the beach littered with bodies and body parts. In this sequence the soldiers are anonymous, and there are no facile heroics—Spielberg evoking just the image of war as abattoir.

However, after providing the audience with this sort of startling realism, Spielberg then aims for patriotic transcendence. He strikes that note when the Armed Forces Chief of Staff, General George C. Marshall (Herve Presnell), upon learning that three of Ryan's brothers had died in combat just that week, orders that the surviving Ryan brother be rescued from combat. To justify his decision he reads a passage from Abraham Lincoln's famous Civil War letter to Mrs. Bixby, a mother who had lost five sons in that war. Sanctified by Lincoln's eloquent rhetoric, *Saving Private Ryan* takes on new meaning. As a result, from the ultimate in combat realism it becomes a brilliantly directed—every off-angle tilt, and every shot-reverse-shot is artfully chosen—relatively conventional combat mission war film.

Before we know it we are following in color the journey of that archetypal World War II squad consisting of a cynical, wise guy from Brooklyn, Private Reiban (Ed Burns), a Bible-quoting southern sharpshooter, Private Jackson (Barry Pepper), a tense, Nazi-hating Jewish kid, Private Melish (Adam Goldberg), a passionate Italian, Private Caparzo (Vince Deisel), a sensitive medic Wade (Giovanni Ribisi), and the loyal, battle-hardened, Sergeant Horvath (Tom Sizemore). If you remember these guys from somewhere else, it's because they've already appeared in such World War II classics as *A Walk in the Sun* (1945), and *The Story of G.I. Joe* (1945). To augment this feeling of déjà vu, there is the battle weary, vulnerable, Captain John Miller (Tom Hanks), who has seen too many beach heads and too many men die. Miller is a wise, small-town high school teacher out of Frank Capra—a heroic, everyman leader free of bloodlust who just wants to finish the job and go home to his wife. And there is Corporal Upham (Jeremy Davies), the awkward, frightened intellectual translator who has never seen action before and whose rite of passage into war's murderousness Spielberg focuses on in the film's final battle. None of the eight men are complex creations, but, at the same time, they are sufficiently individuated to successfully serve the genre.

In their quest for Private Ryan the squad has to destroy the occasional German machine gun nest and radar installation, and have an angry argument over whether or not to kill a captured German soldier whose obsequious odiousness seems to have been culled from some of the worst of the World War II films. There are also moments of repose—a night in a destroyed cathedral—where they recall their pasts or contemplate the war. Much of their talk involves justifying to themselves the possible squandering of the lives of so many to save just one life. Indeed it goes against the philosophy of Captain Miller, who believes that the ninety-four men who died under his command have perhaps saved the lives of thousands. However, in World War II films it's not the philosophy, but the mission and chain of command that matter. Consequently, when they finally find the callow Private Ryan (Matt Damon), and he refuses to leave his post "with the only brothers I have left" they all remain with him to do the good, brave thing and defend a vital bridgecrossing against a furious German counterattack. They are vastly outnumbered and the Germans have tanks, so Sergeant Horvath, Private Melish, Private Pepper, and Captain Miller die in the process. Lives must be lost so the film would be seen as a serious work, not a juvenile action film. Also, much too neatly, the cowardly Corporal Upham must ironically learn about the brutal necessity of killing by shooting the German prisoner whose life he pleaded for in an earlier scene. The sequence's action is choreographed stunningly, but it's melodramatic and interminable, and the squad's fearlessness and courage against impossible odds is really not much different than the behavior of John Wayne and company in countless, less vaunted World War II films.

In the penultimate scene the dying Captain Miller leaves Private Ryan with the moral injunction to "earn this"—to live a life that justifies their sacrifice. Those words seemed less aimed at Private Ryan—who has already demonstrated that he is a man of courage—than at future generations asking them to adhere to Miller's notions of decency and self-sacrifice. The film ends as it begins with a final image of the billowing American flag and Williams' mournful music. In Saving Private Ryan, Spielberg, as in many of his nineties films, sought to confront large historical and moral themes such as American racism and the Holocaust (e.g. Amistad, Schindler's List), bearing witness this time to the heroism of Americans who fought and died in World War II in Lincoln's words (quoted by General Marshall) on "the altar of freedom."

However, except for the film's opening twenty-five minutes, *Saving Private Ryan* often bears skillful witness more to Hollywood's World War II film genre than to the war. The soldiers may kill a few German prisoners after seeing their comrades slaughtered, but these are not the officers and enlisted men from *Platoon*—there are no psychopaths and rapists among them. These are good men fighting a virtuous war against an evil ideology. The war may be horrific, but it's neither meaningless nor futile. This is Spielberg's ahistorical valentine to America and Americans at their best—expunging almost all the contradictions, moral transgressions, and absurdities that exist in any war, even a good and necessary one like World War II.

Released six months after *Saving Private Ryan*, Terrence Malick's *The Thin Red Line* reinforced the return of World War II as a film subject. The two films and two directors, however, could hardly have been more different. Unlike Spielberg who had been in the popular spotlight for over two decades since his first success *Jaws* (1975), Malick had become reclusive after the release of his last film, *Days of Heaven* (1978). Nonetheless, that film and his earlier work, *Badlands* (1973), were critical favorites that turned Malick into a cult figure.

A futher contrast is that Spielberg's film is heroic and patriotic, while Malick's is poetic and philosophical. Based on James Jones' 1962 novel of the same name, Malick, however, eschews Jones' naturalistic treatment of the American invasion and battle for control of Guadalcanal for an evocation of a glorious natural world where Melanesian islanders swim serenely in clear, azure ocean waters and tall green grass waves in the wind. This pastoral idyll is disrupted by the war's savagery, which in turn moves the soldiers to indulge in a great deal of sometimes insightful, other times vaporous and portentous, philosophical and poetic interior monologues about the character of war, nature, and death.

As he does in his previous films, Malick uses extensive voiceovers to portray the emotions and ideas of his protagonists, whose voices and faces often blur and rarely can be individuated. And his portrait of the defeated Japanese is very different than Hollywood's usual conception of them as anonymous cannon fodder or strutting barbarians. Malick humanizes the Japanese, portraying them after being defeated, screaming in fear, begging for mercy or assuming the lotus position as they await their deaths or imprisonment. There are also conflicts that take place between the Americans. One of them depicts the struggle between the idealistic philosophy of Private Witt (Jim Caviezel) and the cynicism, even nihilism of Sergeant Welsh (Sean Penn). They argue over whether the world of our senses ("this rock") is the ultimate reality, or if we are part of a single Emersonian oversoul ("the glory"). A more baleful struggle occurs between the railing, driven Lieutenant Colonel Tall (Nick Nolte) and the compassionate Captain Staros (Elias Koteas) over whether to storm, in a costly frontal assault, the heavily defended redoubts of the Japanese.

Though Nolte's ranting sometimes goes over the top, he successfully captures the desperation of the Homer-quoting, war-loving Colonel who, passed over for promotion, sees this battle as his last chance for vindication. Staros, on the other hand, may be too passive and sensitive—better suited to leading a college seminar than a combat infantry platoon. Malick, however, is less interested in character than in stunning images of light streaming through trees in the rain forest, and close-ups of birds, crocodiles, and lush island vegetation—providing an almost pantheistic view of nature—one that grants life but is also bound by death. If Spielberg's film was the ultimate homage to the Hollywood war genre, Malick's film, though not opposed to our entry into World War II, gives no sense of the historical basis for Guadalcanal, but provides a truly original visual and oral meditation on war.

If enemies from the Cold War, from World War II, and galaxies far, far away didn't suffice, there was always an internal enemy. As a result the nineties were also notorious for their internecine culture wars. And the enemy here was just as likely as not to be the cultural legacy of the sixties. To liberals the radical impulses of the sixties had given way to more traditional politics and more structured, conventional lives as the nineties and middle age closed in on them. For some liberals their new found moderation caused them to wonder if they had betrayed the best of themselves, and perhaps in so doing the future of America.

In the minds of conservative Americans the sixties' challenge to traditional bourgeois ideas about family, sexual relations, and for a brief moment even capitalism itself, was seen as responsible for the climbing divorce rate, the rising number of teenage pregnancies, and soaring drug use. The sixties were viewed as the enemy—an anarchic decade responsible for our collective moral decay, as well as the failure of our national will. Consequently, whatever the political perspective, perhaps the most significant, though generally unacknowledged, legacy of the sixties was a pervasive anxiety about America's destiny.

Oddly enough, a glimpse of that anxiety, though not generated by fear of the sixties, is evoked in *Star Wars: Episode I—The Phantom Menace*—the 1999 prequel to one of the great Hollywood successes, George Lucas' *Star Wars Trilogy* (*Star Wars*, 1977; *The Empire Strikes Back*, 1980; *Return of the Jedi*, 1983)—a film usually numbered in the top ten box office grossing films of all time, and a special favorite of Gen X Americans.

However, despite the fact that the film's narrative revolves around a dispute about the taxation of trade routes in the Galactic Republic, *The Phantom Menace*'s main preoccupation are its special effects. Still, there is frequent reference made to the Galactic Republic's ineffectuality in this crisis, which is alternately assigned to the fact that "the bureaucrats are in charge," and that "there is no civility only politics, no interest in the common good." Of course, one wonders if this is Lucas's way of revealing his anxieties about the state of contemporary affairs or if it is just some nebulous intellectual scaffolding he has constructed after reading too much of Gibbons's *Decline and Fall of the Roman Empire.*

The answer is an obvious one, what really matters to Lucas, as it has since his first film *THX 1138* (1971), is neither politics, character, nor even mythology, but special effects. Unfortunately, those used in *The Phantom Menace* lost their power to excite us as they had in the seventies and eighties. Twenty years of video games, the Internet, and a whole series of the rival *Star Trek* films had dimmed the wonder that once greeted the brilliant effects of the earlier *Star Wars* films. Lucas, also, seemed to be repeating himself with the rocket ship race with its swooping camera that is reminiscent of the rocket fighter attacks in *Star Wars.* Furthermore, although one shouldn't expect political correctness in galaxies far, far away, there is some tin-eared indifference to minorities with bumbling Stepin Fetchit-like characters such as the Jedi knight's valet, Jar Jar Binks, who also speaks with a Jamaican accent.

Despite this *The Phantom Menace* was virtually critic-proof and grossed a record breaking $28.5 million in the first weekend after its release. Consequently, if George Lucas was betraying some small measure of anxiety about the fate of the American Republic in *The Phantom Menace*, he obviously didn't have any at all about the operations of American capitalism.

A much more serious inquiry and response to what had gone wrong with America since the sixties was offered by director Oliver Stone in his presidential films *JFK* (1991) and *Nixon* (1995). Stone's ambitious, brilliantly edited films (flashforwards, flashbacks, flash cuts, jump cuts, a mix of newsreels, still photos, and fiction, black and white and color, etc.) touched a nerve and even before their release journalists, politicians, and assorted literati weighed in with denunciations and critiques of the films. Tom Wicker, the former Op-Ed columnist of *The New York Times* called *JFK*, "paranoid and fantastic, filled with wild assertions, that if widely accepted would be contemptuous of the very constitutional government Stone purports to uphold."[17] Smug conservative pundit George Will anathemized *JFK* as an, "act of execrable history and contemptible citizenship, by man of technical skill, scant education, and negligible conscience."[18] The Nixon family's comment on *Nixon* was the less eloquent, but certainly more succinct description, calling the film, "character assassination."[19]

Stone certainly was not without his defenders too. In an article in *The Atlantic* political and cultural polymath Garry Wills referred to Stone's body of work, saying that, "great novels are being written with the camera—at least when Stone is behind the camera."[20] Norman Mailer, no stranger to the pungent metaphor, said that Stone, "has the integrity of a brute,"[21] and in an especially insightful afterthought commented that *JFK*, "should be seen not as history but myth, the story of a huge and hideous act in which the gods warred and a god fell."[22]

Stone would have readily agreed with at least part of Mailer's estimate. In interview after interview following the release of *JFK*, he consistently argued that, "I'm presenting what I call a countermyth to the myth of the Warren Commission."[23] What was missing in all the controversy over Stone's presidential films was any references to connections between the two films beside the obvious historical links. Nevertheless, there were two essential links between the two films. The first was that in an important sense they were both mysteries, or more precisely one was a murder mystery (*JFK*) and the other a moral mystery (*Nixon*). The second was that taken together they presented Oliver Stone's mythic interpretation of American history and politics since the 1960s.

JFK's status as a murder mystery is most clearly evoked by soft-spoken New Orleans D. A. Jim Garrison (Kevin Costner) in his summation to the jury (one that in actuality Garrison never delivered) in the Clay Shaw trial in which he refers to the Kennedy assassination as, "the murder at the heart of the American dream." The image, however, of D. A. Jim Garrison heroically walking the mean streets of New Orleans in search of the real Kennedy assassins is one that gave critics of the film the most pause. Especially when even die-hard conspiracy theorists considered Garrison's investigation and subsequent indictments, "a grotesque misdirected shambles."[24]

However, for Stone, Garrison's record as a thrice elected New Orleans D. A., his over twenty-year service in the military, and his later career as an appellate judge marked him as a patriot and a Capraesque uncommon common man. Just as significant for Stone was the fact that Garrison was the only American law enforcement official ever to bring indictments in the Kennedy assassination. This allowed Stone to enter the surreal world of the Warren Commission report, giving him the opportunity to present a grand unified conspiracy theory of his own.

In *JFK* Garrison's initial suspicions are aroused by the summer Lee Harvey Oswald (Gary Oldman) spent in New Orleans just before the Kennedy assassination, presumably working for "The Fair Play for Cuba" committee. This inspires Garrison's descent into the lower depths of New Orleans society. Among those he meets among the city's demimonde are the jittery, gay, defrocked priest, and anti-Castro mercenary, David Ferrie (Joe Pesci), and the crudely direct, former homosexual prostitute and prison inmate Willie O'Keefe (Kevin Bacon). The latter implicates the smooth, elegant Clay Shaw aka Clay Bertrand (Tommy Lee Jones) and also regales Garrison with his racist Aryan nation philosophy.

In Stone's version, Garrison's life is one of utter bourgeois respectability. There are frequent cloying, clichéd domestic scenes between Garrison and his nagging wife, Liz (Sissy Spacek), and their clamorous children. And the mixture of his conventionality and his committment to the rule of law have left him poorly equipped to confront the dark side of American life. Still, Garrison's persistence and unwavering courage and integrity bring him more and more into conflict with the immense power of that side of American life, especially its political and economic incarnation—the military-industrial complex.

At the very beginning of the film Stone refers to this colossus in newsreel footage of President Eisenhower's 1960 farewell address warning of its power. However, it isn't until Garrison's meeting with the shadowy former Black Ops agent, Colonel X (Donald Sutherland), that Garrison really begins to fully understand the forces he is confronting: a supposed cabal of high level military men, Mafia dons, oil millionaires, Cuban exile leaders, CIA agents that Colonel X convinces him carried out a "coup d'état."

Using Colonel X as his Virgil, Stone also reveals the political subtext of his film. According to Stone's dubious historical scenario, Kennedy was killed because he wanted to end the Cold War and begin withdrawing American troops from Vietnam. In Stone's view had Kennedy lived we would have been spared the trauma of Vietnam—an assertion that obviously cannot be proven. So for Stone, Kennedy's assassination not only resulted in the loss of a beloved prince, but embodied an end of an era of American innocence and idealism.

This loss of idealism so central to *JFK* is also referred to time and again in *Nixon*. Idealism is of course the last thing one associates with Richard Nixon. Yet for Stone, Nixon is a complex figure, at once a gifted Machiavellian who had a great deal of political hubris, and a man who was equally paranoid, self-pitying, and guilt ridden. The mystery that Stone tries to solve in *Nixon* is the question of what were the personal and moral sources of such a tragic and intricate character. Here Stone is aided by actor Anthony Hopkins, who though bearing scant physical resemblance to Nixon, nonetheless stunningly conveys his physical awkwardness, lack of charm, tight smile, furtive look, and most important of all, his combination of self-conscious, compensatory machismo, and embarrassing mawkishness without ever turning him into a cartoon. In addition, Joan Allen's solitary, long-suffering, sometimes tough-minded Pat Nixon grants her a complicated humanity that all the media images of the smiling, supportive wife never provided.

Hopkins's and Allen's performances are the most striking aspects of *Nixon*. Stone also uses frequent visual references (e.g., newsreels, oblique angles, dark rooms) to *Citizen Kane* to get to the heart of Nixon's character. His appropriation of this classic film as a central metaphor for understanding Nixon was logical given Welles' efforts to penetrate the mysteries of Kane. Indeed this time instead of one "rosebud" there are a host of possible rosebuds that offer clues to the enigma that was Richard Milhous Nixon.

The primary one is Nixon's mother Hannah (Mary Steenburgen), whom he described as a "saint," but whose severity, self-righteous moralizing, and unintentional rejections would have eviscerated the soul of an even more self-confident child than little Richard Nixon, who once referred to himself in a letter to her as "your good dog."[25] Stone also offers tantalizing clues such as, the "four deaths" that Nixon refers to as stepping-stones to his presidency. These included most prominently the deaths of John and Robert Kennedy, and more personally the deaths of Nixon's two brothers (Arthur and Harold); the latter enabling him to attend law school and leaving him with a legacy of guilt.

Stone also allows us to ponder whether or not it could have been psychological and class resentment that motivated Nixon. As John Ehrlichman (J. T. Walsh) says to H. R. Haldeman (James Woods): "You've got people dying because he didn't make the varsity football team. You've got the constitution hanging by a thread because the old man went to Whittier and not Yale." Finally, there is a double-dealing, hypocritical Henry Kissinger's (Paul Sorvino) portentous judgment that, "Imagine, if this man had been loved."

Beside providing a somewhat facile psychological explanation for Nixon's political behavior, Stone also provides an intellectual-ideological rationale for some, albeit not all, of Nixon's political failings. By the time of Nixon, the cancer that Stone had diagnosed in *JFK* had evolved into an invincible all-powerful government, an almost mythic creature that Stone refers to as the "beast"—a creature that no individual, no matter how powerful, can control.

The power of the beast, the hidden government that Nixon hints at, is the penultimate metaphor in Stone's conspiracy-driven vision of American politics embodied in both *JFK* and *Nixon*. It is quite simply, according to Stone, that had Kennedy lived he would have withdrawn from Vietnam, and ended the Cold War. However, the threat of that caused such consternation in the lethal Leviathan/Beast—the military-industrial, CIA-Mafia-Wall Street complex—that they passed a death sentence on him. In the wake of his death there occurred a period of political demoralization, that Richard Nixon, with his combination of relentless political ambition, ruthless pragmatism, and self-destructive vindictiveness brought to its tragic culmination. Or as an anguished Nixon himself puts it one night as he passes before the portrait of Kennedy (the political figure who obsesses him), during the Watergate scandal: "When they see you, they see what they want to be. When they see me, they see what they are."

Oliver Stone's presidential films were certainly not the last word in Hollywood's attempt to come to grips with the last thirty years of American history. Vastly different in style and content was Robert Zemeckis' (*Who Killed Roger Rabbit?*) Academy Award-winning *Forrest Gump* (1994). The center of the film is a low IQ (75), Zelig-like hero, Forrest Gump (Tom Hanks) with an odd stiff-legged walk and utterly flat voice, whose life provides a superficial, magic

realist tour of American society from the fifties to the nineties. A dim Forrest
moves effortlessly and almost unconsciously from All-American football star,
Vietnam War hero, international ping pong champion, seafood mogul, to New
Age guru while also participating in key historical moments like inadvertently
joining the black students who defy Governor George Wallace and integrate
the University of Alabama (the scene using digital computer effects to merge
Forrest with real newsreel footage). Forrest makes this journey armed only with
the truisms of his spunky, loving mamma (Sally Field): "Life is like a box of
chocolates"; and "You never know what you're going to get."

Forrest Gump is a film whose commitment to patriotism, family values, and
entrepreneurial spirit endeared itself to right-wingers. Forrest is devoted to his
suicidal, drug addicted childhood sweetheart, Jenny (Robin Wright), is a loving father to their son, and starts a seafood business as a homage to his black
army buddy, Bubba (Mykelti Williamson)—becoming a millionaire. This led
the Reverend Pat Robertson to observe that the film proves the existence of
"tiny cells of conservatism burrowing deep inside the Hollywood elite."

Still Forrest, like Peter Sellers' Chauncey Gardiner in Being There (1979),
was the kind of blank slate that anyone could project their values on and claim
for their side. If he embodied some conservative values, he also, though named
after the founder of the Ku Klux Klan, Nathan Bedford Forrest, is the only
white in a black gospel choir, as well as maintaining a deep link to Bubba. And
though a Vietnam War hero, he ends up, by accident, addressing an antiwar
rally, and is praised by its Abby Hoffman look-alike leader.

Obviously, the film is no affirmation of the sixties—both the Black Pan-
thers and SDS are seen as radicals who bully, posture, and talk jargon. However, the film's ultimate concern is more philosophical than political. The
embittered, legless Lieutenant Dan (Gary Sinise), whose life Forrest saved in
Vietnam, rants that, "nothing just happens, it's part of a plan." The response to
his fatalism comes from Mamma Gump, who says that "you make your own
destiny." Forrest, in turn, synthesizes the two positions, holding that we both
have a destiny, and float "around accidental like on a breeze."

Forrest's folksy synthesis is another example of the film's sentimental governing notion that he is a holy fool, blessed with great sympathy and an artless
simplicity that makes him a fount of wisdom, capable of moving some of the
despairing characters—Jenny and Lieutenant Dan—to ultimately affirm their
lives. Zemeckis, with the help of Hanks' virtuoso performance, has made a
skillful, manipulative film that substitutes greeting card treacle for real ideas
and emotions.

Unlike Stone's docudramas and Zemeckis' holy fool fable, the western has
always been a barometer of the nation's culture. From the classic westerns of
the twenties and thirties (The Iron Horse, Stagecoach) to the revisionism of the
late sixties (Little Big Man, McCabe and Mrs. Miller) the genre has often illumi-

nated the concerns of American society and culture. And though by the eighties and nineties Hollywood made few westerns, two of those made in the nineties—*Dances with Wolves* (1990) and *Unforgiven* (1992)—were ambitious, serious works that won Academy Awards for best film.

Dances with Wolves, directed by and starring Kevin Costner, who plays the somber, understated, gentle Lieutenant John Dunbar—whose suicidal heroics in the Civil War allow him, by his own choice (he wants to see the frontier, and remove himself from civilization), to be posted out West. Dunbar is transferred to an isolated outpost in Lakota territory, where he comes into contact with Sioux, who, after initial warinesss, accept him as one of their own and name him Dances-with-Wolves.

Dunbar, an observant man, keeps a journal, where he writes: "I had never known a people so eager to laugh, so devoted to family, so dedicated to each other . . ." Costner's Sioux are mythicized—they are in harmony with nature and their sexuality, and blessed with an intuitive wisdom that makes them totally superior to most of the vulgar, murderous, rapacious, and mad whites in the film. There are bad Indians—the feral Pawnees—but the film's real primitives are the whites.

Dances with Wolves' celebration of noble Indians touched an anxious chord among many Americans who felt that in our pursuit of wealth and disregard for our environment we had lost touch with our spirituality. However, this handsome, epic film, filled with long shots of prairies, hills, sunsets, snowscapes, buffalo grazing, is emotionally undeveloped and sentimental, and as mythic in its depiction of the Indians as the old Hollywood was in its stereotyping them as bloodthirsty savages. Modern anthropological studies have shown that the Indians were just as wanton as the whites in their annihilation of the buffalo, and that they almost succeeded in wiping out the continent's deer population.[26] In fact, in contemporary America while some whites attend Indian "sweats" to connect with their spiritual being, many Indian tribes are opening gambling casinos to gain access to wealth.

A more subtle revision of the classic western was Clint Eastwood's noirish western, *Unforgiven*. The film is dominated by black, rain swept prairie nights, morally corrupt characters, and the use of a rich chiaroscuro for interior scenes. Eastwood begins the film with a feminist twist, shooting from the point of view of the prostitutes of a frontier town (Big Whisky), who after one of their number is scarred by a cowboy, offer a reward to anybody who will kill him. From that point on the prostitutes become merely observers (though we are made conscious of their feelings and humanity—a rarity in a western) rather than central figures in a film that centers on William Munny (Clint Eastwood), an aging ex-outlaw, turned failed pig farmer, who has moved away from a life of murderous crime.

Nevertheless, Munny joins forces with a serene former partner, Ned Logan (Morgan Freeman), and a callow, blustery, myopic gunman, the "Schofield Kid" (Jaimz Woolvett), to get the reward. Their journey turns into an ironic view of the American West's cult of violence, and a saga of a redeemed man's momentary resurrection of his past, monstrous self, so he can avenge a friend's killing.

Big Whisky is dominated by a sadistic sheriff, "Little Bill" Baggett (Gene Hackman) who indulges in beatings and summary justice in order to keep the peace. When "English Bob" (Richard Harris), a droll, bullying paid killer, accompanied by his craven, obsequious amanuensis, dime novelist, W. W. Beauchamp (Saul Rubinek) comes to claim the prostitute's reward, "Little Bill" beats and humiliates him—debunking the novels written about Bob's supposed heroic reputation.

The film's power lies in its subverting the romanticization of violence in the Western: "English Bob" is all empty bravado and afraid of Baggett's intimidating games; the inept "Schofield Kid" who after killing his first man, begins to understand the nature of death, and wants no part of killing (e.g., "I'd rather be blind and ragged than dead."); and even Munny while delirious and feverish, speaks about his fear of dying. And in avenging the killing of Logan, the reformed Munny murders "Little Bill" and five of his deputies, vowing to come back and kill every man, woman, and child in Big Whiskey if they follow him. The supposedly exhausted Munny, who at the film's beginning is too inept to hit a can he practices shooting at, has now turned into a coolly, indomitable murderer who exemplifies D. H. Lawrence's judgment that the basic American soul consists of being "cold, isolate and a killer."[27] Unfortunately, Eastwood's practically unrivaled contemporary status as a heroic masculine icon undermined the film's critique of the western's usual romanticization of outlawry—leaving the audience identifying with rather than being repelled by his bloody actions.

One thing missing from all these attempts at evoking American culture's condition was any mention of social class. That, oddly enough, came from an unexpected source—the Academy Award-winning blockbuster *Titanic* (1997). Almost all of the discussion about the film prior to its winning of the Oscar for best picture usually centered on its decor and outstanding special effects such as submersible cameras and the remarkable depiction of the sinking of the supposedly unsinkable luxury ship. Further buzz came from the pre-pubescent girls who flocked to the film numerous times just to drool over young heartthrob Leonardo DiCaprio, who starred as the tragic, androgynously handsome Jack Dawson.

One who did mention the film's class content was Chinese Communist President and party leader, Jiang Zemin, who pronounced the film, "Marxist"[28] (undoubtedly a surprise to media moguls Sumner Redstone of Paramount, and archconservative Rupert Murdoch of Twentieth Century-Fox, who between them invested a record breaking $200 million in the epic tale). The Chinese leader was clearly focusing on the fact that within the flash of the film's dazzling special effects was the tiny germ of a story of love between the classes—the brief but indelible love affair beteen voluptuous, rebellious Rose (Kate Winslet) and impetuous bohemian artist, Jack.

This first class-steerage romance begins when genteely impoverished Rose, engaged, out of economic necessity, to a brutally controlling, sneering, wealthy Cal (Billy Zane), decides that her future as a bird in a gilded cage is more than she can bear, and attempts a rather picturesque suicide plunge from the prow of the doomed ship. Jack, of course, stops her and they begin a whirlwind love affair that incurs the wrath of both Cal and his villainous body guard, Spicer (David Warner), who try to murder Jack. In all this nonsensical, melodramatic derring-do, the rich, with a few exceptions, are depicted as snobbish, greedy, cold, and generally cowardly (Cal survives by getting into the lifeboats with the women and children, while Jack dies saving Rose), while most of the ship's vitality, honesty, and decency seems to reside below decks. Is it any wonder then that Jiang Zemin would applaud this movie?

One cinematic genre that went through a small renaissance was political satire. Possibly because Bill Clinton's behavior as president provided so much comic material for Leno and Letterman, a number of sophisticated political comedies were made in the nineties. They ranged from a roman-à-clef of Clinton's 1992 campaign, *Primary Colors* (1998), an almost prophetic anticipation of strategy employed by Clinton to divert attention from the White house scandals; *Wag the Dog* (1997); a radical, hip-hop inspired farce, *Bulworth* (1998); and a film about a high school class election that becomes a sly metaphor for adult political campaigns, *Election* (1999).

Based on political journalist Joe Klein's pseudonymous novel, *Primary Colors* went over much of the same ground that Chris Hegedus and D. A. Pennebaker's documentary *The War Room* covered back in 1993, with two particularly notable additions. The first was that the witty, politically incisive script was written by Elaine May and directed by Mike Nichols, who as a comedy team in the late fifties and early sixties built a reputation as brilliant satirists of contemporary manners and morals. The other was that *Primary Colors* places Bill and Hillary Clinton, aka Jack and Susan Stanton (John Travolta, Emma Thompson), at the film's center.

Travolta is almost perfect as the Clinton double—Jack Stanton—the governor of a southern state running for the presidency. His politically ruthless and seductive Stanton has the raspy accent, the body language, the empathetic handshake, the populist touch, and the gift for self-destruction that his real life counterpart has. In a similar fashion, Thompson captures Hillary's seriousness, efficiency, aggressiveness, and willingness to turn a blind eye to her husband's inabilty to keep his fly zippered. They operate with a single will when it comes to electing Jack Stanton president. It's that overarching ambition and Stanton's lack of discipline that touches and sometimes destroys all the people that surround them.

It includes Henry Burton (Adrian Lester), the "black George Stephanopoulos," a polite, idealistic grandson of a legendary civil rights leader, who signs on as their deputy campaign director. Henry's perspective is the dominant one in the film, but the character is too pallid to make his moral quandary and consciousness (should he quit or stay with a dirty, negative campaign that has good intentions?) of much dramatic interest.

Primary Colors, like the novel it is based on, is strongest when dealing with political strategies. It has a particularly astute u. Jerstanding of how idealism gets compromised in the quest for political power, and though critical of the Stanton's squalid tactics—it accepts that the political arena is not a place for moralists or those who refuse to be corrupted. Largely passed over by the public, *Primary Colors* may not have the psychological complexity of an *All the King's Men* (1949), but it's a lively, often wittily, incisive portrait of contemporary American politics.

Barry Levinson's (*Rain Man*) *Wag the Dog*, written by David Mamet and Hilary Henkin moves into the black comic, *Strangelove* realm. Its premise is that a sex scandal in the midst of a presidential campaign sends all his aides scurrying to provide damage control. They come up with a sardonic, self-assured, understated spinmeister, Conrad Brean (Robert De Niro), who decides to stage a war to divert attention from the president's problems. To aid him he reaches out to archetypal, narcissistic Hollywood producer Stanley Motss (Dustin Hoffman gives a scene stealing performance) because as Brean says, "war is show business."

The notion that there is no difference between political and media manipulation is not an original one. However, Stanley Motss' unflappable staging of the war with its special patriotic anthem, demonic, archterrorist enemy—"Albania"—and psychotic war hero, Sergeant William "old shoe" Schumann (Woody Harrelson at his most wild-eyed), is truly inspired. The whole production is augmented by songs, a made-for-television-funeral, and an eye for merchandizing tie-ins and back-end-deals (movies, t-shirts, a memorial clock).

About two-thirds through, the film begins to lose momentum and its comic conceit wears thin. Still, there is a clear-eyed view of political spin control, and of Hollywood's gift for manipulating the popular imagination, and the public's willingness to be seduced by it. It is also prophetic about what occurred during the impeachment process when Clinton ordered the bombing of Iraq for defying the United Nations, and was denounced by a number of Congressional Republicans for using a "wag the dog" strategy.[29]

If *Wag the Dog* can be viewed as a synonym for spin control, Warren Beatty's political farce, *Bulworth*, is a model for Hollywood-style radicalism. When we first see California Senator J. Billington Bulworth, Beatty's hero (Beatty directed, co-wrote, and starred in the film), he is unshaven, sleepless, surrounded by discarded junk food cartons, compulsively watching himself on TV campaign commercials, and breaking down. Bulworth was a sixties' left-liberal (there are photos of him with Bobby Kennedy and Martin Luther King, Jr.), and has recently begun to give platitudinous speeches attacking "welfare cheats" and doing obeisance to "family values." In absolute despair he takes out a $10 million life insurance policy, and hires a hit man to kill him.

Freed from the necessity of political caution, Bulworth attacks the Democratic Party's most loyal constituencies, telling blacks that the Party won't take you seriously until you drop O. J., and Hollywood Jews that "it's funny how lousy your stuff is. I guess the money turns everything to crap." However, after a night at a black after-hours club—dancing, listening to rap, snorting cocaine, and becoming infatuated with a beautiful black hit woman, Nina (Halle Berry)—Bulworth is transformed into a comic version of Mailer's white Negro. He then turns into a rap politician, awkwardly using hip-hop rhythms and rhymes to attack corporate dominance of politics and the media and even advocating socialism.

Ironically, this sudden attack on mainstream politics turns Bulworth into a popular hero, an election winner, and echoing the sixties—an assassination victim. Beatty's homily that a popular politician speaks truth to power at one's peril is undeniable. What is dubious in *Bulworth* is the sentimental thesis that the only source of authenticity, vitality, and salvation in America lies within the black inner city, since every other strata is tarnished by the money culture. The inner city ethos transforms Bulworth from a buttoned-down, cynical, political opportunist into a socially committed South Central Los Angeles home boy complete with knit cap, shades, and short pants, who can convince a drug dealing thug, L. J. (Don Cheadle), to magically become a community activist.

The inner city also produces a Nina who, when she stops strutting and scowling, sounds like a Marxist Harvard professor eloquently describing the de-industrialization of the ghetto and the destructive power of a consumer culture built on self-gratification as the reasons for dysfunction in the black community. It is precisely the community's self-destructiveness and fragmentation and the basis in reality of those ominous black street stereotypes that Beatty uses for their comic value (and to sometimes provide a glimpse of the humanity underneath the posturing) that make his vision seem simplistic. Beatty has trotted out the tattered, absurd notion that life on the bottom is intrinsically more decent and more meaningful than the lives of the more comfortable and privileged.

Beatty's banal solution to the racial divide is no better. His idea that we've "all got to keep fuckin each other until we are the same color," is at best simplistic. As a radical solution it sounds remarkably like the one offered by neo-conservative critic Norman Podhoretz's sixties' essay (in his liberal phase), "My Negro Problem and Ours." Similarly, the homeless Rastaman's (the Marxist poet, Amiri Baraka) repeated admonition to Bulworth, "Don't be a ghost! you got to be a spirit," though supposedly a call to action, sounds more like nostalgia for a more confrontational era.

Given Hollywood's usual bland political perspective, a film like *Bulworth*, that attacks capitalism, can be seen, by comparison, as an ambitious, politically radical work. It is also graced with one of Beatty's strongest performances as the vulnerable, despairing Jay Bulworth, and it is alive with farcical humor and truly imaginative moments. Still, its attempt to build tension with a murder plot is lame and intrusive. And, more important, its critique of American politics degenerates into ultra-left, sixties' romanticism.

The political satire *Election*, by not taking clear sides, avoids moving in an ideological direction. Directed by Alexander Payne, whose previous, much less subtle film *Citizen Ruth* (1996) provided a satiric look at both right to life and abortion rights advocates. Set once again in Payne's hometown of Omaha, Nebraska, the film centers on the election of a class president at the almost all-white, ironically named, George Washington Carver High.

The chief and initially unopposed contender is Tracy Flick (Reese Witherspoon), a Liddy Dole clone, all ferocious ambition and self-righteousness. Tracy diligently plans her campaign for class president down to the smallest detail, including how many sticks of gum she can give to each student as a campaign gift. What she doesn't count on is the antipathy of her teacher and the film's prime narrator, Jim McAllister (Matthew Broderick). For McAllister, though he keeps an outwardly controlled demeanor around Tracy, her constant attempts to gain his attention and approval in class are as grating as chalk scratching on a blackboad. So in order to thwart Tracy, McAllister convinces the sweet, dim jock Paul Metzler (Chris Klein) to run against her.

Although the film initially seems to tilt against the comically monstrous Tracy, especially given her blatant drive for success, there is also a strain of pathos in her solipsism and isolation. Payne's gift is to contrast Tracy's blind ambition with the intelligent McAllister's own lack of self-awareness. Trapped in a dead marriage and a dead-end job, McAllister doesn't recognize that some of his malice toward Tracy is also motivated by jealousy of her youth, energy, and promising future—qualities so lacking in his own life. *Election* became more than a just film that uses a high school political campaign as a satiric metaphor for the ego-driven emptiness of American politics—it also turns into an understated, sly depiction of human frailty. The ambiguity of Payne's film derives from his empathy for all his characters' flawed natures.

Though political films like *Primary Colors*, *Wag the Dog*, and *Election* dealt with an important issue—the cynical degradation of our political culture and discourse—it was only *Bulworth* that touched upon the most troubling and seemingly intractible problem of all—race. The race question was exacerbated in the early nineties by conditions in the African-American community which found at least fifty-six percent of black families headed by a woman, forty-five percent of black children living below the poverty line,[30] and black unemployment generally triple the rate of white unemployment. This also had a profound effect on crime levels, which saw over one million black males in prison in the nineties, and the likelihood that one black male in twenty-one would be murdered in their lifetime, most likely by another black man.[31]

These appalling statistics and the culture of social fragmentation and despair they conveyed, inspired the most significant wave of films about blacks that had come out of Hollywood since the blaxsploitation films of the seventies. Indeed one of the curtain-raising films of this trend, John Singleton's *Boyz N' the Hood* (1991), begins with a screen credit that announces the fact the one in twenty-one black males is likely to die as a result of homicide. The film follows up that proclamation with an unsubtle, didactic tale of three young Boyz, Tre (Cuba Gooding Jr.), Doughboy (Ice Cube), and Ricky (Morris Chestnut) growing up on the blood soaked streets of South Central Los Angeles. The film interweaves their rites of passage with the message that the black male's salvation lies in the embrace of patriarchal authority—a strong single mother being insufficient. *Boyz* drives that point home by having the guidance and discipline of Tre's father, the righteous, Afrocentric Furious Styles (Larry Fishburne), saving him from the seductions of street culture and the fate of the promising athlete Ricky, who is murdered, and Doughboy's equally doomed gangstadom.

What was disturbing about the film was that its depiction of drive-by shootings and use of crosscut chase sequences had the most appeal for the young black males in the audience rather than the film's deftly textured evocation of street and neighborhood life and exhortations on black history, neighborhood control, safe sex, the white conspiracy, and the need for black enterprise. In fact, there were numerous incidents of reported gang violence that occurred throughout the country in the wake of the film's theatrical release; a pattern repeated by the Hughes Brothers' *Menace II Society* (1993)—a film with somewhat similar themes and characters.

Menace II Society, however, was as apolitical, dark, and nihilistic as *Boyz N' the Hood* was hortatory. (Neither of the two films was as socially critical and evocative as Spike Lee's *Clockers* (1995), both a powerful lament and attack against the pathology of inner-city life that was much less commercially successful.) The Hughes Brothers' may have seen their frightening and cold *Menace II Society* as avoiding glorifying inner city violence and depicting it as repellent and oppressive. However, the film's casual drug dealing, ripping people off, and arbitrary killing, and the boys' brutal victimization of women elicited cheers and catcalls from inner-city and suburban adolescent audiences. Not only does blood flow as freely as malt liquor in Menace II Society, but there is hardly even a trace of hope to be found in the story of the anti-heroic Caine (Tyrin Turner) and his friends, as there was for the sweet Tre in Boyz. Menace II does include an authoritative black teacher, Mr. Butler (Charles Dutton) who talks to the young men about responsibility and community and a few other characters struggling to get out of the inner city (through playing football or becoming a Muslim), but it is the directionless lives and gratuitous violence ("you are never going to know what's going to happen and when") accompanied by a heavy rap score that dominates the film. In fact, Caine's description of his friend the uncontrolled, murderous O Dog (Larenz Tate) that, "he was America's nightmare, young, black and didn't give a fuck," seems to have been meant to apply to a whole generation of poor black males.

In contrast to Tre's loving parents (his mother is caring, educated, and has a good job), Caine's were drug users, dealers, and murderers, and his mentor, Pernell (Glenn Plummer), was serving a life sentence. Nothing can save Caine—the love of a good woman, the Christian faith of his grandparents, or the black nationalism of one of his friends. Caine's fate seems inevitable. For as Mr. Butler says, "The hunt is on, and you're the prey."

Some of the harshest criticisms of these films came from blacks who felt that films like these projected a distorted image of black life. One black writer wrote that, "The tragedy of the present black film revival is that too many films concentrate on these lost souls at the expense of the truly fascinating stories of thousands of young black people who are succeeding beyond the wildest dreams of my generation."[32]

These critics undoubtedly spoke for a new generation of black men and women who had managed to become middle class. By 1995, aided by affirmative action and the Clinton prosperity that increased black home ownership and wages, at least fifty percent of African-Americans considered themselves middle class. Also, whereas in 1960 only seven percent of blacks had ever been to college, by the nineties that figure was over twenty-one percent.[33] A group this large, however nebulous and uneasy the reality of their middle class status was, provided a sizable audience that was attractive to Hollywood producers. It moved them to make more films, in the mid- and late nineties, directed by both white and black filmmakers, committed to black family values and centering on mobile, middle-class black characters, rather than continuing to produce films focusing on inner city violence and gangbangers.

Many of the films were romantic comedies. They ranged from Forest Whitaker's Waiting to Exhale (1995) to Kevin Sullivan's How Stella Got Her Groove Back (1998) to Malcolm Lee's The Best Man (1999). Waiting to Exhale was a commercial hit, based on Terry McMillan's best selling novel, that equally appealed to both a black middle-class female and white female audiences. The film deals with four black women friends Savannah (Whitney Houston), a TV producer, Bernadine (Angela Basset), a divorced corporate executive, Robin (Lila Rochon), an insurance company executive, and Gloria (Loretta Devine), the owner of a beauty salon, and their man problems. The film is a paean to beautiful, successful, black women, while suggesting that most black men are too insensitive and exploitative to be worth pursuing. *Waiting to Exhale* obviously was meant to appeal to a new black middle-class woman more attracted to the lyrics of a romantic ballad than the nihilism of a rap song, and more likely to be found turning the pages of *Essence* and *Glamour* than the Moynihan Report.

Another film, George Tillman Jr.'s *Soul Food* (1997), eschews romantic comedy for an extended homily on the need for black family solidarity and black male pride. When family matriarch, Big Mama Jo (Irma P. Hall), an earthy, wise character that anyone familiar with Lorraine Hansberry's *A Raisin in the Sun* would recognize, goes into a coma and dies, her family consisting of her three beautiful daughters, Maxine (Vivien Fox), Terry (Venessa Williams), Lady Bird (Nia Long), and their husbands begins to self-destruct. However, little Ahmed (Brandon Hammond), Big Mama Jo's doting grandson, cannily brings the feuding sisters and their husbands together by reviving the family's forty-year-old tradition of a Sunday soul food dinner. *Soul Food's* aims are salutary, and it touches perceptively on some aspects of black middle-class life, but the film is essentially no more than sentimental soap opera centering on black rather than white characters.

Fortunately all black films weren't either hood films or mediocre homages to the new black middle class. Black independent filmmakers such as Julia Dash's stylized *Daughters of the Dust* (1991) explored the Gullah heritage of blacks, evoking the oral tradition of the sea islands that lie off the coast of South Carolina and Georgia. Similarly, Charles Burnett's fresh *To Sleep with Anger* (1990) combined black folk material and a touch of mysticism and prose poetry with a realistic depiction of Los Angeles black middle-class life, in the tale of a friend, from their rural Southern past, the charming, devilish Harry (Danny Glover), who insinuates himself into the family and nearly destroys it. Later in the decade, a film like Kasi Lemmon's *Eve's Bayou* (1997) dealt with a child's eye view of her parents' troubled marriage in a self-enclosed black enclave in 1960s Louisiana. Although these films achieved deserved critical acclaim and even some international festival awards, none of these films captured the imagination of a wider audience, either black or white.

What was equally surprising was the failure of two highly touted films about the African-American experience from two of the most successful entertainers of the nineties, Oprah Winfrey and Steven Spielberg. Winfrey, whose syndicated TV talk show was virtually the television bible of legions of American women, seemed practically a shoo-in to attract a large cross-over audience. However, her production of Nobel Laureate Tony Morrison's poetic and bleak *Beloved* was a failure both with audiences and critics. Part of the problem was due to the difficulties in translating Morrison's metaphor and symbol-clogged novel to the screen. One may also attribute its failure to the bleakness of a film dealing with a former slave Sethe's (Winfrey) memories of the child she killed to gain her freedom being resurrected by the appearance of a mysterious black woman (Thandie Newton), who embodies the spirit of that child. Unfortunately, it was probably too much of an emotional stretch for an audience that associated the positive thinking talk show hostess with the hugs of absolution and tears of renewal that were regular features of her highly rated TV show.

In the same way, Spielberg, who succeeded with almost everything he touched in the nineties, failed with his attempt to tell the story of the *Amistad* (1997), the Spanish slave ship that was taken over by a slave mutiny, and which became a symbolic battle ground for abolitionists and slaveholders in the antebellum United States. Spielberg's film was graced by two impressive performances from Djimon Hounsou, as Cinque, the acknowledged leader of the revolt, and Anthony Hopkins, as former President John Quincy Adams, who defended the slaves before the Supreme Court. However, with its repetitious courtroom scenes, its demonization of the pro-slavery forces, and its inability to have the slaves and their defenders really communicate with one another, the film lacked dramatic energy, preventing it from rising beyond the level of an interesting historical tableau.

Though a critical and box office failure *Amistad* was only a modest blemish on the directorial reputation of Spielberg, who had risen to a point somewhere between genius and sainthood as a result of his 1993 film, *Schindler's List*. Adapted from Thomas Keneally's semi-documentary novel about Oskar Schindler, a Nazi Party member and wartime profiteer, who became a "righteous gentile" by saving the lives of over 1100 Jews in Poland during World War II. *Schindler's List* not only won Spielberg an Academy Award for best director, it also established him in Hollywood, as a morally serious artist, who at same time, demonstrated that he could be perfectly at home with the bottom line.

Grappling with the theme of the Holocaust presented problems for any artist, even one as talented and singularly knowledgeable about the cinematic and dramatic potential of film as Spielberg. First and foremost of these was the terrible fear of possibly trivializing and vulgarizing such an apocalyptic and horrific event. There were critics like George Steiner who had written that "the world of Auschwitz lies outside of speech as it lies outside of reason."[34] Still, there was the compelling need, despite the utter desolation and hopelessness of the experience, to bear witness to these crimes, which had inspired such stylistically and intellectually different documentaries as Alain Resnais' elegant, understated *Night and Fog* (1955) and Claude Lanzmann's much harsher, more trenchant and unadorned *Shoah* (1985), and Joseph Losey's hauntingly ambiguous fictional film, *Mr. Klein* (1976). Even Hollywood had produced credible Holocaust works such as Sidney Lumet's powerful evocation of the Holocaust survivor in *The Pawnbroker* (1965) and Alan J. Pakula's earnest but melodramatic version of William Styron's novel, *Sophie's Choice* (1982).

Spielberg succeeded in walking a tightrope between what might have become crass exploitation and what is a hightened realistic representation, shot in a formally virtuosic and self-conscious manner—dramatic lighting, a voluptuous black and white mise-en-scène, cross-cutting, fluid montage, hand-held camera shooting, and Yiddish folk songs on the sound track. Most of these formal elements are artfully used in the powerful sequences depicting the destruction of the Krakow ghetto and the selection process (the apotheosis of Nazi objectification), where the Nazis made everybody undress, and decide who was able-bodied enough to become slave laborers and shipped off the others to die in the death camps. There are emotionally stirring touches such as the little girl in the red coat (seen from Schindler's point of view)—a vivid contrast to the film's black and white footage—who wanders innocently amidst the ferocious clearing of the Krakow ghetto, only to wind up later as a limp, crumpled tiny body on a pile of corpses. Spielberg turns her into a striking symbol for all the innocents that the Nazis annihilated.

Despite Spielberg's skill at classical narrative construction and genius for emotionally moving an audience, the film is not free of problems. A central difficulty is the mystery of Schindler's character. Liam Neeson may have star looks, and shot from a low angle tends to overwhelm all the other characters, like the heroic protagonists of many Hollywood films, but he is utterly convincing as the womanizing, hedonistic conman turned courageous humanitarian. Nonetheless, the film grants no real insight to what moves Schindler to do what he did, or shed much light on a character who before the war was almost arrested on his wedding day, and who after the war ended, appropriated charitable contributions meant to help his wife. The film never gets inside his psyche, and beyond Schindler's suggested moral revulsion with Nazi genocide, we never truly learn what inspired his selfless humanity and often reckless heroism.

Perhaps Spielberg and his co-screenwriter Steve Zaillian felt that an explanation might emerge in the contrast between Schindler's mere roguery and the demonic murderousness of German SS officer Amon Goeth (Ralph Fiennes). The psychopathic Goeth, who is placed in charge of the Plaszow concentration camp (created as a slave labor camp after the clearing of the Krakow ghetto) is practically Schindler's double in his corruption, and love of wine and women. However, in contrast to Schindler who as his connection with the Jews increases so does his commitment and protectiveness of them, Goeth brutally revels in his power of life and death over the camp inmates and treats the Jews as vermin whom he can kill on a whim. One difficulty with Fiennes' performance and Spielberg's conception of Goeth, is that however depraved he is, he emanates a romantic, larger-than-life aura along with his monstrous villainy.

Since Spielberg focuses so intensely on the German characters, the Jewish ones, with the exception of the shrewd, disciplined Itzhak Stern (Ben Kingsley), are less individuated and depicted mainly as characters in swiftly moving anecdotal vignettes, in order to personalize the Holocaust for the movie audience. Their presence provides the audience with virtuous victims to identify with, but they remain basically opaque figures who look more like Hollywood actors rather than people living close to the abyss. On the other hand, Stern is portrayed as a man of great self-control whose business skill is necessary and complements Schindler's talent for making contacts and his more imaginative personality. At first, Stern is wary and resentful of Schindler, but as Schindler's plans become clear to him his feelings blossom into respect and finally warmth. Stern is the one Jewish hero in the film, for it's his mastery of detail and quiet courage that keeps the factory going and helps save the lives of the 1100 Jews.

What's more troubling about Schindler's List were the moments of Hollywood kitsch that run through the film. There is the heavily ironic scene (civilization merged with barbarism) during the liquidation of the Krakow ghetto where a SS officer plays classical piano as the round-up and murder of the Jews continue. And there are cliff-hanging moments where a heroic Schindler rides to rescue a trainload of his Jews who have been wrongly sent to Auschwitz-Birkenau. Another scene melodramatically builds audience tension and fear (in a quasi-Hitchcock mode) by having Schindler's terrified women workers think they are entering an Auschwitz gas chamber, but then finding themselves in a shower room. Finally there are the crass moments of Schindler's lachrymose farewell speech (much of it shot in close-up and theatrically lit) to his rescued workers just before their liberation, and his teary guilt-stricken breakown over the fact that he didn't save more of them. It's almost as if the Holocaust occurred so Schindler could be morally redeemed. All of these scenes, and others where music is used on the soundtrack to heighten feeling, are rendered to wring the most sorrow and tears out of events that could be shot in a less manipulative, artificial manner and still arouse profound emotion.

One can go on picking holes in a film that sacrifices character for visual power and beauty, and narrative excitement and the creation of a world of good and evil for a meditation on the complex nature of the Holocaust. Though given Spielberg's penchant for using the whole arsenal of film technique, Schindler's List is in comparison to his other films, a work of social real-

ism. It is also one of the most optimistic films made about the Holocaust—
centering on survivors rather than the millions who went to their deaths.
However, the fact is that it is Spielberg, working in the mainstream Hollywood
tradition, not Lanzmann's great interview-based *Shoah* (Lanzmannn refused to
use any direct representation of the past), who has made the larger public conscious of the horrors of the Holocaust. If we view *Schindler's List* as a work of
popular culture not documentary realism or high art, Spielberg's achievement
is a considerable one.

The film also did raise the whole issue of the Holocaust and its use in American life. For one thing many critics objected to what they perceived as an
"Americanization of the Holocaust,"[35] the film emphasizing American cultural values such as the need of our popular culture to create heroes, especially
in an event which was noteworthy not so much for its heroes as its victims.
Others objected to the film's suggesting that the emergence of the State of Israel was in some way the logical outcome of the Holocaust—a theme that
Spielberg repeats in the final moments of the film when the surviving
Schindlerjuden, accompanied by actors and extras in the movie, place stones
on Schindler's gravestone in Israel. Many also saw the symbol of the Holocaust
being used as a means of perpetuating the image of Jewish "victimhood," when
the reality is that they are one of America's most successful minorities. In addition, the memory of the Holocaust helped sustain a group consciousness for a
generation of Jews whose religious and ethnic ties were generally weakening
because of both intermarriage and the general prosperity, opportunity, and
power that Jews enjoy in America.

There were those who even challenged the right of Jews to monopolize the
use of the term holocaust, and that the notion of genocide applied exclusively
to the murderous behavior that had occurred in Europe between 1939–45. For
example, some African-American scholars referring to the millions of blacks
who died in the "middle passage" or were worked to death on American plan-
tations, as a "black holocaust."[36] And the 1.5 million Armenians massacred by
the Turks during the First World War generally perceived themselves as the
first victims of twentieth-century genocide. As a result, the words genocide
and holocaust seemed above all to take on an expanded meaning, and became
part of the sacralization of victimhood in the nineties. No better place was this
on display than in the use of the word genocide that some gay activists appropriated to describe the effect of the AIDS plague on the gay community.

For most of its history Hollywood's relation to gays and lesbians was best described by critic Vito Russo (himself a victim of AIDS) as the "celluloid
closet."[37] However, though overt depictions of gay characters or gay themes in
films were taboo, they often appeared in covert fashion in dialogue, double en-
tendres, and characters whose physical and personal characteristics were so
blatant that only the dimmest audience members would miss what was being

suggested. Being closeted extended from screen depictions to the lives of a long list of homosexual actors, directors, and producers who were forced to live double lives to survive professionally.

In the eighties, Hollywood, confronted by the more open evidence of homosexual lifestyles produced by the growth of the gay and lesbian movement, responded with tepid films such as *Making Love* (1982), about the coming out of a repressed gay doctor. However, the AIDS epidemic (known as the "gay cancer"), that started in the early eighties, presented filmmakers with a challenge. On the one hand, it was a headline story with almost daily casualty counts, including famous Hollywood names such as Rock Hudson publicly succumbing to the disease. Consequently, films that made people aware of the disease almost constituted a public service. It was also a topic filled with just the kinds of dramatic emotions and triumphs over adversity that was stock in trade for Hollywood filmmakers. However, on the other hand there was the fear that these films would repell the more religious and homophobic members of the audience, and it would show up in what Hollywood revered more than topicality, public service, or sentiment—their profit margins.

One of the early films dealing with AIDS was the generally critically well-received, *Long Time Companions* (1990), (it even garnered an Academy Award nomination for one of its leads, Bruce Davison). The film sympathetically traced the lives of a group of upper-middle-class gay friends from their first hearing about AIDS until it tragically alters all their lives. It was a small budget, straight forward film—a touch too sanitized—that didn't receive the audience response it deserved. In contrast, Jonathan Demme's—an idiosyncratic director whose best work (e.g., *Something Wild*, *Citizens Band*) identified with individuals at odds with the social system—$25 million production of *Philadelphia* (1993) reached into the mainstream. His film gained for Tom Hanks, who played the AIDS-stricken lawyer Andrew Beckett, his first Academy Award for best actor. However, *Philadelphia* is much less about AIDS, or homosexual lifestyles, than it is about homophobia. Denzel Washington playing Joe Miller, a macho, quick-witted, ambulance-chasing lawyer, is hired by Beckett to take his case against his WASP, white-shoe law firm for wrongful termination, and is the movie's real center.

Beckett, a personable, up and coming star at his firm, had been summarily dismissed when evidence of his AIDS became unmistakeable. While Miller takes the case, perhaps because as a black man he can sympathize with the kind of discrimination that Beckett is confronted with, he's unprepared for the scrutiny that his own homophobic attitudes soon come under. From taking jibes about his own sexual preferences, to even another black gay man trying to pick him up, as well as fears that contact with Beckett might place his own family in jeopardy, Miller has to confront his own ignorance and prejudices about homosexuals and AIDS. Miller is the surrogate for the movie audience that is supposed to identify with him exorcising his homophobic demons and achieving some form of liberal tolerance and understanding.

Throughout it all the even-tempered Beckett maintains a strangely imperturbable stoicism quite at odds with his scene-by-scene physical deterioration. There is one scene in the film, however, where Beckett conveys intense feeling, and the film rises to high art. When Beckett and Miller meet to discuss the former's upcoming testimony, the film's frames go red with a passionate glare, and seem from a high overhead angle, Beckett glides around his loft with an IV in his arm ecstatically listening to Maria Callas' aria "O Mamma Morta" from Giordano's *Andrea Chenier*. He translates the words for Joe, especially its brilliant chorus, "I am oblivion . . . Ah! I am love." In that moment, Joe, moved by Beckett's sensitivity and heartache, starts to transcend his own discomfort with gayness, and begins to grasp their shared humanity.

Unfortunately, not everything in *Philadelphia* is quite as brilliant as that moment. For example, Beckett's old law firm colleagues are portrayed as kind of patrician devils, especially it's gay-loathing senior partner (Jason Robards). In contrast Andrew's suburban family, with Joanne Woodward as his mother, is practically a hallmark card of unconditional support and love, as is his non-sexual relationship (the film carefully avoids dealing with gay sex) with his nurturing partner, Miguel (Antonio Banderas). Demme has made a simplified, conventional (a great many courtroom confrontations) thesis film that is both moving and extremely safe. Andy Beckett is merely a nice man who happens to be gay and is suffering from a deadly disease. The film never goes any deeper than that in characterizing him, or in evoking the gay social world. It's the type of skillful, emotionally manipulative, self-congratulatory film that Hollywood often makes so it can display its liberalism while simultaneously leaving the audience emotionally and intellectually undisturbed.

The antithesis of being a safe and simplified film was Kimberly Pierce's gender bending *Boys Don't Cry* (1999). The film is based on the 1993 murder of Brandon Teena, a cross dresser, who was killed because she/he had stolen the affections of the girlfriend of a Nebraska ex-con. *Boys Don't Cry* is a direct, emotionally honest film, and Hillary Swank, who won a 1999 Academy Award for best actress for her performance as Brandon Teena/Teena Brandon, captured the recklessness, eroticism, and pathos of Brandon Teena, who could no longer bear her life as a woman and decided to pass as a man.

At first, Brandon seemingly lives out her dream by linking up with two young thuggish sociopaths, John Lotter (Peter Sarsgaard) and Tom Nissen (Brendan Sexton III), and Lotter's girlfriend, the tough, deadpan, but dreamy Lana (Chloe Sevigny), who works in a spinach factory. Ironically, it is Brandon's feminine characteristics, especially her/his gentleness, which stand in such marked contrast to the cruelty of Lotter and Nissen, that first gain Lana's attention and then her love. It is this tenderness that also marks their lovemaking scenes in which Brandon somehow manages to get away with his masquerade.

When Brandon/Teena's impersonation is revealed, Lotter and Nissen's subsequent brutal rape and murder of her is almost too difficult to watch. In the process Brandon/Teena is turned into an almost sainted victim, albeit one that is a petty criminal and whose pitiable fantasy life consists of wanting to go to Graceland with Lana. Furthermore, not since Richard Brooks' production of Truman Capote's *In Cold Blood* (1967) has a film captured, in its depiction of Lana's dysfunctional family life and its portrait of a social world consisting of shabby homes and trailers, cheerless roadhouses, and roads stretching out to nowhere, the bleakness of middle-American life. (Though there are times when the characters talk hopefully about the future where Pierce, by using striking lighting, grants the barren landscape an eerie beauty.) *Boys Don't Cry* is an unsentimental film that avoids condescending to its intellectually limited, socially marginal characters, and feels both psychologically and socially true.

Images of victimization were hardly the exclusive province of gays and blacks in the nineties. While the images of women projected by Hollywood were decidedly more positive, they were nonetheless permeated with ambiguity. On the one hand, Hollywood recognized the commercial potential of films that presented a positive image of women; on the other, it all to frequently presented those images in traditional genre packages that could subtly undermine that positive image. Two films, *A League of Their Own* (1992) and *Thelma and Louise* (1991), illustrate this paradox.

Penny Marshall's *A League of Their Own* depicts a neglected chapter in American sports history—the women's baseball league that was founded during World War II to help satisfy Americans' craving for the national pasttime while many of the male ballplayers were away at war. The film centers on the creation and rise of the Rockford Peaches, one of the premier teams in that league. At the center of this contrived, sentimental story is the tension between the Hinson sisters. There is Dottie (Geena Davis), the married, totally professional, and highly talented catcher for the Peaches, and her angry younger pitcher sister, Kit (Lori Petty), who is petulant and clearly jealous of her sister's superior athletic ability. However, this film's only real virtue is capturing the bonding that went on among these female ballplayers who had to confront all sorts of male condescension and contempt because they just wanted to play ball. For example, the league had the players take charm lessons, and a number were recruited more for how they looked in short skirts rather than their baseball skills. They also had to endure the sexist jeering of male fans and promotional slogans such as, "Catch a foul ball, and get a kiss."

Despite its feminist perspective, the film all too frequently lapses into stereotypes (the team owner is a miser, the chief scout a boor, and the manager

[Tom Hanks] a sexist drunk who predictably is transformed into a proponent of women's baseball). Ugly girl jokes abound, and the film even has Madonna playing a promiscuous character called "all the way May." The film is well-intentioned, but permeated with cliches and patronizing stereotypes that subvert its supposed purpose.

It was controversy rather than condescension which surrounded flashy, high concept director Ridley Scott (*Alien, Bladerunner*) and first-time scriptwriter Callie Khourie's *Thelma and Louise*. The film revolves around two women whose weekend getaway turns into a violent chase through an endless highway of motels, diners, and gas stations, and a stunningly shot American Southwest landscape of plains, deserts, and John Ford's Monument Valley. Some critics charged that the adventures of the initially dizzy, guileless, and oppressed housewife Thelma (Geena Davis), and the tough, wary, independent waitress Louise (Susan Sarandon), whose violent response to an attempted rape send them on a cross-country crime- and male-chauvinist-pig-bashing spree, were examples of "toxic feminism," "a paean to transformative violence," and female "fascism."[38]

Much of the angry critical response to *Thelma and Louise* was engendered by the violence committed by the two women. However, it really exemplified the double standard at work from critics who barely raised an eyebrow when Arnold Schwarzenegger blew away dozens of people in *Total Recall* (1990) or who seemed to prefer women depicted as prostitutes transformed by a man into a Cinderella in the romantic comedy hit, *Pretty Woman* (1990).

Critical outbursts aside, *Thelma and Louise* was a shrewd, entertaining, seamlessly constructed work of pop feminism. Both Thelma and Louise free themselves of the constraints of home, husband, and society, and turn themselves into tough female outlaws. Feckless, sloppy, and a passive doormat for her idiotic, philandering husband Daryl (Christopher McDonald), Thelma is magically transformed (by a man) from bimbo into an erotically charged desperado who takes charge of her own destiny. Louise, a bit less stereotyped and more self-aware, is at first rigid and controlling, but learns to loosen up and take life on its own terms.

The most frequently raised criticism of the film was its male bashing. The film contains a multitude of female revenge fantasies involving punishing would-be rapists, crude truckdrivers, and gestapo-like state troopers. The other male characters are also simplistic and include Thelma's aforementioned husband, a cartoonish male chauvinist, and handsome J. D. (Brad Pitt), the manipulative convenience store bandit-hitchhiker who steals Thelma and Louise's money (not, however, before he treats Thelma to her first orgasm). More interesting and a touch more complicated is the character of Jimmy (Michael Madsen), Louise's hard-drinking, flawed, commitment-shy musician boyfriend, who loves her enough to let her go, even after he proposes. Finally, there is the one and only truly good male, the sympathetic detective Hal Slocumbe (Harvey Keitel), who develops a paternalistic affection for Thelma and Louise—whose lives he wants to save.

The most oft criticized aspect of the film even by feminists was Thelma and Louise's suicidal ending. Cornered by a posse of state troopers and FBI agents, the outlaw pair affirm their friendship with a kiss, and opt to drive off a cliff rather than surrender. While some feminists saw it as a symbolic liberating gesture—the only choice for women in a male-dominated, oppressive society—many others saw the finale as overdetermined, and the notion that a woman's freedom is discovered in death as absurd.

However, Thelma and Louise were trapped by more than just society or a posse; most of their actions were determined by the conventions of the road movie. Like *Bonnie and Clyde* (1967), *Easy Rider* (1969), and *Butch Cassidy and the Sundance Kid* (1969), death was inevitably the outcome of the journeys taken by the films' protagonists. Still, *Thelma and Louise* is the kind of genre film that remains open to multiple and often contradictory interpretations. One could even see the film's objectification of men as a sly, ironic comment on how countless Hollywood action films have treated women.

Although *Thelma and Louise* is open to manifold interpretations—it's a film without much intellectual or emotional depth. What is significant about the film, however, is not its complex treatment of feminist consciousness, but its gift for creating powerful pop images of female independence.

That the genre conventions didn't always have to act as a straitjacket was demonstrated by Quentin Tarantino's *Pulp Fiction* (1994). Tarantino, a movie autodidact, whose film school was a Southern California local videostore, directed the relentlessly energetic, heist-gone-bad film, *Reservoir Dogs* (1992), whose virtuoso profanity and multitude of pop culture references vaulted it almost overnight into an independent film cult classic. His less linear, larger scale *Pulp Fiction* was an ironic, postmodernist reworking of familiar film noir cliches such as the boxer who refuses to take a dive in a fixed fight, the gangster's moll with a roving eye, and the camaraderie of two professional killers.

Tarantino's postmodernist style was characterized by putting aside the traditional linear story line in favor of four overlapping stories that contain characters from each story as well as moving back and forward in time. His arch, self-conscious dialogue was filled with comic riffs such as hit men Vincent Vega (John Travolta) explaining to his volatile, born-again partner Jules Winnfield (Samuel L. Jackson wearing an Afro wig) that the cheeseburger in the Paris McDonald's was called a "Royale with cheese." There are also scenes where grisly violence explodes only to turn into moments of black humor, such as when Vincent accidentally and literally blows a victim's brains out, and the duo have to turn to Jules' hen-pecked nervous friend Jimmie (Tarantino) and the avuncular, ultra-fastidious fixer, Wolf (Harvey Keitel), to help them clean up the mess. Playing Jimmie, who's married to a black woman, Tarantino self-consciously demonstrates how hip and beyond conventional liberalism he is, by tossing the word "nigger" around every chance he can get.

Nor does the film stint on pop culture references. For instance, Vincent takes his boss' glamorous, coke-sniffing wife, Mia (Uma Thurman), to Jack Rabbit Slim's, a fifties retro restaurant that features Douglas Sirk steaks and a Buddy Holly martini, served by a waiter who looks like James Dean, and includes a twist concert introduced by an Ed Sullivan impersonator. There are also clear narrative references to films like *Kiss Me Deadly* (1955) and *Deliverance* (1972), and television shows like *Charlie's Angels*. In addition, to the delight of postmodernist theorists, Vincent dances a self-reflexive twist with Mia that resurrects memories of Travolta's greatest hit, his star-making role as Tony Manero in *Saturday Night Fever* (1977).

Tarantino's film is smart, entertaining, stylish (striking camera angles, 360-degree pans), and permeated with macho posturing. There are also moments where Tarantino's gothic, horror comic touches, such as the sado-masochism and male rape scenes where Butch and the black, mob boss Marcellus Wallace (Ving Rhames) are imprisoned by a couple of redneck neo-Nazis, go over the top. What is most disturbing about Tarantino's films are their rejection of the real world, and their lack of moral center. His films are about nothing more than words and images that, with originality and wit, parody Hollywood and television genres for audiences who are so insulated from the world that they desire nothing more.

In contrast to Tarantino's work there were films, particularly in the early and late nineties, that tried to consciously say something about American culture and society and about the emotional state of angry white males. Whether that male's anger stemmed from the loss of economic and social status as a consequence of the economic downturn that hit middle-class, mid-level management males particularly hard in the beginning of the decade, or the existential malaise that entrapped some middle-class suburban males in the more prosperous second half of the nineties, the results were usually the same—self-destruction.

In Joel Schumacher's *Falling Down* (1993) Michael Douglas plays a laid off defense worker, William Foster—an exasperated and volatile man just waiting to explode. On an extremely hot day in Los Angeles, he takes a murderous journey across a sun-baked nightmare city violently acting out what the director views as the fantasies of many ordinary urban dwellers. Confronted with a compendium of irritating to profound urban ills—from traffic jams, graffiti, jostling crowds, and general boorishness, to smog, gangbangers, homelessness, and the omnipresence of guns—the film's brush-cutted Everyman strikes out at a variety of urban stereotypes including dour Korean grocers and Latino thugs. (It is interesting that blacks and gays, who make up significant portions of Los Angeles's population, are left untouched by his rampage.)

Falling Down is an exploitative, cartoon-like film that tries to have it both ways. Foster or D-FENS (his monicker) is enough of an abusive father and trigger-happy sociopath to repel audiences with his behavior, but also someone whose confusion over his loss of economic viability and social marginality and his desire for revenge they can identify with. The film makes D-FENS more sympathetic by juxtaposing him with a neo-Nazi, homophobic manager of an Army Navy surplus store (played by Frederick Forrest) who he rejects as "a sick asshole." The film also suggests that D-FENS' fury is clearly more justifiable than the white trash racist's. Schumacher's film ultimately illuminates little about the condition of American cities or the resentment and rage of an economically displaced Everyman—sacrificing social meaning for a fast-paced narrative and kinetic violence.

English theater director Sam Mendes' first film, the Oscar-winning *American Beauty* (1999), also focuses on an angry white man who wants out—the sour, ironic Lester Burnham (Kevin Spacey, who delivers every line with dazzling and subtle mockery). He's the sardonic center of a dysfunctional suburban family that includes his self-hating, up-tight, materialistic wife Carolyn (Annette Bening does a nice bitchy turn) and their sullen teenage daughter Jane (Thora Birch). There is nothing left to their marriage but contempt and recriminations, and Lester, who has lost his odious job and his place in the family, finds solace only in salivating day dreams (rose petals floating out of her open sweater) about Jane's absurdly vain, nymphet friend, Angela (Mena Suvari). There is also a family of new neighbors, even more disturbed and alienated than the Burnhams. It consists of a rigid, homophobic, brutal ex-Marine Colonel father (who turns out predictably to be gay), his catatonic, servile wife, and their son Ricky (Wes Bentley)—an eerily perceptive drug dealer and voyeuristic loner who becomes involved with Jane.

American Beauty provides the blackest of comic portraits of American suburban life. There is nothing nuanced about this film—over-the-top caricatures being the rule and the social reality of the suburbs reduced to a few motifs—cheerleaders, selling real estate, jogging, and growing roses. There is also no reason to believe that the film's characters were ever happy and empathetic, and that the distorted and disconnected lives they now lead are a consequence of America's destructive values.

The film is witty and contains striking and sometimes haunting imagery (the product of cinematographer Conrad Hall's keen eye)—like a plastic bag floating in the wind or Rick and Lester standing, a distance from each other against a blank wall, smoking pot. At the same time, it doesn't feel that different in its heavy-handed, melodramatic skewering of suburban lives than another black comedy permeated with loathing for a similar milieu, Tod Solondz's *Happiness* (1999).

What is most distinctive about *American Beauty* is Kevin Spacey's Lester, who is the one complex character in a gallery of basically one-dimensional figures. The cynical man who feels he's dead already renews himself as an aggressive adolescent—smoking dope, building up his body, blackmailing his boss, and becoming sexually turned on. Spacey's discovery of some personal peace before being killed may be self-consciously poeticized, but it's much more imaginative than Mendes' social satire of suburban life.

The world of Mendes' *American Beauty* is a bitingly comic mirror of Stanley Kubrick's final film (he died at seventy before its release), *Eyes Wide Shut* (1999). It's a film that provides a fitting movie coda to American cinema's fin de siècle.

Kubrick had already peeked across the millennial divide in his mystical and socially critical *2001: A Space Odyssey* (1968), and the violent, nihilistic *A Clockwork Orange* (1971). Kubrick's coldly cerebral, ironic, formally imaginative films were always eagerly awaited. This was the case with *Eyes Wide Shut*, his first feature since the Vietnam War film, *Full Metal Jacket* (1987). The expectations of the film were accentuated by rumours flying about dozens of takes, continuous reshooting, and the absolute secrecy required by Kubrick of all its participants. None of these production problems and personal tics were new for a perfectionist like Kubrick. Nevertheless, the usual anticipation was heightened by his death and the advanced hype that began to build up around the film, which now also took on something of the weight and significance of a last testament.

Disappointment was bound to result from such high expectations. Stanley Kauffmann, in *The New Republic*, titled his review of *Eyes Wide Shut*, "Kubrick: A Sadness,"[39] and said the film was "a castastrophe." Other critics attacked Tom Cruise's performance, and Kubrick's inability to convincingly capture the relationship between a man and woman. There were, however, a few critics who differed. For example, Janet Maslin wrote a rave review in the *The New York Times*, stating that "This astonishing film is a spellbinding addition to the Kubrick canon."

The fact that *Eyes Wide Shut* evoked such widespread condemnation and such passionate praise is less a sign of failure than the film touching on some profound critical nerve.[40] Perhaps it was Kubrick's treatment of sexuality in this film—a mixture of cold, voyeurisitic interest (a great many shots of female nudes) and utter revulsion—connected, on a deeper level, to the linkage of sex and death in so many of his works. For example, it was a repeated motif in *Dr. Strangelove*'s scene of airplanes copulating and in *Full Metal Jacket*'s drill sergeant urging his men to treat their rifles like their mistresses. The film also projected a view of bourgeois marriage that saw it as a mixture of tenderness, loyalty, boredom, spite, and alienation.

The inspiration for *Eyes Wide Shut* was Arthur Schnitzler's 1926 novella, *Traumnovelle*. Schnitzler's work, though rarely read or staged today, was highly regarded in his day. Sigmund Freud, who was his contemporary in Vienna, considered Schnitzler his equal in the understanding and acknowledgment of sexuality as a singular force in the human condition. Though Kubrick was probably aware of Freud's high regard for Schnitzler, it could hardly have been the deciding factor in his attempt to adapt the novel to the screen. His use of the novella probably had more to do with its investigations of sex and dissection of the ways in which dreams and the irrational erupted into reality.

Actually Kubrick's attempt to do a film about sex and sexuality went back to the sixties when he tried to adapt Terry Southern's novel *Blue Movie* to the screen. Ironically, *Blue Movie* dealt with a highbrow director's efforts to make a big budget porn movie with famous stars. With Tom Cruise and Nicole Kidman as his stars in *Eyes Wide Shut*, Kubrick seemed to be turning Southern's fiction into a reality.

Of course, *Eyes Wide Shut* is not porn (Warner Brothers made absolutely sure of that by digitally censoring some graphic sexual imagery in the film's orgy scenes). It is, however, a string of dream-like sequences—all of them beautifully shot with a stately tracking camera, strikingly eerie lighting, and emotionally resonant long shots of the protagonist walking down abandoned streets and long, empty halls and corridors—a man who has lost his moorings. However, the few scenes that are psychologically incisive alternate with scenes so labored and self-conscious that they made one wonder if someone other than the driven perfectionist, Kubrick, was responsible for its final cut.

Eyes Wide Shut focuses on a young, beautiful, moneyed upper-middle-class New York couple, Dr. Bill Harford (Tom Cruise) and his wife Alice (Nicole Kidman), who are invited to a Christmas Eve party at the home of a millionaire friend (whose conventional, easy-going persona belies his corrupt nature), where they both engage in sexual flirtations. After smoking some pot, Alice cruelly confesses having had, the previous summer, a wild sexual fantasy about a young naval officer. This admission and the midnight summons to the home of a dying patient sends Bill out on a long night's journey where he has a series of sexual encounters that range from the mysterious to the absurd, and finally to the dangerous and forbidding.

What links Bill's encounters is their heavy coupling of sex and death and their dream-like quality. Thus, Marion (Marie Richardson), the tremulous daughter of his dead patient, whom Bill has hardly ever spoken to, peremptorily confesses her passionate love for him at her father's death-bed. The scene is exquisitely lit, and the two of them, seen in two shot, seem like characters in a powerful, soft-focused dream. Then the friendly prostitute (Vinessa Shaw), who Bill has a casual and interrupted encounter with, and whom Bill attempts to visit the next day, turns out to be HIV positive. Finally, the mysterious naked hooker who saves Bill's life, at an orgy he contrives to attend, is found dead of an overdose.

The linkage of sex, danger, and death is harnessed to Kubrick's theme of the ways in which the irrational erupts into and disrupts life, as in *The Shining* (1980) where a writer's inner demons prompt him to murder. In *Eyes Wide Shut* it is Alice's recounting of her sexual fantasy and then later of a nymphomaniacal nightmare that disrupt the complacency of their supposedly harmonious marriage and are replayed compulsively like black and white pornographic films in Bill's mind. Later, Bill visits the costume shop of a sly, bearded Milich (Rade Sherbegdia), who self-righteously excoriates the Japanese tourists playing sex games with his daughter, only later to sell her sexual services to them, as well as offering them to Bill.

It is the lengthy orgy scene that aroused the most intense criticism. With its masked and costumed participants, almost naked models in masks and thongs, ominous music, and couples engaged in sex, the sequence is stiff, nonsensical, overly-solemn, and despite its bizarre surface, lacking in sexual and emotional energy. Nonetheless, it provides a dramatic dénouement for what otherwise might have been a loosely connected series of sexual misadventures. More important, the orgy scene with its combination of pagan mystery and Black Mass is in keeping with Kubrick's sexual vision, where sex has almost nothing to do with erotic pleasure and everything to do with chilling cynicism about the human condition. For example, Alex, the Droogie, in *Clockwork Orange* refers to sex as a sterile, mechanical act—the "old in and out." In *Eyes Wide Shut* Kubrick connects sex with almost everything that seems corrupt and frightening.

It is this collision with the nightmarish world of their sexual fantasies and decadent sex that send Bill and Alice scurrying back to the safety and complacency of their bourgeois marriage. In the film's final moments they speak of their desire to start over, but first, in Alice's words they have to do something important, "fuck." For Kubrick this is a relatively happy ending. Kubrick makes it clear that their once shut eyes have opened a bit. They have awakened to the complex longings and darker undercurrents of marriage—to the existence, in symbolic terms, of the orgy mask (that in one scene lies on a pillow next to the sleeping Alice) in their lives.

Despite most critics viewing *Eyes Wide Shut* as an abject failure, it is an ambitious, deeply problematic film, that despite its profound flaws, is a memorial to a filmmaker's lifetime obsessions and themes. One might point to it as evidence that Kubrick was still capable of change even at this late stage of his career, since *Eyes Wide Shut* is the first film in which he ever really attempted to deal with human intimacy. (Though Cruise's character remains a cipher, and the relationship between him and Kidman lacks any heat or depth.) More significantly, Kubrick's *Eyes Wide Shut* stands as a fitting monument to the cinema, which reached its hundreth anniversary in the nineties. Indeed *Eyes Wide Shut*, with its evocation of dreams and fantasies and the role they play in our everyday life, provides a parallel to the impact of film illusion and fantasies on our own psychic landscapes. American films have allowed us to roam far and wide in time and space. They have also permitted us, as we have argued throughout this book, some consciousness and understanding of the spirit of the times and the culture. One has little reason to doubt that that American film will continue to supply the same opportunity for entertainment, escape and even insight in the millennium to come.

NOTES

1. Eric Hobsbawm, *The Age of Extremes: A History of the World, 1914–1991* (New York: Vintage Books, 1996), pp. 1–17.

2. Michael R. Beschloss and Strobe Talbott, *At the Highest Levels: The Inside Story of the End of the Cold War* (New York: Little Brown and Co., 1994), pp. 475–93.

3. Hobsbawm, *The Age of Extremes*, pp. 461–99.

4. Thomas L. Friedman, *The Lexus and the Olive Tree* (New York: Anchor Books, 2000), pp. xi–xxii.

5. George Stephanopoulos, *All Too Human: A Political Education* (New York: Little Brown and Co., 1999), pp. 81–107.

6. Martin Walker, *The President We Deserve: Bill Clinton: His Rise, Falls and Comeback* (New York: Crown, 1996), p. 347.

7. Jonathan Chait, "The Slippery Center," *The New Republic* (November 16, 1998), pp. 19–21.

8. Lars-Erik Nelson, "Clinton and His Enemies," *The New York Review of Books* (January 20, 2000), pp. 18–22.

9. Stephanopoulos, *All Too Human*, pp. 51–80.

10. Ibid., pp. 64–67.

11. Jeffrey Toobin, *A Vast Conspiracy: The Real Story of the Sex Scandal that Nearly Brought Down a President* (New York: Touchstone, 1999).

12. Friedman, *The Lexus and the Olive Tree*, pp. 3–28.

13. John Pierson, *Spike, Mike, Slackers and Dykes: A Guided Tour Across a Decade of American Independent Cinema* (New York: Hyperion, 1997), pp. 6–20.

14. Peter Bart, *Who Killed Hollywood? . . . and Put the Tarnish on Tinseltown* (Los Angeles: Renaissance Books, 1999), pp. 64–65.

15. Louis Menand, "Independence Day," *The New York Review of Books* (September 19, 1996), pp. 14–16.

16. Mel Gussow, "A Child (and an Adult) of War: A Military Historian Puts a Vivid Cast on World War I," *The New York Times* (July 3, 1999), p. B11.

17. Tom Wicker, "Does 'JFK' Conspire Against Reason," *The New York Times: Sunday Arts and Leisure* (December 15, 1991), pp. 1, 18.

18. James Petras, "The Discrediting of the Fifth Estate: The Press Attacks on JFK," *Cineaste*, vol. XIX (Winter 1992), p. 15.

19. Bernard Weintraub, "Nixon Family Assails Stone Film as Distortion," *The New York Times* (December 19, 1995), p. C18.

20. Garry Wills, "Dostoyevsky Behind a Camera: Oliver Stone is Making Great American Novels on Film," *The Atlantic Monthly* (July 1997), pp. 96–101.

21. William Grimes, "What Debt Does Hollywood Owe to Truth?" *The New York Times* (March 5, 1992), pp. C15, 22.

22. Norman Mailer, "Footfalls in the Crypt," *Vanity Fair* (February 1992), pp. 124–129, 171.

23. Lance Morrow and Martha Smilgis, "Plunging into the Labyrinth," *Time* (December 23, 1991), pp. 74–76.

24. Anthony Summers, *Conspiracy* (New York: Paragon, 1989), p. 11. This book has been reissued with the new title, *Not in Your Lifetime: The Definitive Book on the JFK Assassination* (New York: McGraw-Hill, 1998).

25. Fawn Brodie, *Richard Nixon: The Shaping of His Character* (Cambridge: Harvard University Press, 1983), p. 76.

26. Nicholas Lemann, "Buffaloed: Was the Native American Always Nature's Friend?" *The New Yorker* (September 1, 1999), pp. 98–101.

27. D. H. Lawrence, *Studies in Classic American Literature* (New York: Doubleday and Co., 1951), pp. 43–73.

28. "Titanic Praised by Chinese President Jiang Zemin as Politically Correct Class Warfare," *Wall Street Journal* (May 15, 1998), p. 11.

29. Frank Bruni, "Wagging Tongues in 'Incredibly Cynical Times,'" *The New York Times* (August 21, 1998), p. C19.

30. Andrew Hacker, *Two Nations: Black and White, Separate, Hostile, Unequal* (New York: Charles Scribner's Son, 1992), pp. 67–92.

31. Ibid., pp. 179–98.

32. Playthell Benjamin, "These Boyz Lives: Let Us Now Praise (or Pan) Menace: Six Critics Speak," *Village Voice* (May 25, 1993), p. 23.

33. Stephen and Abigail Thernstrom, *America in Black and White: One Nation Indivisible* (New York: Touchstone, 1997), pp. 183–202.

34. Berel Lang, *Act and Idea in the Nazi Genocide* (Chicago: University of Chicago Press, 1990), p. 151.

35. Norman Finkelstein, *The Holocaust Industry: Reflections on the Exploitation of Jewish Suffering* (New York: Verso, 2000).

36. Randall Robinson, *The Debt: What America Owes to Blacks* (New York: Dutton, 2000), p. 216.

37. Vito Russo, *The Celluloid Closet: Homosexuality in the Movies* (New York: Harper and Row, 1987).

38. "Why Thelma and Louise Strike a Nerve," *Time* (June 24, 1991), pp. 52–56.

39. Stanley Kauffmann, "Kubrick: A Sadness," *The New Republic* (August 16, 1999), pp. 30–31.

40. Graham Fuller, "Is *Eyes Wide Shut* a Genius's Final Erotic Masterpiece? Over to the U.S. Critics," *The Observer* (July 18, 1999), p. 6.

SELECTED BIBLIOGRAPHY

Dean Acheson, *Present at the Creation* (New York: W. W. Norton, 1969).

Renata G. Adler, *A Year in the Dark* (New York: Berkeley, 1969).

James Agee, *Agee on Film: Reviews and Comments* (Boston: Beacon Press, 1966).

Hollis Alpert and Andrew Sarris (eds.) *Film 68/69: An Anthology by the National Society of Film Critics* (New York: Simon and Schuster, 1969).

Rick Altman (ed.), *Genre: The Musical* (London: Routledge & Kegan Paul, 1981).

Stephen Ambrose, *Rise to Globalism: American Foreign Policy 1938–1970* (Baltimore, MD: Penguin, 1971).

Albert Auster and Leonard Quart, *How the War Was Remembered: Hollywood and Vietnam* (New York: Praeger, 1988).

Alan G. Barbour, *John Wayne* (New York: Pyramid, 1974).

Eric Barnouw, *Tube of Plenty: The Evolution of American Television* (New York: Oxford University Press, 1977).

Peter Bart, *Who Killed Hollywood? . . . and Put the Tarnish on Tinseltown* (Los Angeles: Renaissance Books, 1999).

Michael Beschloss and Strobe Talbott, *At the Highest Levels: The Inside Story of the End of the Cold War* (New York: Little, Brown and Company, 1994).

Donald Bogle, *Toms, Coons, Mulattoes, Mammies and Bucks* (New York: Bantam, 1973).

Fawn Brodie, *Richard Nixon: The Shaping of His Character* (Cambridge: Harvard University Press, 1983).

Tim Bywater and Thomas Sobchack, *Film Criticism: Major Critical Approaches to Narrative Film* (White Plains, NY: Longman, 1989).

Lou Cannon, *Ronald Reagan* (New York: G. P. Putnam's Sons, 1982).

Frank Capra, *The Name Above the Title* (New York: Bantam, 1972).

Terry Christensen, *Reel Politics: American Movies from Birth of a Nation to Platoon* (New York: Basil Blackwell, 1987).

Michel Ciment, *Kazan on Kazan* (New York: Viking, 1973).

Alistair Cooke, *A Generation on Trial* (Baltimore, MD: Penguin, 1952).

Pam Cooke (ed.), *The Cinema Book* (New York: Pantheon, 1985).

Philip Davies and Brian Neve (eds.), *Cinema, Politics, and Society in America* (Manchester, UK: Manchester University Press, 1981).

Barbara Deming, *Running Away from Myself: A Dream Portrait of America Drawn from the Films of the Forties* (New York: Grossman Publishers, 1969).

Morris Dickstein, *Gates of Eden: American Culture in the Sixties* (New York: Basic Books, 1977).

Thomas Ferguson and Joel Rogers, *Right Turn: The Decline of the Democrats and the Future of American Politics* (New York: Hill and Wang, 1986).

Norman Finkelstein, *The Holocaust Industry: Reflections on the Exploitation of Jewish Suffering* (New York: Verso, 2000).

Frances Fitzgerald, *Fire in the Lake* (New York: Vintage, 1973).

Gerald R. Ford, *A Time to Heal* (New York: Berkeley, 1980).

Hugh Fordin, *The World of Entertainment: Hollywood's Greatest Musicals* (Garden City, NY: Doubleday, 1975).

Brandon French, *On the Verge of Revolt: Women in American Films of the Fifties* (New York: Frederick Unger, 1978).

Phillip French, *Westerns* (New York: Oxford University Press, 1977).

Thomas Friedman, *The Lexus and the Olive Tree* (New York: Anchor Books, 2000).

Neal Gabler, *An Empire of Their Own: How the Jews Invented Hollywood* (New York: Crown, 1988).

Nicholas Garnham, *Samuel Fuller* (New York: Viking, 1971).

Charlie Gillett, *The Sound of the City: The Rise of Rock and Roll*, rev. ed. (New York: Pantheon, 1984).

Eric F. Goldman, *The Crucial Decade—and After, America 1945–1960* (New York: Vintage, 1960).

Walter Goodman, *The Committee: The Extraordinary Career of the House Committee on Un-American Activities* (Baltimore, MD: Penguin, 1969).

Joseph G. Goulden, *The Best Years, 1945–1950* (New York: Athenium, 1976).

Gordon Gow, *Hollywood in the Fifties* (New York: A. S. Barnes, 1971).

Andrew Hacker, *Two Nations: Black and White, Separate, Hostile, Unequal* (New York: Charles Scribner's Sons, 1992).

David Halberstam, *The Best and the Brightest* (New York: Fawcett, 1973).

Stuart Hall and Paddy Whannel, *The Popular Arts* (New York: Pantheon, 1965).

Jon Halliday, *Sirk on Sirk* (New York: Dell, 1980).

Molly Haskell, *From Reverence to Rape: The Treatment of Women in the Movies* (Baltimore, MD: Penguin, 1974).

Venable Herndon, *James Dean: A Short Life* (New York: Signet, 1975).

Charles Higham and Joel Greenberg, *Hollywood in the Forties* (New York: Paperback Library, 1970).

John Hill and Pamela Church Gibson (eds.) *Film Studies: Critical Approaches* (Oxford: Oxford University Press, 1998).

Eric Hobsbawm, *The Age of Extremes: A History of the World, 1914–1991* (New York: Vintage Books, 1996).

Godfrey Hodgson, *America in Our Time: From World War II to Nixon, What Happened and Why* (New York: Vintage, 1978).

Diane Jacobs, *Hollywood Renaissance: The New Generation of Filmmakers and Their Works* (New York: Delta, 1980).

Garth Jowett, *Film: The Democratic Art* (Boston: Little, Brown, 1976).

Pauline Kael, *Going Steady* (New York: Bantam, 1971).

Pauline Kael, *Kiss, Kiss, Bang, Bang* (New York: Bantam, 1969).

Norman Kagan, *The Cinema of Stanley Kubrick* (New York: Grove Press, 1975).

Norman Kagan, *The War Film* (New York: Pyramid Publications, 1974).

Stuart M. Kaminsky, *Don Siegel: Director* (New York: Curtis Books, 1974).

Judith Kass, *Robert Altman: American Innovator* (New York: Popular Library, 1978).

Doris Kearns, *Lyndon B. Johnson and the American Dream* (New York: Signet, 1976).

Siegfried Kracauer, *From Caligari to Hitler: A Psychological History of the German Film*, 3rd ed. (Princeton, NJ: Princeton University Press, 1970).

Godfrey Berel Lang, *Act and Idea in the Nazi Genocide* (Chicago: University of Chicago Press, 1990).

William L. Langer, *Political and Social Upheaval, 1832–1852* (New York: Harper and Row, 1969).

Christopher Lasch, *The Culture of Narcissism* (New York: Warner Books, 1979).

D. H. Lawrence, *Studies in Classic American Literature* (New York: Doubleday and Company, 1951).

Norman Mailer, *Armies of the Night* (New York: Signet, 1968).

Gerald Mast and Marshall Cohen (eds.), *Film Theory and Criticism* (New York: Oxford University Press, 1974).

James Monaco, *American Film Now: The People, the Power, the Money, the Movies* (New York: Oxford University Press, 1979).

Joseph Morgenstern and Stefan Kanfer (eds.), *Film 69/70: An Anthology by the National Society of Film Critics* (New York: Simon and Schuster, 1970).

Victor S. Navasky, *Naming Names* (New York: Viking, 1980).

John E. O'Connor and Martin A. Jackson (eds.), *American History/American Film: Interpreting the Hollywood Image* (New York: Frederick Unger, 1979).

William L. O'Neill, *Coming Apart: An Informal History of America in the 1960s* (New York: Quadrangle, 1971).

John Pierson, *Spike, Mike, Slackers, and Dykes: A Guided Tour Across a Decade of American Independent Cinema* (New York: Hyperion, 1997).

Sidney Poitier, *This Life* (New York: Ballantine, 1980).

Gerald Pratley, *The Cinema of John Frankenheimer* (Cranbury, NJ: A. S. Barnes, 1969).

Barbara Koenig Quart, *Woman Directors: The Emergence of a New Cinema* (New York: Praeger, 1988).

Randall Robinson, *The Debt: What America Owes Blacks* (New York: Dutton, 2000).

Peter Roffman and Jim Purdy, *The Hollywood Social Problem Film* (Bloomington: Indiana University Press, 1981).

Deborah Silverton Rosenfelt (ed.), *Salt of the Earth* (Old Westbury, NY: Feminist Press, 1978).

Robert A. Rosenstone, *Romantic Revolutionary: A Biography of John Reed* (New York: Alfred A. Knopf, 1975).

Richard Rovere, *Senator Joseph McCarthy*, rev. ed. (New York: Harper and Row, 1973).

Vito Russo, *The Celluloid Closet: Homosexuality in the Movies* (New York: Harper and Row, 1987).

Michael Ryan and Douglas Kellner, *Camera Politica: The Politics and Ideology of Contemporary Hollywood Film* (Bloomington: Indiana University Press, 1988).

Kirkpatrick Sale, *SDS* (New York: Vintage, 1974).

Nora Sayre, *Running Time: Films of the Cold War* (New York: Dial Press, 1982).

Thomas Schatz, *The Genius of the System: Hollywood Filmmaking in the Studio Era* (New York: Pantheon, 1988).

Jonathan Schell, *The Time of Illusion* (New York: Alfred A. Knopf, 1976).

Frederick F. Siegel, *Troubled Journey: From Pearl Harbor to Ronald Reagan* (New York: Hill and Wang, 1984).

Robert Sklar, *Movie Made America: A Cultural History of American Movies* (New York: Vintage, 1975).

Susan Sontag, *Against Interpretation* (New York: Dell, 1969).

Donald Spoto, *Stanley Kramer: Filmmaker* (New York: G. P. Putnam's Sons, 1978).

George Stephanopoulos, *All Too Human: A Political Education* (New York: Little Brown and Company, 1999).

Anthony Summers, *Not in Your Lifetime: The Definitive Book on the* JFK Assassination (New York: McGraw-Hill, 1998).

Stephen and Abigail Thernstrom, *America in Black and White: One Nation, Indivisible* (New York: Touchstone, 1997).

Jeffrey Toobin, *A Vast Conspiracy: The Real Story Behind the Sex Scandal that Nearly Brought Down a President* (New York: Touchstone, 1999).

Diana Trilling, *We Must March, My Darlings* (New York: Harcourt Brace Jovanovich, 1977).

Irwin Unger, *These United States: The Questions of Our Past Since 1865*, vol. 2 (Englewood Cliffs, NJ: Prentice-Hall, 1989).

Martin Walker, *The President We Deserve: Bill Clinton: His Rise, Falls, and Comeback* (New York: Crown, 1996).

Robert Warshow, *The Immediate Experience* (Garden City, NY: Anchor, 1964).

Edmund White, *The Beautiful Room is Empty* (New York: Ballantine, 1988).

Raymond Williams, *Communications*, 3rd ed. (London: Pelican, 1976).

Garry Wills, *Reagan's America: With a New Chapter on the Legacy of the Reagan Era* (New York: Penguin, 1987).

William Julius Wilson, *The Truly Disadvantaged: The Inner City, The Underclass, and Public Policy* (Chicago: University of Chicago Press, 1987).

Michael Wood, *America in the Movies: or, "Santa Maria, It Had Slipped My Mind!"* (New York: Basic Books, 1975).

Robin Wood, *Arthur Penn* (New York: Praeger, 1969).

James Wooten, *Dasher* (New York: Signet, 1978).

INDEX

Nicholson, Jack, 92
Nixon, 181–82
Nixon, Richard M., 68, 72, 87; American credibility, 97; image promotion, 98–99
Nolte, Nick, 177–78
Norma Rae, 112
Norris, Chuck, 144–45
North Atlantic Treaty Organization (NATO), 15
North by Northwest, 48
North, Oliver, 129
Nosferatu, 24
No Way Out, 59
Nuclear arms race, 42, 62–64, 68, 75–76

Oates, Warren, 88
Objective Burma, 19
O'Brien, Edmond, 89
O'Brien, Margaret, 35
O'Brien, Tim, 119
Obsession, 103
Odets, Clifford, 62
O'Donnell, Cathy, 22
Oklahoma, 52
Omen, The, 117
O'Neill, Eugene, 138
On the Beach, 63–64
On Golden Pond, 136
On the Town, 4, 36
On the Waterfront, 46–48, 56
Optimism, 52
Ordinary People, 132–33
Our Daily Bread, 6
Our Man Flint, 79

Pakula, Alan, 109, 114
Panofsky, Erwin, 2
Parallax View, 114
Paramount, 16
Parenthood, 3
Parker, Alan, 153
Parsons, Estelle, 83
Partisan Review, The, 41
Patch of Blue, A, 81

Paths of Glory, 62–63
Patriotism, 17
Pawnbroker, The, 80
Payne, Alexander, 189
Peale, Norman Vincent, 41
Pearson, Beatrice, 32
Peck, Gregory, 64
Peckinpah, Sam, 7, 87–89
Penn, Arthur, 82–84, 89–90
Perez, Rosie, 154
Pesci, Joe, 180
Petty, Lori, 199
Petulia, 89
Philadelphia, 10
Pickens, Slim, 78
Pierce, Kimberly, 198
Pigeon, Walter, 75
Pillow Talk, 64
Pinky, 32
Place in the Sun, A, 56
Places in the Heart, 143
Platoon, 4–5, 146–48
Plummer, Glenn, 191
Poindexter, John, 129
Poitier, Sidney, 59–60, 80
Political issues, 2, 4–5, 45–46; in *Nashville*, 105–7; 1950's, 40–41; 1960's, 74–79, 81
Pollack, Sydney, 114
Pollard, Michael, 83
Polonsky, Abraham, 20, 28, 33–34
Port of Shadows, 24
Possessed, 25
Postman Always Rings Twice, The, 28
Postwar adjustment, as theme, 19–24
Preminger, Otto, 24, 75
Presnell, Herve, 175
Pride of the Marines, 19–20
Primary Colors, 186–87
Pryor, Richard, 113
Psycho, 74
Psychoanalytic interpretation, 7–8
Pullman, Bill, 173
Pulp Fiction, 201–2
Purple Heart, The, 17
Puzo, Mario, 103

ABOUT THE AUTHORS

LEONARD QUART is Professor of Cinema Studies at the College of Staten Island and at the CUNY Graduate Center. His essays and articles have appeared in *Film Quarterly*, *Dissent*, *The Forward*, and *London Magazine*, among others, and for over twenty years, he has been an editor and contributing editor of *Cineaste*. He is the co-author of books including *The Films of Mike Leigh* and *How the War Was Remembered: Hollywood and Vietnam* (Praeger, 1988).

ALBERT AUSTER is Associate Professor in the Department of Communication and Media Studies at Fordham University and a research associate at the McGannon Communications Research Center. He is a frequent contributor to *Television Quarterly*, *The Journal of Popular Film and Television*, and other journals, and is the author or co-author of books including *How the War Was Remembered: Hollywood and Vietnam* (Praeger, 1988).